PSYCHIC HOOKS
AND BOLTS

PSYCHIC HOOKS AND BOLTS
PSYCHOANALYTIC WORK WITH CHILDREN UNDER FIVE AND THEIR FAMILIES

Maria Emilia Pozzi

KARNAC
LONDON   NEW YORK

First published in 2003 by
H. Karnac (Books) Ltd.
6 Pembroke Buildings, London NW10 6RE

A subsidiary of Other Press LLC, New York

Copyright © 2003 Maria Emilia Pozzi

The rights of Maria Emilia Pozzi to be identified as the author of this work have been asserted in accordance with §§ 77 and 78 of the Copyright Design and Patents Act 1988.

All rights reserved. No part of this publication may be reproduced, stored in a retrieval system, or transmitted, in any form or by any means, electronic, mechanical, photocopying, recording, or otherwise, without the prior written permission of the publisher.

British Library Cataloguing in Publication Data

A C.I.P. for this book is available from the British Library

ISBN 1 85575 907 1

10 9 8 7 6 5 4 3 2 1

Edited, designed, and produced by The Studio Publishing Services Ltd, Exeter EX4 8JN

www.karnacbooks.com

Dedicated to the memory of my aunt Gaspara Stampa Baj, who always took part in the accounts of my life with sympathetic joy, and would have loved to have shared my pleasure in publishing this book.

"Midway along the journey of our life
I woke to find myself in a dark wood,
for I had wondered off the straight path.

How hard it is to tell what it was like,
this wood of wilderness, savage and stubborn
(the thought of it brings back all my old fears),

a bitter place! Death could scarce be bitterer.
... ...
And when I saw him standing in this wasteland,
... ...
"Are you then Virgil, are you then that fount
from which pours forth so rich a stream of words?"
I said to him, bowing my head modestly.
... ...
"You are my teacher, the first of all my authors,
... ...
You see the beast that forced me to retreat;
save me from her, I beg you, famous sage,
she makes me tremble, the blood throbs in my veins."

Dante, *Inferno*, vv. 1–7; v. 64; vv. 79–81; v. 85; vv. 88–90;
The Indiana Critical Edition, translated by Mark Musa,
Indiana University Press, 1995.

CONTENTS

ACKNOWLEDGEMENTS xi

FOREWORD
Lisa Miller xiii

BIOGRAPHICAL NOTE xvii

SUMMARY xix

PART I THEORETICAL BACKGROUND

Introduction 3

CHAPTER ONE
The importance of infant observation in under fives' counselling 7

CHAPTER TWO
Outlines of psychodynamic under fives' counselling and theoretical background 11

Theoretical influences on under fives' counselling
1. Melanie Klein, Wilfred Bion, and Donald Winnicott 12
2. Other influential approaches: short psychodynamic psychotherapy, parent–infant psychotherapy, attachment theory and family therapist John Byng-Hall, and neurosciences 20
3. Setting and technique 32

PART II CLINICAL CASES

Introduction   51

CHAPTER THREE
Post-natal maternal depression   55

CHAPTER FOUR
Separation difficulties and parental input   63

CHAPTER FIVE
Eating problems   81

CHAPTER SIX
The little girl who could not sleep, or psychic bolts   89

CHAPTER SEVEN
Soiling   101

CHAPTER EIGHT
Gender identity   115

CHAPTER NINE
Bereavement and loss   121

CHAPTER TEN
Learning disabilities   133

CHAPTER ELEVEN
The borderline child and the establishment of internal reins   143

CHAPTER TWELVE
Hyperactivity and Ritalin   149

CHAPTER THIRTEEN
Mental illness in the family   161

CHAPTER FOURTEEN
The use of under fives' counselling as parental guidance with
     severely developmentally delayed children   171

CHAPTER FIFTEEN
Under fives' counselling as a form of assessment   179

CHAPTER SIXTEEN
Consultation to a nursery school   189

CHAPTER SEVENTEEN
Parents' line   195

Concluding remarks   201

REFERENCES   203

INDEX   213

ACKNOWLEDGEMENTS

I would like to express my warm thanks to my innumerable families. First of all my family of origin: my late father, my living mother, and two brothers, who provided the emotional background and impetus to my interest in children and family dynamics. Then there are the families of friends and supporters, colleagues, teachers, and especially my analysts. They all contributed in different and important ways to the creation of this book; in particular, Jan Poulter, who befriended me when I first moved to London to train as a child psychotherapist. We remained friends until her untimely and most sad death in 1995. Brett Kahr always encouraged me with enthusiastic appreciation to write about my work and linked me with people who supported my endeavours. Bob Monzo provided me with home security and space to write. Sue Reid and Lisa Miller nourished me professionally through my child psychotherapy training at the Tavistock and afterwards. Daniela Ostinelli typed a lot of my work through the years and I appreciate her faithful and humorous friendship. Frances Tustin was more than a teacher and gave so much of herself. Ajahn Upekka and the Amaravati Buddhist Monastery, where I wrote parts of this book, have offered me existential and philosophical wisdom and containment. Andrew

Briggs contributed his thoughts to the first part of the book, while Hannah Kanter and Miranda Whyte offered their thorough editorial skill. This book could not exist without my patients and I expand on this in the introduction.

Additionally, I wish to thank the *Journal of Child Psychotherapy*, *Psychoanalytic Psychotherapy*, Whurr Publishers and Indiana University Press for giving permission to quote from and reproduce papers and chapters previously published by them. Leena Häkkinen from Karnac Books has assisted me with friendly ease in the phase of getting the manuscript in order.

FOREWORD

Maria Pozzi was for many years an untiring member of the Tavistock infant mental health team. She worked in the Under Fives' Counselling Service that was set up in the early 1980s. Since then she has carried her work forward, as she shows in this book, but without straying too far from the general principles established during her time in the Under Fives' team. The following chapters exemplify, illustrate and develop the work she began there. They are a very personal and individual account of her efforts.

Although Maria Pozzi herself describes the work pioneered at the Tavistock, it may be useful to summarize here its fundamental components. The Under Fives' Counselling Service offers up to five sessions when there is a concern focussed on the baby or the young child. Experience tells us that at the early stages of development there is considerable potential for change in a family; the family system has not been set in a particular mould; the child or children are not yet established personalities to the extent they become as the school years approach; and relationships within the family always need to shift with the birth of a new baby. Perhaps what we often see are families where a new baby has not been fully assimilated into the family system, whether that system consists of a single mother on her own or a far more elaborate one. The new relationships which need to be formed have met difficulty in the process, whether the difficulty stems from a problem internal to the child, a problem hanging over from a parent's childhood, problems in the parental relationship, external blows like bereavement, or indeed some more chronic difficulty such as a disability. In many cases, of course, we see multi-determined complexity.

However, simply by coming, the family announces its readiness to seek help. At the Tavistock we felt, and feel, that in cases where there is an infant or small child, there should be no delay; and we have prided ourselves on a rapid response service. (Maria Pozzi describes a very fascinating and useful development of this in telephone consultation.) It has not been at all uncommon to hear a baby's mother crying as she telephones—an indication of how close to the surface the emotions are in people who care for their small children, often in somewhat unsupported circumstances. Because some parents are in an emotionally charged state, it is a good time to provide them with a worker who aims, as a priority, to be emotionally receptive. Our method of working starts here. We look on ourselves as somewhat privileged; free of the central responsibilities carried by doctors, health visitors or other nurses for the physical health and well-being of the baby, we are able to put the questions of what the family (including the baby, if there is one) are thinking and feeling at the top of our agenda.

As Maria Pozzi says, a training in infant observation is most helpful to those who undertake this kind of parent-infant work. Indeed, the practice of infant observation forms an essential part in the training of child psychotherapists and many other professionals, and the Tavistock model of under fives' work draws inspiration and practical aid from it. It is easy to see that the same qualities of emotional responsiveness and resilience which infant observation develops are of the greatest use in brief encounters with a therapeutic intent.

The other source of thinking from where the Under Fives' model grew was the extensive work done in the Child & Family Department (and of course elsewhere) with the parents of all referred children. Whether the family is treated by a systemic family therapist or a worker whose thinking is primarily psychodynamic, the child is seen in the context of its family life and relationships.

When the treatment of choice is individual therapy for a child, it is essential for the parent or parents also to be regularly worked with. And whether that work concentrates on discussing the child's problems and progress, or whether the discussion widens to take in the parents' characters and pathology, the point is that they, the parents, must be attended to. Otherwise it is all too likely that an uprush of feeling and conviction, probably negative or confused, will surge out from some aspect of the parents' infantile selves that is giving them trouble and interfere, perhaps totally, with their child's treatment. We have to attend methodically to the negative side of their response to the Clinic: after all, they come with both hopes and fears, and both may be realized. In work with parents it is important always to keep their child in mind, but also to look out for child-aspects of the parents themselves, while at the same time forming an alliance with the adult side which is responsibly seeking help. In the counselling service we thought of ourselves as having a strong link with the adults, the people who come to consult us about their baby, but tried to be vigilant in observing those moments when the adult is overwhelmed by infantile anxiety and unconscious phantasy.

Evidence for some of these moments where unconscious feelings are communicated often comes from the countertransference, the emotional experience of the workers. It is probably true to say that what distinguishes the under fives' work which evolved at the Tavistock from much other excellent work is the firm reliance on transference and countertransference, those essential tools in the psychoanalytic apparatus. Workers like Maria Pozzi do not just rely upon what their patients tell them and what their patients do in the room, but on what they make the therapist feel. Unconscious communication may be very powerful. For many families, as we see in this book, a prime part of the relief they gain is from communicating something about their lives—their inner lives or their external lives—that nobody has quite heard before. It is as though some of them have been going about for some time with a message to deliver, and have not found anyone quite capable of receiving it until they met someone—in this book Maria Pozzi—with the equipment needed to received and decode the message.

This equipment includes a grasp on transference and counter-transference, a readiness to accept that families will certainly have strong negative feelings about the therapist as well as positive ones and a strong stomach for some of the extreme feelings which characterize infancy, early childhood and families overall when the children are small. In this book we also see how the therapist is helped by her capacity to observe and remember details and to put it all together into a coherent narrative. She holds in her mind the natural history of the treatment. For the space of time that the family is engaged in work they have a time in her week, and a place in her mind. She struggles to make sense of what they convey, and to find a way to use the understanding that she has which will be based upon receptive observation. Then the difficulty lies in how to communicate understanding to the family in a way which they find makes some sense to them. If it makes no sense, it is worse than useless.

In this book it is made plain that complex and powerful understanding can take place in brief work. The baby's development is carried forward, the family re-groups differently, understanding brings a change in behaviour. One might say that the families arrive in pain and anxiety, pushed to enact internal states. That is to say, they do not know why they are all behaving as they would not wish to behave. The are taken over by forces which they feel they cannot control, whether the uncontrollable thing is the child itself, or the parents' reaction to it. The therapist's task is to see whether thinking about things will help. Will it be possible to substitute a more ordinary feeling of people in charge of their lives? In other words, will ego-functioning be enhanced and will the adults start to regain their rightful place as guardians and fond protectors of the children?

It is interesting to note that another book reflecting on this field of work is forthcoming, this time to be published in the Tavistock/Karnac series. It will be edited by the current chairs of the Infant Mental Health Workshop and will attend in depth to the matters I have briefly raised here—the history, philosophy and practice of the service in general. Maria Pozzi is a determined and experienced proponent of this sort of work, and this book, which describes her particular approach, satisfies our desire for rich clinical detail. She will also contribute to the forthcoming volume a chapter on research work in this area.

Lisa Miller
15 November 2002

BIOGRAPHICAL NOTE

Maria Pozzi was born in Italy in the fifties and later moved to England where she trained as a child and adolescent psychotherapist at the Tavistock Clinic, then as an adult psychotherapist with the British Association of Psychotherapists. She has special interests in treating children with autism, Asperger's syndrome, and mental handicap, and in brief work with children under five and their families. She has been working in Child and Family Clinics since 1984 and also privately. Presently she is a visiting tutor at the Tavistock Clinic, the B.A.P., and the London Centre for Psychotherapy. She also teaches and lectures in Italy and Switzerland on topics related to child and adolescent psychotherapy. She is at present involved in research that focuses on the process of change in brief work with families of children under five. Her publications include papers on topics such as A.D.H.D. and Ritalin, Asperger's syndrome, mother–child separation, and under fives' counselling. She has contributed chapters in books on narcissism, social responsibility, and autistic states, and is the winner of the 1999 Frances Tustin Memorial Prize.

SUMMARY

This book describes a method of brief and focused psychoanalytic counselling of children under five, seen together with their parents and siblings. The first part of the book covers theoretical ideas used in this approach, and technical aspects of this work. The second part is made up of clinical vignettes and case histories which give flesh to the theory.

This type of work is shown to be brief, but deep and effective, and can access the heart and mind of the participants in a few sessions. The book aims to inspire interested professionals and to offer parents new ideas on difficult, but familiar, problems in child rearing.

PART I
THEORETICAL BACKGROUND

Introduction

In this book, I focus on young children up to the age of five and the parents and siblings with whom they live. My aim is to explore the deep, unconscious connections between children and parents, especially in those cases where symptomatic behaviour develops and turns a potentially pleasant and satisfying family life into hell.

When psychotherapists and psychoanalysts write about their work they are usually grateful to their patients and their families. This is particularly so in the case of child analysts, as children and their families constitute one of the essential ingredients of the work of writing. Through our therapeutic work and our relationships with patients, we continue to learn about human nature, suffering, and the functioning of the mind.

The word "patient" stems from the Latin "*patior*" which means to suffer. In the cases I describe in later chapters, the patient, or more often the patient's family, are the sufferers. They come into treatment to find ways, with the help of the analyst, to reduce or to give up that suffering. The patients present themselves with emotional, neurotic or existential suffering. It can be a consequence of trauma, abuse or physical or mental illness, but is usually a lonely and meaningless type of suffering. It differs from the psychic pain that the patient will hopefully be able to experience and tolerate by the end of therapy. The Latin word *subferre* is the root of the verb to suffer and means to go below or under. The patient then, from being a sufferer, someone who bears the weight of life events and is a victim of this somewhat unhealthy state, becomes able to understand, to take charge and to turn that lonely suffering into the psychic pain that is part of the human condition. It is what Freud meant by his famous reply to a hypothetical patient questioning him about his imability to change the circumstances and events of the patient's life. Freud replied: "But you will be able to convince yourself that much will be gained if we succeed in transforming your hysterical misery into common unhappiness" (Breuer & Freud, 1893–1895, p. 305).

The inspiration for the title of this book came from two families whose small children needed help. Four year old Claire and her mother had an idyllic relationship during the first two years of Claire's life. The external world had been excluded, in some inexplicable way, from this tight dyad. However, when mother became pregnant with her second child and the "no" phase was ushered in, Claire became contrary, angry, and intolerable. She was no longer the delightful child she had been and clearly felt deeply betrayed and let down by her mother. She had not yet begun to master the presence of the "third person", when the new baby arrived, despite father having been involved in her upbringing. Mother on her part felt guilty for giving her beloved "princess" such a harsh experience and was hurt by Claire's reaction. She also felt hooked onto her daughter's anger and disappointment and in the session she demonstrated this feeling by hooking her two index fingers together. This became a metaphor that we continued to use through the family sessions and I still use it, ten years later, in my current practice. It is the equivalent of the state of collusion where the child's feelings and states of mind resonate and latch on to the parents' feelings. The latter react in turn, without processing the events. The child and the parent, or both parents, are caught up with each other in a relationship that becomes like a tug-of-war, and is far from being the container–contained relationship described by Bion (1962a).

The concept of "psychic bolts" also emerged during family counselling with another four-year-old girl, Susan, who had not been able to sleep properly since she was an infant. The parents, the newborn baby, and Susan were distraught by lack of sleep and in a counselling session, the parents, out of exasperation, expressed the conflicted wish to put bolts on Susan's bedroom door. "Psychic bolts could be enough," I suggested. This metaphor stood for firm boundaries that could be opened and closed and it defined the separateness, which had never been properly achieved between Susan and her parents. It worked indeed, as we will see in the chapter on sleep. The term "psychic bolts" has also become part of my tool kit and has indeed alleviated the pain of many more unhappy families when too many "hooks" exist between children and parents and prevent the evolution of a containing relationship.

As often happens in psychoanalytic writing, this book is also inspired by my personal family history and vicissitudes. It focuses on the infant or small child's world within the wider context of family relations and interactions. It is born out of my desire to continue thinking and to share with the reader the exciting work and achievements that can be obtained in psychodynamically-based work with small children, seen together with their parents, siblings, and occasionally also with the grandparents. It is a psychological work that aims to examine this young age within its family context, when so much can still be done to achieve relative stability and resolution of conflicts, even in just a few sessions. The widening of our knowledge and research about this early age and what affects it, have been confirmed by statistical evidence. In turn, this confirms the theories and ideas that have informed our work which, in the past, has also relied greatly on intuition, clinical judgement, and personal experience.

The first part of the book explores the theoretical thinking relevant to this work, as well as the method of psychoanalytic observation and enquiry that is applied, and the technical aspects and problems that are encountered. The second part consists mainly of the clinical work with families of young children and it is organized around some common difficulties and problems typical of this age group. The last two chapters demonstrate how this type of work can be applied more widely in a consultation to a nursery school and to a telephone advice line for parents of young children.

Phantasy is spelt in this way throughout the book, to refer to the psychoanalytic concept of an unconscious phantasy in contrast to fantasy, which is used to indicate a conscious process.

Names, locations, and other circumstances have been changed to preserve confidentiality as best as possible.

CHAPTER ONE

The importance of infant observation in under fives' counselling

The infant observation method was first introduced by the Polish psychoanalyst Esther Bick in 1948. It consists of weekly observations of an infant and his or her mother within the home environment from birth to the end of the second year of life. It is now a well-established method by which we can learn about the development of the child's mind, his emotional and cognitive life, his personality, and interactions (Bick, 1964; Lubbe, 1996; Magagna, 1987; Miller et al., 1989; Perez-Sanchez, 1968; Pontecorvo, 1986; Reid, 1997; Winnicott, 1941). Infant observation is an essential tool in training child and adult psychoanalysts and psychotherapists, as well as other professionals who are involved in human relationships. It studies the emergence of archaic and unconscious body and mind states, of feelings and emotions, and of needs and communication, at their very origins. It also opens the observer's inner eye to his or her own emotional responses to what is being observed. The observer is in the active position of being emotionally receptive and tuned in to the actions, the atmosphere, and the feelings of the people observed. At the same time, the observer learns to refrain from action and to pose him or herself as a friendly and benevolent presence, ready to receive whatever the family offers, in terms of both verbal communication and the intimacy of family life that revolves around the infant. A space is created in the observer's mind to give a home to the detailed scenario, with the baby and his surroundings at the centre. Meanings gradually emerge from the repeated patterns that are observed in the mother–infant interactions, as a result of some essential attitudes of the observer.

Firstly, there is the "negative capability", as the Romantic poet Keats, in a letter to his brother, defined the attitude that bears uncertainties, not knowing, and the anxiety about new and unpredictable situations. In this frame of mind the observer does not act but witnesses events (Keats, 1952). Secondly, there is the capacity to identify with the many people who are present during the observations; for example, the hungry baby, the jealous sibling, the competitive father, the exhausted mother, the interfering grandparents, as well as the supportive figures in the family scenario.

This capacity for many and almost simultaneous identifications, is what Bion called "binocular vision" and "multiple vertices". Meltzer clarified this concept as being "the natural mode of experience of an individual, who by contact with different parts of his personality, is able to identify with different roles in human interaction and perception" (Meltzer, 1978, p. 6). The capacity to be familiar with one's own different aspects enables the observer to take up the different points of view of the characters in the observations. At the beginning of his observation, an observer developed a great capacity to identify with the infant, but failed to identify with the untidy mother, since he had declared himself to be a rather orderly person. As a result he lost the chance to observe that family. He unconsciously communicated his hostile and competitive feelings to the mother and this prompted her to stop the observation.

Observational skills and training are the foundations for working with families and small children. In the clinical part of the book, I will show that great fluidity in taking up different identifications is needed by the therapist.

An exciting aspect of the infant observation method is that the understanding of the developing emotional, mental, and interactive life of the infant, which is being inferred through pragmatic observations, is also being confirmed and corroborated by recent research and discoveries in neuroscience. Emotions and affects have important biological components, such as heart rate, blood pressure, respiratory rate, and glandular secretions, which can be observed and exist universally throughout human culture and even in preliterate cultures (Amini *et al.*, 1996). According to Ekman and Izard, the perception and expression of affect are "innate capacities and part of the genetic endowment from our phylogenetic heritage" (*ibid.*, pp. 214–215). This implies that feelings are not just subjective, internal experiences, but have complex, physiological processes rooted in the history of human evolution. Affects have a survival function of communication, as we can observe in babies within their families as well as in studies in the laboratory, through the analysis of mother–infant video recordings (Beebe, 1982; Stern, 1971). The intensity, subtlety, and effectiveness of the communication of a baby, who turns away from mother's intrusive gaze, or screams to draw her attention to his needs, is as powerful as the lack of any emotional expression in the depressed or autistic infant, who is dead to the world of feelings.

A sharp observer can begin to weave the thread of a family story even from the first encounter with the family in the waiting room of the clinic. Worries and feelings about coming to the clinic with a problem child, the problem itself that has prompted the parents to seek help, and the main family dynamics are often displayed in the waiting room through facial expressions, body postures, general demeanour, and activities. The following vignette illustrates this idea and emphasizes the value of observation in work with the under fives.

The family had arrived a few minutes early for their first appointment. The therapist introduces herself in the waiting room and invites them to go with her. She notices that mother and father are sitting next to each other on armchairs. Father holds a baby in his arms while mother slouches passively and looks distant and withdrawn. The three-year-old boy, referred for his aggressive and unmanageable behaviour, sits at some distance on the floor by the toy cupboard and turns his back to his family and the room. It takes them a long time to gather themselves together. Father tries to convince the boy to put the toys away and talks patiently and firmly to him. Mother looks as if she has given up. The boy eventually complies and they all follow the therapist along the corridor to the therapy room, with the solemnity of a religious procession. The impression of a depressed mother, a very involved father, and an angry and stubborn toddler is what the therapist has gathered from a photographic view of this family in the waiting room. The impression gained through the initial observation of the family dynamics and behaviour in the waiting room is later confirmed in the course of the session.

Working with under fives, whether in the first or last session, relies greatly on the observation and understanding of the here and now. The therapist elicits an account of the problems, concerns, symptomatic behaviour, and the child's early history as well as the parents' own experiences in their families of origin. The therapist also sharpens his or her attention to and observation of the nuances of the child's play and the interactions with the parents, the siblings and *vice versa*. As it appears appropriate, one can just listen silently, or offer a descriptive commentary of the emotions, fears, worries, and conflicts that are expressed by the family members, or can make links with what is being recounted.

Interest, curiosity and a capacity to observe are paramount in this work, as in all psychological work. The receptive and non-intervening role of the observer during the infant observation can influence the parents' curiosity and interest in their own baby as well as lead to many other, useful realizations. For example, a couple who had been observed with their baby for two years by a Swiss psychologist, decided to pursue marital therapy as a result of the observation experience. The experience of observing, absorbing, and processing the family scenario, often has a greater therapeutic function than one may imagine, before one embarks on an infant observation.

CHAPTER TWO

Outlines of psychodynamic under fives' counselling and theoretical background

Introduction

The model I describe in this book is based on the Under Fives' Counselling Service founded at the Tavistock Clinic in the eighties. It is rooted in the belief, the experience, and knowledge that early intervention has a curative, as well as a preventative, effect. The emotional difficulties of young children are expressed in physical and behavioural symptoms that are closely linked with the developmental phases of infancy and early childhood. Parents come to Child and Family Psychiatric Clinics or consult child psychotherapists privately with a variety of complaints. We encounter infants who do not feed, cry incessantly or never settle into a sleep pattern. We see children who do not learn to talk, cannot be toilet-trained, refuse to separate from their mother or do not settle at playgroup. We also see children who are hyperactive, violent, isolated or excessively shy.

The Under Fives' Counselling Service offers up to five sessions to the parents and child, who can refer themselves to the clinic directly or be referred by their health visitors or doctors. Most of the families I discuss in the book have been seen in N.H.S. services or privately in

England and abroad. The therapeutic model is also rather flexible (Miller, 1992), as it reflects and adapts to the needs of families of this age group. Flexibility and improvisation are often required by parents to deal with the intensity of passions and urgency of needs of their under fives. Similarly, although it is preferable to meet the whole family and work with both parents, the counselling accommodates individual needs of attendance and frequency. The gap between sessions also varies according to the needs of each family and such issues are carefully explored together with the therapist.

The symptomatology of infancy and early childhood usually has a particular poignancy and can cause great distress, anxiety, confusion, and discomfort to parents and carers. Infancy is a vulnerable age and small children, being malleable and open to the world without having strong defences, are easily affected by what happens to them. They are still not equipped to defend themselves and are totally reliant on those adults around them for appropriate protection and adequate parenting. Therefore a prompt intervention is required when this age group is in need. Early intervention, even in a few encounters, can resolve the presenting difficulties and unblock complex situations. It can prevent things from getting worse or becoming entrenched or, when necessary, it can open the situation up to other therapeutic interventions. To respond to parents in need, often at the end of their tethers, quickly mobilizes a therapeutic alliance. When motivation is high, emotional availability and openness are also at their utmost. It is heartening to see how many families can benefit from short counselling and can strive to keep to the number of sessions initially offered.

Theoretical influences on under fives' counselling

In this section, I explore some of the theoretical ideas that have inspired my particular style of work and on which the model of under fives' counselling is based.

Melanie Klein

Melanie Klein, together with Anna Freud and Donald Winnicott, was a pioneer in the psychoanalytic understanding and treatment of children. Her ideas were clearly influenced by Freud's theory of childhood sexuality, which was confirmed in his treatment-by-proxy of Little Hans (Freud, 1909a). Klein traced the emotional development of the child back to birth and introduced interesting concepts regarding two major developmental emotional phases in the child's first year of life. The first few months are dominated by extreme states. On the one hand there is body–mind pleasure, satisfaction, bliss, and tranquillity and on the other are extreme states of unhappiness, fear, terror, pain, confusion, and need. The infant relates to separate aspects of the mother and of the world around. The mother, or the person who cares for the infant and satisfies his or her needs and requests, is perceived as a good person. However, when the infant's needs are not responded to immediately, the mother is seen as a bad person. The infant does not recognize these opposite versions of the maternal figure as belonging to the same and whole person. The infant also relates to aspects of the maternal care or to parts of the mother's body separately, as if they did not belong to the same and whole person. Klein called this phase of infantile emotional development "paranoid–schizoid", since its main purpose is the survival of the infant in a confusing, contradictory, split, unknown world where extremes are not integrated. Threats and dangers hover around and within the infant and fragmentation and disintegration shake the powerless and totally dependent child. During normal development, in the second part of the first year of life, the child achieves some sort of integration where the maternal figure is recognized as one whole person, who can be both the satisfying and the frustrating mother. The child develops concern and longing for the mother, and these feelings are unknown in the hell-or-heaven states of the infant. This phase of emotional development Klein named "depressive", a term that should not be confused with depression. By "depressive position" (Klein, 1935) Klein meant a state of mind characterized by a preoccupation for the survival and welfare of the other person or "object" and by a responsibility for one's own feelings.

Klein's discovery of the existence of an unconscious phantasy (Klein, 1952a, 1959) being present in any bodily and mental activity is another useful tool which can be used to understand the evolving mind and body of the child. In the feeding situation, the infant, who sucks the nipple to satisfy an instinctual need, also performs a mental activity. The activity regards the contact of the mouth with the nipple, the flow of milk in the mouth and stomach, the feeling of satisfaction and the contact of the cheek with the warm breast or the tactile feel of the soft breast or clothes. All this becomes compounded in a good experience which, when it is repeated many times, establishes itself and is internalized inside the child. Equally, if the instinctual needs are not satisfied, the physical and psychological discomfort of the empty mouth and stomach are accompanied by the mental impressions of something bad and hurtful happening inside the infant. The mind and the body are an undifferentiated whole at this early stage. Freud wrote of bodily ego (Freud, 1923) and Isaacs of a "... single undifferentiated experience of sucking and phantasising" (Isaacs, 1948, p. 92n).

From these early unconscious phantasies based on parts of objects, the child progresses to phantasies of characters interacting and behaving according to his emotional age. For example, the phantasies of a generous and kind mother or a cruel, abandoning one, give way to phantasies of siblings stealing the goodness from the child, who may be wanting to keep mother all for himself. The rivalrous father may also gang up and exclude the child from the treasure. Successful hunts to discover the buried richness representing the good mother, may confirm the toddler's sense of potency. Unconscious phantasies inhabit the child's world like real stories on a theatre stage or painted on a wall, as in prehistoric cave paintings. In pretending to be different characters in his phantasies, the boy may act as the glorious knight who defeats the enemies and conquers the imprisoned princess kept in a tower. Meanwhile the girl may escape the witch mother and bad sisters to finally meet the prince, who will marry her, as fairy tales tell us. In their phantasies children get rid of unpleasant and unwanted aspects of themselves and pretend to be someone else, even if only an ordinary mum or dad and not just an ideal or heroic figure. Klein called these mechanisms splitting and projective identification and assumed that they are part of normal development. We can say that these mechanisms are necessary to foster the capacity to put oneself in other people's shoes, to empathize with and to understand our fellow human beings. These mechanisms are linked to that of role reversal, often observed in small children, for example, the child who pretends to be the nursery teacher telling his mum or dad, now turned into children, which puzzle to do, or the patient who makes the therapist the hungry baby, while he or she acts as the feeding mother in charge.

Guilt and reparation are two other extremely useful ideas upon which Klein expanded. The mind can be in an anguished state of conflict and, according to the stage of emotional development, Klein talks of persecutory or depressive guilt. Parents may believe that they have a bad and naughty child who is not growing up according to plan. They feel they have done everything right and it is the child who is to blame. Other parents are very contemptuous and angry for not having been treated well by professionals, whom they blame for their child's unhappiness and difficulties. The disposition of mind that Klein called paranoid–schizoid is based on the early mechanism of splitting and projection: the subject is good and right, while badness resides in the other person. These parents usually feel the guilt so intensely and so punishingly that they have to rid themselves of it, by depositing it in their child or into the professionals, in order not to be overwhelmed by it. It is only with emotional maturity that guilt becomes more bearable and takes the shape of a wish to put things right in oneself and in one's child. Parents, who humbly feel they need help and new ways of thinking and dealing with their small children to ameliorate their family life, are in the mental disposition that Klein called depressive. This implies a sense of guilt, a real concern, and a curiosity to explore different ways and skills in parenting children in order to help them and to take responsibility for change. We will see how the parental couple usually presents both these states of mind and types of guilt, at least in a small amount. The presence of a depressive sense of guilt and disposition of mind allows change to occur and the therapeutic work to become effective.

Wilfred Bion

The notion of container and contained introduced by Bion (Bion, 1962a) is the cornerstone of my therapeutic work and also applies to under fives' counselling. It implies an emotional experience between the mother and her infant, where the mother is in touch with and open to receive the infant's states of mind, sensations, and feelings of any sort, without being submerged in them. Maternal reverie, which Winnicott called holding, is the attitude of being able to feel and think of the feelings, needs, and states of the infant and then to act accordingly by providing an emotional, not just a practical response. When things go well and the mother is not too overwhelmed by her own infantile needs and guilt, and is well supported by her husband and family, she is able to receive and process inside herself all that her baby demands of her and communicates to her. She can respond to the baby in a way that conveys her understanding and this satisfies the baby's psychological and physical needs. Bion used the feeding relationship as the prototype of any interaction between mother and infant, or of any two people where there is an emotional exchange. When this exchange happens many times, a good experience is established safely inside the baby and this fosters growth by nourishing both the body physically and the mind psychologically.

In the families described in this book, the container–contained function of the mother, or more widely speaking of the parental couple, is somehow lacking, due to a variety of circumstances, and the healthy development of the child has been interrupted. Through the experience of an understanding therapist, who acts as a container for the family's distress and disturbance, a transformation can be achieved and the obstacles to the child's growth removed.

According to Bion, thinking can develop and learning from experience can occur through this container–contained function. An infant, who has experienced understanding and satisfaction over and over again, grows an idea that goodness exists and is available. Therefore the infant becomes progressively able to withstand longer moments of absence of that good experience and can rely on the certainty that it will return. We can often see this in the observations of babies and their mothers within the family context. The infant learns from experience that needs are satisfied and he or she can tolerate a temporary absence and begin to imagine the return of the satisfying mother. However, when things do not go well, the child does not take in the experience of a good provider being available. The child will rely more and more on his own devices including his body. He may freeze, tense up or move excessively in the attempt to hold himself together, or to evacuate unpleasant sensations. The child can also perpetuate being in a state of mental omnipotence and omniscience, states that are part of normal development and are a defence from the dependence, vulnerability, and separateness that cannot yet be tolerated by the immature psyche.

Children can get stuck in believing that they can do and know everything, beyond the age when the reality of their separateness and dependence on the adult should be accepted. The tough, intimidating, tattooed father of a three-year-old girl confessed in a family session that she was acting as an extremely powerful and frightening "monster". Bion proposed that when omnipotence and omniscience predominate, reality is not seen for what it is, and true and false are confused and not discriminated (Bion, 1967, p. 114). In the example above this led to a mad state of unreality in which the three-year-old ruled the family and a reversal of values and roles occurred. The child's unconscious hooked onto the father's unconscious need and what followed was an inability on the adult's part to understand the child's communication and to put it into perspective. The therapist is trained to experience emotionally the chaotic communications or projections from the family unit, to make sense of them, and to be able to give words to them, transforming a previously distorted state into true feelings.

Painful and undigested emotional traumas from the parents' past can re-emerge, and prevent them from acting towards their children with what Bion called "common sense". The intimidating father, who was terrified by his three-year-old daughter, had never overcome his childhood terrors. He himself had been terrorized by his parents' violence towards each other but had never been able to talk about it. His defiant, provocative, and boundary-testing three-year-old had reminded him of his impotence as a child in the past and he could not deal with her in the present. He feared becoming violent himself and the only way he knew of dealing with her was to give in to her demands and wishes. He now defended against the unbearable psychic pain he had experienced in his childhood by having tugs-of-wars with his daughter. Neither he nor she was any longer a parent and a child, as reality had become distorted in this family.

The painful, unconscious conflicts that can emerge in this short counselling can be tolerated through the help offered. Bion wrote:

> ... the implicit aim of psycho-analysis to pursue the truth at no matter what cost is felt to be synonymous with a claim to a capacity for containing the discarded, spilt-off aspects of other personalities while retaining a balanced outlook. [Bion, 1967, p. 88]

This sums up the parental function and the therapeutic role performed by the analyst once such function has not occurred in the patient's family.

Donald Winnicott

Winnicott has inspired me in my work with small children and their parents. A number of aspects of his work are particularly relevant to under fives' counselling. Winnicott was at great ease in talking to children and parents and was a skilled observer of the infant/child–mother dyad. The psychic unit of the child–mother dyad particularly interested him through his working life. He trained and worked as a paediatrician and a psychoanalyst during which time he saw innumerable infants and children with their mothers. Winnicott combined his medical and psychological insight and vast knowledge in the most creative way, building up an enormous experience in treating many problems, most of which are still extremely relevant in bringing up children today. He developed a unique way of assessing symptoms associated with the child–mother dyad and of talking to children and of assisting parents in the difficult task of rearing children. The fact that he addressed mainly mothers in his work probably reflects his cultural and historical era. Fathers were far less involved in childcare and were busy earning a living for the family or fighting for their country.

Small children often use the body to express mental states of discomfort and so the combination of paediatrics and psychoanalysis is a particularly fortuitous one. Winnicott was in a unique and privileged position to deepen our understanding and treatment of illnesses and symptoms.

The spatula technique extensively described by Kahr (1996) permitted Winnicott (1941) to make a rapid diagnosis and treatment in the case of seven-month-old Margaret who suffered from asthmatic wheezing. Winnicott used to place the spatula or tongue depressor within reach of the baby and observed her response.

> ... Margaret spent a full five minutes of hesitation before reaching out for the object. During this important period of observation, Winnicott noticed not only Margaret's reluctance to grasp at the spatula but also the way in which her mother clasped her hands

around the child's chest. He became very aware of how Margaret developed a bronchial spasm during the period of hesitation in reaching for the desired object. When Margaret finally did approach the spatula and take hold of it, the asthmatic wheezing disappeared. [Kahr, 1996, pp. 335–336]

After that single consultation, the baby no longer suffered from asthma, but her mother became bronchially asthmatic. Already in 1941, when this event occurred, we can see a form of parent–infant psychotherapy in embryo. Winnicott pioneered the idea of parental projection, which has recently become a widely accepted way of looking at some of children's psychological difficulties. In Margaret's case he illustrated very powerfully how infants and children become the vessel of their parents' symptoms and unresolved conflicts.

Winnicott was a courageous man who fostered great freedom in parents. He believed that it was necessary to be aware of one's hatred towards one's own children or towards patients, in the case of psychoanalysts and psychotherapists. The hatred does no harm as long as there is awareness of it. What is deeply harmful, Winnicott wrote, is the effect of the repressed or unconscious death wish towards the baby, as it is beyond the baby's capacity to deal with it and it may lead to autism or infantile schizophrenia (Shepherd et al., 1996). In *Therapeutic Consultations in Child Psychiatry* (Winnicott, 1971, pp. 12–27) Winnicott introduced the squiggle technique. He would draw a line with closed eyes and then invite the child patient to turn that line into whatever he wanted. They took it in turns to start and to complete the pictures. This put the child at great ease and revealed what was nearest to his heart and concern. Nine-year-old Iiro communicated immediately his infirmity which he had inherited from his mother. In the session with mother alone, she admitted to having hated and rejected her son when he was born and she saw his deformed fingers. She only began to accept him when she made plans to repair the damage at any cost. She persisted in submitting him to many operations with the unrealistic hope of repairing the deformity completely. She ended up loving him more than her other children to compensate for the original hatred. Both mother and child benefited from their single and separate encounters with Winnicott. Mother modified her unrealistic expectations and the boy became free to live his life.

The expression of negative feelings that took the form of overcompensation in Iiro's mother was reduced. Her hatred for her child had to become conscious before she could adopt a healthier and realistic view of the situation.

By giving permission to parents to feel negative emotions and not just love towards their children, the risk of acting out hatred or violence is greatly reduced and the child is allowed freedom to exist. In under fives' counselling, parents are given permission to feel and to talk about their negative and ambivalent feelings towards their children. The therapist does not blame the parents, but accepts their feelings.

Other influential approaches

Short psychodynamic psychotherapy

The history of short psychoanalytic treatment is as old as psychoanalysis itself. Freud treated some of his early patients like Anna O., Dora, and The Rat Man (Breuer & Freud, 1983–1995; Freud, 1905, 1909b) for a limited period of time. He obtained permanent improvements despite the seriousness of the symptomatology at the onset of treatment. Later on he became preoccupied with the interminability of some analysis (Freud, 1937) and, as Malan reported (Malan, 1975, p. 14), experimented setting an ending to the treatment in the case of "The Wolf Man" (Freud, 1918). He was dealing with individual adults, as were Ferenczi, Balint, and Malan who, too, had an interest in pursuing the study and research into Brief and Focal Psychotherapy.

Ferenczi was interested in shortening psychoanalytic treatments and wrote papers on this topic, but later abandoned this project.

Balint, who pioneered focal, psychoanalytic therapy with individuals, was keen to extend the favourable outcome of long-term psychotherapy to a wider number of people for whom long-term psychotherapy was not possible. He, together with a group of psychoanalysts, set up to explore and research brief psychotherapy. The outcome of their research is part of a book (Malan, 1975). The authors found out that focal work required enthusiasm and an active stance on the part of the analyst as well as a capacity to formulate "circumscribed therapeutic plans" (Malan, 1975, p. 277).

The patient suitable for this treatment has to be highly motivated to explore feelings and able to relate easily, so that a relationship with the therapist can be established quickly. Moreover, in the authors' view, the patient has to be able to mourn, and to bear sad feelings. The workshop found out that, technically, even severe and long-standing psychopathologies could benefit from brief, focal therapy and that transference interpretations were essential from the beginning. In my model of under fives' counselling, I elaborate on some of these ideas such as the transference interpretation and the patient's capacity to mourn. I have found out that transference interpretations are necessary and essential tools, especially in the case of the patients who have negative feelings towards the clinic and the therapist.

In the next section, I will consider short-term psychotherapy in the work with infants or small children and their parents.

Parent–infant psychotherapy

Under fives' counselling is inspired by the ideas and findings of clinicians who founded and developed psychodynamic psychotherapy with parents and small children.

In 1975, Selma Fraiberg and co-workers wrote the seminal paper, "Ghosts in the nursery: a psychoanalytic approach to the problems of impaired infant–mother relationship", which was to become the manifesto of parent–infant psychotherapy. She believed that the repetition of the parents' past childhood experience of violence, abuse, and neglect persisted but the affect, i.e. the emotional experience of such events, had undergone repression. The parent repeats the past, "identifies with the aggressor of the past" (Fraiberg, 1975, p. 194) and acts it out with his or her baby/child in the present. The ghosts from the past inhabit the nursery. It is through the re-experience—in the present, therapeutic context—of the early anxieties, sufferings, and feelings that the parent becomes emotionally re-connected with the affects of the original experience. He or she is freed of the repetition of the past and becomes able to identify with a protector figure and to become a loving parent for his or her own child.

Stern (1998), Brazelton and Cramer (1991) have combined child development with a psychoanalytic approach that focuses on the parental representational world, projected into the infant. It is a form of therapy that utilizes both a Freudian model for treating neuroses, not major affective disorders or character disorders (Stern, 1998, pp. 121–124), and attachment theory with its different patterns of attachment. The therapeutic gain is to modify such internal representations and projections both by an understanding of these interactions and by providing an experience of an alternative, good parental figure in the person of the doctor, i.e. by a positive transference to the therapist (*ibid.*, p. 125). It is a valuable model that has been shown to achieve changes in a relatively short period of time, as Stern reports in his book, *The Motherhood Constellation* (Stern, 1998). However, in my view, it lacks the richness and the depth of the unconscious phantasies, that populate the worlds of children and parents and can become alive in the therapeutic setting as child psychotherapists inform us. They give much attention to the child's inner world, to the parents' projections, and also to the negative transference (Acquarone, 2002; Baradon, 2002; Barrows, 1999; Brafman, 2001; Daws, 1997; Gallo, 1997; Hopkins, 1992; Miller, 1992).

Stern acknowledges the difference between the Geneva group and the San Francisco group with Fraiberg, who "rely on post-Freudian psychoanalytic models" and have evolved a model "better designed for treating character disorders, affective disorders, and even psychosis". Their clinical cases are "more like cases from the British object relation school, [...] who treat borderline patients" (*ibid.*, p. 124). He suggests that the Geneva clinical cases belong to a more advantaged social group and are mostly "intact nuclear families of middle socio-economic status, who seek psychotherapy of their own volition". In his book he does not mention the contribution of child psychotherapy from the London schools to parent–infant psychotherapy.

Manzano and Palacio-Espasa (1998) think similarly to Cramer and Stern regarding the maternal negative pre-transference, which is seen as a counter-indication for short psychotherapy. However, they differ on the issue of the maternal, psychodynamic, mental configuration, as they call it. They believe that the mothers who do best at short psychotherapy, are the ones for whom the birth of the baby—who will become the referred patient—brings new hope to deny the loss of an object they had not been able to mourn. The baby becomes a sort of substitute for the mother's lost object. On the other hand, the mother who does not try to regain a lost object through her baby, but tries to expel some unwanted part of herself into the baby, as she feels paranoid about that part, is not a good candidate for short therapy. This finding is in line with my own experience of the family depressive mental disposition versus a paranoid–schizoid disposition. In the section on Klein, I have mentioned parents' different attitudes: some want to know more about their children's problems and how they can help to change things; others only need to blame the child or other people for such problems. The latter are indeed the hardest to treat and to alleviate from their burdens and pains.

Palacio-Espasa and Manzano's type of therapy is nearer to the one practised by child psychotherapists, who see the whole family and include the children in their observation and interpretative work. Psychoanalytic child psychotherapists are well trained and experienced in working with negative emotions and transference of both children and parents as well as with early psychotic and paranoid–schizoid states of mind. This model facilitates reaching deep layers of the mind in a short time and allows expression of primitive anxieties and fears within the transference relationship, often leading to lasting modification and improvement.

There are many other schools of thoughts and clinicians, who have contributed to the thinking and practice in the field of parent–infant and under fives' psychotherapy. In London there are: the School of Infant Mental Health; the Infant Mental Health Workshop at the Tavistock Clinic and also in Bristol and the Parent Infant Project at the Anna Freud Centre. I also want to mention the international and multi-cultural contributions from: Acquarone (2002), Ben-Aaron *et al.* (2001), Baradon (2002), Barrows (1999), Berg (2000), Blos (1985), Lebovici (1983), Norman (2001), Pawl & Lieberman (1997), Thomson-Salo & Paul (2001), Trad (1993) and Watillon (1993).

Attachment theory and family therapist John Byng-Hall

In 1969, John Bowlby introduced a new language and a specific way of looking at relationships, which stemmed from his psychoanalytic training. He wrote:

The understanding of the response of a child to a separation or loss of his mother-figure turns on an understanding of the bond that ties him to that figure. In psychoanalytic writings, discussion of this theme has been conducted in terms of object relations. Thus in any description of traditional theory the terminology of object relations must often be used; in the presentation of a new theory, however, terms such as "attachment" and "attachment figure" are preferred. [Bowlby, 1969, p. 177]

Holmes writes about the attachment theory as being, "essentially a spatial theory in which the care-seeker is constantly monitoring and adjusting his distance from the care-giver depending on the level of perceived anxiety and the strength of the drive to explore" (Holmes, 1993, p. 155).

Mary Ainsworth developed laboratory tests based on this theory (Ainsworth *et al.*, 1971). The "strange situation" is designed to evoke and then categorize attachment behaviours. Twelve-month-old children are separated from their mother figure for two brief moments and then are left in an unfamiliar laboratory with an unfamiliar person and observed at moments of separation from, and reunion with, their mothers. Three different groups of attachment were initially observed. The securely attached child protests at separation, but searches for mother's comfort at reunion and is quickly consoled and can let go of her easily. The insecure/avoidant child does not appear bothered when mother leaves and turns away from her at reunion. The insecure/ambivalent child clings to mother, protests strongly at separation and is inconsolable at reunion. Ainsworth later introduced a fourth group of attachment, the insecure/disoriented type. This child has no coherent response in the "strange situation" and may feel threatened by his mother, hence he both approaches and avoids her. (Ainsworth *et al.*, 1978).

Main and colleagues devised an Adult Attachment Interview (AAI), which explores the parents' childhood experience of attachment to their respective parental figures. They found that in 78–80% of cases the type of parental attachment predicts their children's attachment to them (George *et al.*, 1996; Main *et al.*, 1985).

At present I am not using the AAI in the counselling of the under fives. However, the attachment categories inform both my diagnostic thinking, when I gather the parents' family histories, and my therapeutic interactions, when I draw parallels between the parents' past experiences as children and their present experiences with their own children.

John Byng-Hall developed and used the attachment theory in his family work and has adopted a model that encompasses systemic and psychodynamic family therapy (Byng-Hall, 1986). He has come to see the referred patient's symptoms as something that has evolved to regulate the relationship between parents, i.e. by bringing them together when they have drifted away, or by getting in between them if their closeness has become dangerous. This explains familiar situations seen in under fives' counselling. A child's problem can be a reflection of either a difficult relationship with the child's internal object or of an unconscious parental way of expressing their early attachment. Often it may lead to the problem in the child and may cover up marital disharmony. For example, a father who was uncomfortable with his relationship with his mentally unstable wife had encouraged a close Oedipal relationship with his four-year-old daughter, excluding mother. However, the child had become unmanageable and thus attracted the adults' attention to their marital unhappiness. It frequently occurs that, once the child's symptomatic behaviour subsides in the course of counselling sessions, the parents are faced with having to look at their relationship closely. In my experience, it is not uncommon for parents to decide to undertake individual or marital therapy after ending the under fives' counselling work.

My work with the under fives has also been influenced by Byng-Hall's concept of family scripts. Families tend to replicate or correct old scripts, i.e. "the family's shared expectations of how family roles are to be performed within various contexts". Alternatively, they improvise new scripts of family life.

> Often family members see things differently and vary in their wish to change the pattern either now or in the next generation. For example children vow to themselves to follow different patterns when they become parents. No one, however, acts in a way that successfully breaks the current pattern. Hence, family expectations of what will happen, remain the same. [Byng-Hall, 1995, p. 4]

Parents often talk about their own parents. For example, a mother who had a violent father tried to resist being put in a similar position by her unmanageable four-year-old daughter. However, for fear of repeating a similar story of violence with her child, she could not have ordinary boundaries with her. Father on his part, wanted to perpetuate the permissive relationship he had with his father and the self-idealized position he had occupied amongst his siblings. He maintained this old script, to use Byng-Hall's phrase, and colluded with his wife's difficulties and unconsciously encouraged their daughter's rebelliousness.

Children play-act the roles of being mum, dad or the younger baby. It helps them to express their unconscious phantasies, wishes, anxieties, frustrations, and feelings of dependency, rivalry, and smallness. However, when these roles extend out of the play arena and into family relationships and the child really acts and becomes the parentified adult, leaving the parent to be the incapable and impotent child, then something has gone wrong. It is at this point that some parents ask for help. Children with insecure, ambivalent or disorganized patterns of attachment have parents who are unpredictable and unavailable to the child's needs. The child becomes the one who constantly watches out for the parent's reaction and presence and who adapts his own needs to those of the parents. It is a topsy-turvy world where the parentified child supports, comforts or stimulates the parent. In the language of object-relations, the child's unconscious, omnipotent phantasies of both control and dominance over the adult, or of magic resolution of painful feelings and conflicts become reality and take over family life. In addition, parental projections of anxiety, phantasies, expectations or experiences combine with their children's phantasies. For example, in the case of the sexually abused father who saw in his young daughter his own abusing grandmother, he was unable to have any firm authority with her.

It is through the patient and sensitive work of unravelling intergenerational attachment patterns and object-relations, that freedom is given back to the child and the family through the establishment of new and healthier object relations and models of identification.

The contribution of the neurosciences to under fives' counselling

Frances Tustin was a pioneer in the psychoanalytic treatment of children with autism and was well aware that she was dealing with very primitive mental states. Autism, in her view, implied the absence of both a mind and an ego. She treated these early proto-mental states, in which mind and body are recognized to be a whole and to be very closely interdependent on each other. In her latest thinking, Tustin formulated the hypothesis that autism was a defensive reaction to a precocious separation from the suckling mother at a time when the infant had not yet developed either a mental or a neuro-physiological apparatus to deal with such trauma (Tustin, 1994). She was a pioneer in her intuitions and thinking about the undeveloped neurological apparatus, and in her wish for more knowledge and research, that was soon to become available in the field of neuroscience. She lived and worked on the edge of a new and exciting era, in which neurosciences were beginning to flourish and to build bridges between our understanding of the development and growth of the human brain, the world of emotions, and the patterns of attachment behaviour in children. Perhaps we are now re-discovering, with research-based evidence, the wholeness of the human person, versus the duality of mind and body, of emotions/phantasies and brain, which has characterized the western world and philosophies since Cartesian times.

The findings of neuroscientists such as Schore, Perry, and Amini are extremely relevant to under fives' counselling in its aim to integrate emotional disturbances and physical symptoms through an early intervention in the child–parent relationship and interactions.

A number of authors have studied affects, their location in the brain, their origin and functions, and how early, interactive emotional patterns are imprinted in the brain of infants and small children. I will not discuss the details of brain physiology and anatomy, but would recommend an explanatory paper by Amini *et al.* (1996). In short, affects are complex physiological processes, with their roots in evolutionary history, which perform functions that enhance survival, fitness, and communication. Developmental psychologists have studied babies using videos, and psychotherapists have used direct observations. They have shown that, from birth, babies have an extraordinary competence in communicating with their mothers in non-verbal ways. Babies can recognize and discriminate between different facial expressions within the first few days of life and are sensitive and responsive to facially expressive signals in their mothers (Brazelton *et al.*, 1975; Field *et al.*, 1982; Miller *et al.*, 1989). They regulate the relationship either by turning away when they feel impinged upon by their mother's gaze and affectivity (Fraiberg, 1982; Stern, 1977; Trevarthen, 1984; Tronick, 1989), or by stimulating a maternal response, as in the case of depressed mothers (Cooper & Murray, 1997).

Recent "attachment research suggests that social mammals and therefore human beings, regulate each other's neuro-physiology and alter the internal structure of each other's nervous systems through the synchronous exchange of affects" (Amini *et al.*, 1996, p. 229). It is at a very early time in the infant's life "that implicit memories of the experience of the attachment relationship are laid down, ... encoded and stored ... in a process that may be somehow analogous to the learning of motor skills" (*ibid.*, p. 229). This implies that in later life people enact the attachment patterns based on their early experience without having conscious knowledge of why they do so. The adult attachment interview confirms this idea (Main *et al.*, 1985) and shows that parents tend to repeat the same or similar patterns of attachment with their children as they themselves experienced as children. Early "attachment relationships, transacted in the universal language of affect, result in the establishment of an enduring neural structure in implicit memory that exerts a long-lasting influence on emotional self-regulation and behaviour related to relatedness" (Amini *et al.*, 1996, p. 284). In object relational language, we could say that the infant's experience of being understood, satisfied, and contained by the parental object or figure becomes internalized and somehow sets the way for the child to learn to relate to people. In contrast, the experience of an inadequate attachment figure or of object relations that are lacking will result in an inner structure incapable of self-regulation and an incapacity to contain one's emotions and to manage conflicts appropriately.

The well-known phenomenon described by psychoanalysts as "repetition compulsion" and ascribed to intra-psychic conflicts, also has a neuro-biological component. Individuals become attached to those attachment figures in the present who are similar to those of the past and have affected the neural structure of the brain and become encoded in memory (*ibid.*, p. 231).

Schore linked the critical period of the maturation of the prefrontal cortex of the infant's brain, which is essential for the regulation of affects through life and spans between ten–twelve and sixteen–eighteen months, with the infant's early object relation with the mother which is: "indispensable to the development and organization of the psychic structure responsible for self-regulation and adaptation" (Schore, 1994, p. 27). Schore and colleagues' research confirms that the normal maturation of the brain, even as early as ten months of life, is "experience-dependent and directly influenced by the care-giver infant relationship" (ibid., p. 30).

Tustin spoke of the shock absorber function of the mother, who mediates the world of psychological and physiological experiences for her infant (1990, personal communication). Neuroscientists are well aware that at birth:

> the human organism is ill-equipped to cope with the variations and excitations of its new environment ... and it lacks the means of modulation of behaviour which is made possible by the development of the cortical control. The role of the higher structure is played by the mother: she is the child's auxiliary cortex. [Diamond, B. & Diamond, 1963 in Schore, 1994, p. 30]

It seems that psychoanalysts and neuroscientists are coming together on extremely relevant and basic issues about the development of the human mind and body.

Even the concept of the "black hole", which psychoanalysts refer to as a very early or primitive psychotic experience of catastrophic terrors, chaos, nothingness, of falling for ever and of leaking out (Grotstein, 1990; Tustin, 1972, 1986, 1990; Winnicott, 1954), now finds a corresponding place in the impairment of particular areas in the brain, which are involved in the maintenance of body images, visual images, and auditory sensations (Schore, 1994, p. 422). Schore examines the aetiology of borderline and narcissistic personalities from a neuro-physiological perspective, and links it to a pathogenic relationship with the care-giver, who cannot "mediate psychobiological state transitions in herself and her infant" (ibid., pp. 426–429). Both borderline and narcissistic personalities do not evolve neurologically, and their structural growth is stilted as result of a dyadic dysfunction between their care-giver and themselves in the first six months of life.

Perry *et al.* (1995) follow similar lines of thinking about the effects of the external environment and primary carers on the developing and maturing brain of the infant, focused on the effects of trauma during early infancy. The brain mediates threats and traumas with different responses of a neurobiological, neuroendocrine, and neuropsychological nature and the infant or the young child shows specific behavioural responses, which have a survival function. The first response to a traumatic or threatening event produces a state of fear or terror with hyper-arousal and increased body activities, such as heart rate and breathing and production of stress hormones. This is followed by a dissociative reaction in which the infant cuts off; stares with a glazed look and is generally inhibited and frozen. The production of stress-hormone inhibitors such as cortisol is also increased. This toxicity of the brain chemistry impairs the growth of the brain itself especially if there is a genetic, constitutional predisposition. Traumas affect the brain, which in turn affects the behaviour and the production of symptoms.

Possibility of changes in the brain

The brain is apparently a rather plastic organ and can continue being affected by experiences throughout life and therefore has the potential for change (Perry *et al.*, 1995; Schore, 1994).

The question of whether the child's internalized care-giver's regulatory functions can be changed and recreated in the course of a psychotherapeutic relationship, has received positive answers. Schore quotes a number of authors in support of the view that the treatment of the early right hemispheric attachment pathology involves the socio-affective experience-dependent development in the patient of an internalized image of the therapist that counters the one generated in interaction with an early "psychotoxic" mother (Schore, 1994, p. 466). This fairly recent way of thinking, which is based on the study of the brain and on the effect of psychotherapy on it, is extremely relevant to work with small children. Although changes can occur throughout life, permanent changes in the neurophysiology of the brain are most likely to occur at this young age. In my work, I am aware that the younger the children are when they are referred to us, the more likely it is that their brain will develop normally rather than abnormally through the perpetuation of depriving and traumatic circumstances.

Through the re-experience of the symptomatic behaviour, thought distortions, and emotional difficulties in the transference relationship with the therapist in the sessions, an emotional understanding and an alternative model of relating and parenting from those experienced in the child's life can be achieved. In this way a different object relation can become internalized and hopefully supersede old ones. Schore writes: "Advances in our understanding of the developmental neurobiology of corticolimbic regulatory structures now enable us to more precisely characterize the nature of such structural changes" (1994, p. 467). It appears that changes in affects and representations of self-and-object images that occur during psychotherapy, are not just a symptom removal but reflect structural changes of patterns in the patient's nervous system.

Moreover there are other very important aspects in any psychotherapeutic treatment. These include the analyst's reverie and intuition and unspoken bodily, affective, and atmospheric communications between patient and analyst, particularly with patients affected by early developmental disorders such as autism (Tustin, 1986). To speak about intuition and reverie has always been looked down on as a non-scientific approach to treatment. Nowadays, the neurosciences are providing a different view that supports the validity of such aspects of any therapeutic treatment. Schore and other authors propose that the "almost exclusive focus of research on verbal and cognitive rather than non-verbal and affective psychotherapeutic events has severely restricted our deeper understanding of the dyadic therapy process" (*ibid.*, p. 469). He suggests that studying only the left hemispheric activities cannot explain the "socioemotional disorders that arise from limitations of the right hemispheric affect regulation" (*ibid.*, p. 489). Chaos therapy is now beginning to study the psychotherapy processes and the chaotic dynamic states and mental control processes occurring during psychoanalytic psychotherapy sessions. "They conclude that certain therapeutic interventions perturb patients from the "incarceration" in certain pathological mental states, leading to healthier trajectories during and after psychotherapy" (*ibid.*, p. 470). During sessions with individual patients or with families, what brings a modification to the problem are both the intellectual and the emotional contact with either a parent or a child, when the therapist's interpretation touches or switches on something in the patient. It is extremely valuable to learn that, even in the brain, changes are also happening.

I have often been asked whether the improvements seen in my work are maintained or if relapses occur. I can say with some confidence, based on long-term follow-up sessions with families, that when a real emotional realization has occurred, the changes are maintained and new symptoms do not replace the original ones. The changes occur within the parent–child relationship and the vicious circle of parental projections and past pathological experiences is interrupted. It is not only the parent's deep-seated problems and personality that are modified, but the relationship with their children.

The emotional availability and receptivity of the mother to her infant also appears to have a neural substrate. Neuroscientists describe a right hemisphere–right hemisphere transaction between mother and infant and *vice versa* (Schore, 1994, p. 463) that one can easily recognize in the unconscious disposition that Bion called "reverie" and Winnicott "maternal preoccupation". For example, Hammer, quoted by Schore (*ibid.*, p. 452) describes his mental and physical posture when seeing patients:

> leaning back, to let the mood, the atmosphere, come to me—to hear the meanings between lines, to listen for the music behind the words. As one gives oneself to being carried along by the affective cadence of the patient's session, one may sense its tone and subtleties. By being more open in this manner, to resonating to the patient I find pictures forming in my creative zones... An empathic channel appeared to be established which carried his state or emotion my way in a kind of affective "wireless". This channel, in turn, carried my image back to him, as he stood open in a special kind of receptivity. [Hammer, 1990, pp. 99–100]

Schore thinks that this kind of non-verbal communication between patient and therapist occurs between the right hemispheric orbitofrontal zones of them both and is the same process that occurs in the infant–care-giver psychobiologically attuned state.

Setting and technique

The setting

The under fives' counselling I describe is based on a psychoanalytic model and on some fundamental principles that are applicable to any psychoanalytic treatment. It also incorporates other thinking drawn from attachment theory and family therapy, such as the notion of the inter-generational transmission of patterns of attachment.

In *Beyond the Pleasure Principle*, Freud wrote that the aim of psychoanalysis was that "what was unconscious should become conscious". This was achieved by the patient free-associating and repeating in the transference relationship with the analyst, "the repressed material as a contemporary experience" (Freud, 1920, p. 18). The parents of referred children may already be aware of what is upsetting their relationship with their child. For example, the father of nine-month-old Ross knew of his hostility towards his baby. However, his unconscious rivalry had to be unburied in the family sessions, before he could give up battling with his baby.

The setting, in which the analytic encounter takes place and where problems emerge to be worked through with each individual patient or a whole family, is an essential part of any psychoanalytic treatment. I like to think of the setting as formed by the physical setting and by the mental setting of both the analyst and the patient's mind. First of all, I will define my setting with regard to the use of language. I refer to the child, the patient, and the psychotherapist in general, as male and I use psychoanalytic psychotherapist and analyst interchangeably. I am aware that different psychoanalytic groups and societies use different terms, with similar rigour in theoretical, professional, and ethical standards of training and practice. I take the liberty of using either term, when I refer to this work.

Another characteristic of psychoanalytical work is the absence of advice given to the patient. Freud said "we do not make use of direct suggestion in psychoanalytic therapy" (Freud, 1917c, p. 448) as this will stop the analyst from learning anything about the sense and the meanings of symptoms and will only have "a cosmetic effect", not a permanent improvement (*ibid.*, p. 250). In the work with under fives, the therapist does not prescribe or prohibit certain behaviours in the child or actions in the parents, but rather observes, tries to understand, and when appropriate, draws the parents' attention to his or her observations. This can move the parents' curiosity and spur them to a free associative mood. However, an indirect suggestion can be made after the original conflict or anxiety has been unveiled and alternative solutions may be discussed together with the parents. For example, the mentally and verbally hyperactive mother of a physically hyperactive three-year-old boy realized that at the root of her reactivity to her son lay a conflict with her mother. They had had an exclusive and symbiotic relationship with no space allowed to a third person, i.e. the father or a sibling. This realization made her think of a different way of relating to her child, facilitated by my input in the session. She held back and observed her boy before jumping into an explosive reaction every time he did something.

The physical setting

The consulting room used for psychoanalytic treatment has to be the same, modestly furnished, and well insulated to provide privacy and reliability. The toys provided for the child are kept in a box, which is entirely personal to that child. The time offered is usually around an hour for family work, although some flexibility is appropriate in working with small children. The first session may be longer than an hour to gather important family information, to establish some meaningful contact with at least one or more family members and to allow the family dramas to begin to unfold. Other sessions may be shorter, as was the case when a sudden episode of projectile vomiting managed to propel a family out of the room, despite the acceptance of this event on my part, followed by my interpretative work. These are extreme circumstances, more likely to occur with small children, when physical needs may take over the thinking space. However, as Dilys Daws suggests, persuading the family to stay in the room, and balancing the reality of urgent needs and requests, for example to leave the room even to go to the toilet, is an interesting issue which can be explored together in the session and can open up the family to difficult feelings (Daws, 1999, p. 265).

The physical boundaries of the room are there to be preserved, stretched, tested, and even broken. For example, in the case of a two-and-a-half-year-old boy affected by a rare, genetic, and badly handicapping disease, his father walked out of the therapy room in a rage. The father's acting-out was the prelude to a long wished-for parental separation, which turned out to be very painful, but also necessary for the growth of the whole family.

Another aspect of the physical setting is the possible presence of a co-therapist, a practice which some therapists have and which I occasionally adopt, for training purposes. Both therapists become part of the setting and need to be present for the entire treatment. In a follow-up session that took place six weeks after the satisfactory end of therapy, the registrar who had co-worked with me had by then left the clinic. The parents and myself were taken by surprise when, in the middle of that follow-up session, the little boy became rather pensive and, uncharacteristically, noticed that the person who had occupied the empty chair in the room, was not there. It was a reminder of the impact that small changes can have on children even when therapy has finished and some time has elapsed.

The mental setting

The analyst's mind

In my view, the attitude and state of mind of the analyst are the most important aspects of the therapeutic setting. They defy the boundaries as well as the nature and quality of the work and can also make up for possible lacking aspects in the physical setting. Bion advocated that the analyst be devoid of "memory and desire" (Bion, 1967) and open, receptive, and observant. The freedom from preconceptions, expectations, and feelings facilitates a genuine therapeutic relationship, because the analyst is in a position to tune into and to absorb the multitude of conflicts, concerns, and emotional turmoil with which he is presented. The function of the analyst is similar to that of the mother, who is receptive and open to receive and contain what her baby expresses in terms of bodily and psychological states and needs. The analyst picks up what is presented openly and also what is concealed and unconscious to the patient, and tries to make sense of it in his mind. The "reverie" (Bion, 1962b) or "holding" (Winnicott, 1960) that the analyst performs is an understanding that contains distress and that is processed silently in the mind. The analyst can then communicate back to the patient this understanding in different ways. At times, a simple descriptive comment or a question can help the patient, the family or one of its members to feel understood and to shift emotionally. At other times, it is enough for the analyst to have metabolized something, without having to express it. Communication happens at many levels, just like between a baby and a mother. Both detect unspoken cues and respond as if in a mutual dance (Stern, 1977).

Another type of communication is the verbal interpretation of conflicts expressed in the here and now of the therapeutic situation.

Freud in *Analytic Therapy* wrote: "In psychoanalysis we act upon the transference itself, resolve what opposes it, adjust the instrument with which we wish to make our impact" (Freud, 1917c, p. 451). In under fives' counselling, the analysis of the transference and countertransference is part of the work, a work that begins in the analyst's mind. I personally find it necessary to interpret possible negative feelings about coming to the clinic as soon as they are noticed. More examples of this are reported in the clinical section of this book.

The therapist becomes aware, not only of intra-personal and inter-personal conflicts, but also of the situation, which is re-enacted in the session, and of his own feelings and thoughts as a reaction to the situation. A tall, tattooed, truculent-looking man seen at the clinic late one Friday afternoon, when hardly anybody was around, disquieted a female therapist from his first appearance in the waiting room. The man had managed to project his feelings into those around him at home and also into the therapist in the clinic. She was able to address the man's fears, by understanding her own countertransference feelings rather than being overwhelmed by the fear. Eventually, the father revealed that he was scared of his puny, two-year-old daughter. She reminded him of his own powerlessness and fears as a child, when he had witnessed his violent parents fighting.

Finally, a thought about the analyst's versatility and availability to identify, just like the observer in infant observation, with many people and generations. Those who come to therapy sessions to play and to talk, are not just the children and the parents physically attending the sessions, but their internal objects in the form of grandparents, relatives, siblings, friends, teachers, and other relevant figures in their lives. To be able to step fast into identification with these different characters is an important skill and is a reminder of the psychotherapeutic work done with people with multiple personalities (Mollon, 1993; Sinason, 1994).

The patient's mind

The patient represents the third essential element of the setting. In under fives' counselling, the patient is the whole family unit, whether all members come for treatment or not. Absent members can still be in the minds of the ones who are present.

Over the years, I have come to accept for treatment families that present a severe psychopathology. In line with Malan's thinking, I have found that even parents with a history of psychiatric illness and paranoid features have benefited from under fives' counselling and have improved their relationship with their symptomatic children. Bonny's mother had suffered from repeated mental breakdowns before coming to the clinic with her husband and their uncontrollable four-year-old daughter. Mother was unable to look at me and felt a great deal of hostility towards me. She felt threatened by me as she had by other professionals. However, she wanted help for Bonny and it was through her husband that she could eventually change her way of being with Bonny and with me. He became the interpreter between us. It is necessary for at least one person in the couple, or even the child when both parents are resistant to thinking, to be somewhat receptive. At least a small part of the patient has to be in a depressive mental predisposition. It allows the patient to be interested in looking at himself and in understanding how things could be managed differently, without feeling too overwhelmed by guilt, self-blame or blame for others. Families usually arrive at the clinic with intense emotions of anxiety, confusion, and despair, having tried many other paths unsuccessfully. The accumulation of confused, raw experiences, and preoccupations is deposited into the analyst's mind to be disentangled in the session.

The point of contact with the patient can be via any of the adults or the child when the parents are stuck in an obstinate entanglement. For example, three-year-old Rosy helped the therapist to hold onto hope and meaning when she played with a ball. The ball popped in and away from behind her bottom, thus reproducing the situation of control she had in going or not going to the toilet. Rosy, with her extraordinarily appropriate play, provided an area of curiosity in the parents and an opening to the therapist's comments. Family therapists often see the child as the symptomatic person in a dysfunctional family, but it is often that child who manages to summon help for the whole family.

Transference and countertransference

Freud discovered the phenomenon of transference when, for the first time in 1895, he wrote about the patient being "frightened of finding that she is transferring onto the figure of the physician the distressing ideas, which arise from the content of the analysis. [...] Transference on to the physician takes place through *false connection*" (Breuer & Freud, 1893–1895, p. 302). Later in 1905, in a more elaborated view of transference, he wrote:

> They are new editions or facsimiles of the impulses and fantasies which are aroused and made conscious during the process of the analysis; but they have this peculiarity, which is characteristic for their species, that they replace some earlier person for the person of the physician. To put it in another way: a whole series of psychological experiences are revived, not as belonging to the past, but as applying to the person of the physician at the present moment. [Freud, 1905, p. 116]

At first Freud thought of transference as being a hindrance to the treatment but soon realized that it was "an inevitable necessity", which was not to be evaded but was to become the "most powerful ally [to psychoanalysis...] if its presence can be detected each time and explained to the patient" (*ibid.*, p. 17). He maintained that Dora's treatment was broken off prematurely because he did not understand her warning dream and did not master the transference in good time. He was certain that both loving and aggressive feelings were being transferred onto the therapist and that these feelings needed to be interpreted to the patient. Transference was to become "the main battlefield of treatment", as Freud called it. He also realized that transference is a phenomenon of the human mind and occurs in most relationships. In the analytic relationship, particular attention is given to transference and attempts are made by the analyst to uncover the existing transference.

In 1910, Freud also spoke of the phenomenon of countertransference, the analyst's own feelings stirred up in himself by the patient. His thoughts about it remained consistent even in his later writings. He wrote: "We have become aware of the countertransference which arises [in the analyst] as a result of the patient's influence on his unconscious feelings, and we are almost inclined to insist that he shall recognize this countertransference in himself and overcome it" (Freud, 1910, pp. 144–145). Freud considered this phenomenon to be a hindrance and an interference in the analytic work of understanding the patient's unconscious, due to some residual pathological element in the analyst.

The concept of countertransference has undergone great evolution in the course of the years and there are many controversies amongst the different psychoanalytic schools on how to understand and use, if at all, the analyst's countertransference.

The Kleinian and Independent Group have come to consider countertransference as an important and necessary aspect of the analytic process. Paula Heimann wrote that the analyst's "emotional response to his patient within the analytic situation represents one of the most important tools for his work" (Heimann, 1949/1950, p. 74). However, she stressed, "the analyst's countertransference is not only part and parcel of the analytic relationship, but it is the patient's creation, it is a part of the patient's personality" (*ibid.*, p. 77). Heimann implies that the patient has projected something of himself into the analyst, thus creating or stimulating a response in the latter. In her later paper, she concluded, in line with Freud, that the countertransference must be recognized and overcome and that when it occurs "it must be turned to some useful purpose" (Heimann, 1959/1960, p. 160).

Racker dedicated a whole book to the topic of transference and countertransference, which he saw as "a unity mutually giving life to each other and creating the interpersonal relation of the analytic situation" (Racker, 1968, p. 59). He expanded on Freud and Heimann's view, when he wrote:

> it is mainly through the countertransference that we feel and can understand what the patient feels and does in relation to the analyst and what he feels and does in face of his instincts and feelings towards the analyst. Hence the principal interpretation, the transference interpretation, springs from the countertransference. [*ibid.*, p. 60]

In 1956, Money-Kyrle wrote about two types of countertransference. The normal countertransference is based on concern for and identification with the patient. This is reminiscent of Freud's "benevolent neutrality", a tolerant but neither indulgent nor indifferent involvement with the patient. Money-Kyrle studied a second form of countertransference, which he called "deviated countertransference". This occurs when the material becomes obscure and engenders conscious or unconscious anxiety in the analyst and consequent decrease in understanding, frustration and despair. However, if during these "less satisfactory states" (Money-Kyrle, 1956, p. 31) the analyst can analyse his own reactions silently without becoming defensive or depressed, then his insight can increase and he can learn more about his patient.

I came to recognize a form of deviated countertransference in the despairing clinical work with Rosy and her parents, which I write about in detail in the chapter on soiling.

I have already mentioned the importance of the capacity to be aware and to bear a whole range of emotions and states of mind when we practice psychoanalytic counselling with the families of under fives. However, it is worthwhile expanding on Winnicott's view expressed in his 1947 paper "Hate in the countertransference" to the British Psycho-Analytic Society. Winnicott recognized the necessity of being aware of one's own hatred and similar difficult feelings experienced during the analysis of psychotic patients. He also expanded this idea to other professional and parental figures such as psychiatrists, adoptive parents, and ordinary mothers with their newborn babies. He reported the maddening and hateful feelings engendered in him by a nine-year-old boy, whom his wife had generously looked after for three months. The boy had run away from his current hostel. Winnicott, who had had an emotionally meaningful single consultation with him, described this episode of hate as something justifiable in ordinary life situations. The boy had experienced a hopeful contact with Winnicott and had then attempted to test the environment and its capacity to love him, as well as to hate him. In the same paper, Winnicott specified the many reasons that any mother might have to hate her baby. He proposed that it was necessary for integration into reality and for a complete ending of any analysis that the patient knew what the analyst had done and felt for the patient.

Nowadays, many analysts from many schools and different continents seem to agree that countertransference is no longer an obstacle to treatment and it is seen as a:

> complex entity containing the analyst's subjective responses fused and mixed with projected aspects of the patient's inner world. [...] countertransference not only exerts a continuous influence on the analytic process but constitutes an invaluable pathway for the investigation of the process. [Jacobs, 1999, p. 591]

Transference and countertransference in working with under fives

In my work, I recognize different types of feelings in myself, which could fit in with the "normal and deviated" forms of countertransference as postulated by Money-Kyrle (1956). The identification with the various aspects of oneself, which we see embodied by the different people in the session, seems rather straightforward. It is the healthy or the sick child; the proper or abusive parent; the idealized, the strict or the denigrated professional aspects of the therapist that emerge rather easily. However, it is another aspect of the countertransference that I find particularly interesting and somewhat mysterious. Bion wrote that, in treating psychotic patients, the communication between patients and the analyst could not be based on verbal thought for a long time. "The analyst who essays, in our present state of ignorance, the treatment of such patients, must be prepared to consider that for a great proportion of analytic time the evidence on which an interpretation can be based is that which is afforded by the countertransference" (Bion, 1955, p. 224). He goes on to describe the growing sense of tension, anxiety, and fear felt by the analyst sensing that a patient was meditating an attack on him. The analyst interpreted this as the fear of murdering the analyst being pushed by the patient into the analyst. The effect of the interpretation was a decrease of tension in the room. This led the patient to re-own the fear that he had communicated to the analyst in a non-verbal manner. Bion used the countertransference in a rather humble way suggesting something impalpable and yet almost concretely palpable in the room and in the person of the analyst.

I have had sessions in which an adult patient was lying calmly on the couch or a family was talking to me in a friendly way. Gradually, I have become aware of phantasies and feelings in me that were apparently unrelated to the presented material. Once I was able to link these countertransference productions with the patient's material, the atmosphere changed. I felt relieved of that wave of destructive thoughts and feelings and the patient also somehow changed. He became more agitated or engaged with mental thoughts expressed in the next associations, or play activity, that seemed related to the interpretation given.

Bion puzzled on how a patient can succeed in imposing a phantasy and its affect upon the analyst and yet deny it in himself.

Bion recognized the effort needed to differentiate between what belongs to the analyst and what to the patient.

In under fives' psychoanalytic counselling, the therapist is at the centre of transference and countertransference phenomena coming from all directions. Some clinicians do not refer to the transference relationship with the analyst, as they would do in individual analytic treatment. They deal with phantasies and projections between mother and child (Manzano & Palacio-Espasa, 1999). In order to adopt a multidimensional approach to the analytic situation, it is worthwhile asking oneself the following questions, as Heimann suggested: "What is the patient doing at this very moment? Why is he doing it? Whom does the analyst represent at this moment? Which past self of the patient is dominant? In what manner does this represent a response to a former interpretation?" (Heimann, 1959/1960, p. 160).

The mother of three-year-old Jonas, an insightful woman already familiar with counselling, became rather disturbed by my interpretation of the boy's murderous jealousy for the baby brother, a jealousy which had been diverted onto mother. The interpretation had been based on the observation of the boy's play and also of his verbal associations. Mother's disturbance was not expressed openly in that session and I was left somewhat uneasy. A few days later, mother telephoned me saying that she wanted to interrupt counselling, but she was able to agree to return with her husband and without the children. She complained that I had put murderous ideas into her son's head, but she was also able to hear me say that it was a rather common and healthy feeling for children of that age. Later in the session she revealed, in horror, that she had often felt murderous toward Jonas. He had provoked and driven her mad ever since the second baby was born. In the previous session, the boy had responded affirmatively to my interpretation of his "killing" feelings. Mother, in a moment of non-separateness from Jonas, had become disturbed by her own "killing" feelings, which were by then mixed up with her son's feelings. In this case, I did not interpret the transference, the maternal attempt at murdering both the counselling and my interpretation, but I did not let her destroy the counselling by having her interrupt the sessions.

I write more about this case in the chapter on under fives' counselling as a form of assessment. My understanding of transference and countertransference only informed my work in this case while, at other times, I do interpret the transference, as it seems the only way for treatment to go on or even to begin.

Technique

In this section of the book, I describe some of the techniques I apply in the work with under fives. I have already touched upon some of the ideas in the previous sections, but I will also introduce new concepts.

Initial assessment through telephone conversation

An important aspect of my work begins on the telephone. At the moment of reading and discussing the referral letter, the therapist begins to think, feel, and speculate about the child and his family. A pre-transference or mental space is beginning to be created inside the therapist. When children under five are referred to the clinic, I, or other child psychotherapists, have a telephone consultation. This consultation consists of a telephone conversation of up to thirty minutes with one of the parents. It aims to begin to explore the problem, how the parents perceive it, and how it affects the family. It is also a useful way to begin to assess the capacity of the parents to think about the child, the extent of parental involvement and availability to the thinking of the therapist, and the urgency of the situation. After over ten years of experience and practice, it has now become a vital procedure, although not yet validated by research. I will discuss this approach in further detail in the section on Parents' Line.

Meeting the family

Firstly, I briefly introduce myself to the family in the waiting room and begin to observe the family as a whole, then continue to do so as we walk towards the therapy room. I have already described the value of observation in Chapter One. Once we have sat down, a more thorough introduction of all the family members follows, before beginning to explore the reasons for coming to the clinic and the feelings about it. I do so by addressing and involving all the present members as soon and as much as possible. I have noticed that while the adults mostly control or contain their anxieties about this first visit, the children tend to be more in contact with their fears. For example, some children expect to be told off for being "naughty", others wish to be the centre of attention or dislike being put in the hot seat. These feelings, as well as the parents' more unconscious ones, need to be addressed and shifted to less persecuted, less critical ones. When the child leaves the close proximity of the parents, who sit on the couch, and feels free to move to the table with toys and to start playing, it is a sign that some anxiety has been lifted and contained in either the child or in the parents.

Different stories, which at times sound like an outpouring of complaints about the child, the nursery-school, and the professionals, are recounted by the parents and may be mirrored by the child's play or drawings. The stories centre on the problems parents come with and how these manifest at home or at nursery. In the first or next sessions, we talk about the parents' families of origin and how authority, discipline, feelings, and pleasant activities occur and were dealt with then and also now, in their present family life.

The here and now are closely observed and I occasionally comment on what I observe and link it with what goes on at home and at nursery, with the parents' own experience as children. As I have mentioned in Chapter One, on observation, it is vital for the therapist to be able to take up many different identifications and to be in touch with aspects of his or her own personality and mind to be able to identify with all the people present.

First sessions with families of under fives are often:

> very intense and difficult for the therapists, as well as for the family. Raw, unthinkable, undigested and chaotic experiences, which have affected the family for many months or years, are brought out and violently or subtly projected onto the therapist. Also, and this is different from individual sessions with patients, it is the gamut of experiences of the various members of the family which can bombard the therapist. The experiences result from the many relationships involved: mother–child, mother–father, father–mother, father–child, child–mother, child–father etc., to mention only a few and to speak only about the present generation. [Pozzi, 1999, p. 54]

The use of transference and countertransference

The transference and countertransference are also closely scrutinized by the therapist in his mind and occasionally verbalized, especially when a negative transference creates an impasse in the work. Both positive and negative countertransference are very useful tools and the negative transference can be very obvious, especially with more disturbed families. The children's drawings, play, activities, and silences are also observed and occasionally interpreted in their deep meanings to both the child and the parents. This can be well received by children of this age group and it may stimulate the parents' curiosity and interest or suspicion. In the best cases, a link between the child's perception of the difficulty and the parent's talk about it can be established. A three-year-old boy affected by signs of an early eating disorder drew fat and greedy animals while mum and dad spoke of his food refusal. A link was made between the boy's anxiety about his greed and his wish to overeat, on the one hand and his refusal of food, on the other hand, which interested the parents and reached the boy.

Working with the negative transference and being able to bear the negative projections from the family members and if necessary to verbalize them, can sometimes be the only way to connect emotionally with the family. At other times the therapist just needs to stay with and absorb the emotional atmosphere of the session without being more overtly active, until permission to intervene with descriptive comments or with interpretations is given by the parents.

Guilt responsibility and blame
Coming to the clinic often requires an act of courage and humility on the part of the parents. It can stir up feelings of guilt and blame about one's parenting capacity or failure. "Am I a bad mother? Am I a bad father? Have I failed my child?" are questions that betray some of the parents' feelings. Others blame the child or professionals who have not been helpful. I have noticed that what makes the work possible is for at least one of the parents to be in a self-reflective, depressive disposition of mind, rather than in a persecuted state characterized by the tendency to blame others and to evacuate responsibility. If the parents are not available to be reached, the child can become a point of entry and gradually will help the parents, as we will see in the case of Bonny. I have also come across families who could not come to the clinic when things were too bad and hopeless. Only when the parents regained a glimmer of hope, were they able to consider searching for help.

I have found that working on the parents' guilt either by verbalizing it, if appropriate, by linking it with the material in the session, or by bearing it in mind can be extremely important. It can both alleviate guilt and open up trust towards the therapist or pre-empt splitting and projection onto the therapist. If blame is projected on the therapist, he or she is perceived as the one who blames the parents and makes them feel bad. Bobby's mother realized that her short fuse had contributed to her three-year-old son's hyperactivity and she blamed me for making her feel bad. However, when she was able to confront her feelings towards me openly, we could understand that she was seeing me as her critical mother. It helped her to re-own her critical, internalized mother, and to try and modify her own response to her son, who had also become the object of her impatience and criticism. The change in mother propelled the passive and despondent husband to abandon his stance and to involve himself more actively with their difficult child. I will discuss this family in more detail in the chapter on the borderline child.

Parental hooks and feelings

In a previous paper, I explored a technical point that I find very valuable in my under fives' work. "Helping parents to understand that their feelings towards their child may have also to do with their child's feelings towards them can be a useful tool in this work" (Pozzi, 1999, p. 56). "I take seriously the complaint that a two-year-old becomes the tyrant or the monster in the family and the parents are reduced to feeling frightened or bossed about" by their young one (*ibid.*, p. 57). I realize that their potency and authority has been projected into the child and a role reversal is taking place in the family. I tend to share this thinking with surprise and puzzlement, which can help the parents to reflect how this has happened. When they begin to see the whole scenario as almost humorous, I remind them of how their small child may have felt small, impotent, frightened or cross until he found a way to make the parents have such feelings instead. Four-year-old Peter had managed to make mum extremely cross with his persistent soiling since the arrival of his baby brother some months earlier. Otherwise, he had not shown any sign of jealousy towards the baby and he was said to be very good with him. But mother was fuming with rage and felt completely fed up. She had two babies to clean and change and could not make sense of Peter's behaviour. I invited both parents to imagine how Peter may be feeling now that a new boy was in the family and he had to share mum's individual attention with him. They eventually could realize that their anger might be a reflection of his anger, which he was not expressing more directly. I suggested that, in a strange sort of way, he had found a way to rid himself of his feelings and to have mum feeling the anger instead of him. We addressed Peter's anger in the session and I suggested that the parents also talked to him at home, whenever the situation presented itself.

This technique aims to help parents observe their feelings and reactions towards their children and is rooted in the concept of projective identification. The child projects his states of minds and feelings into the parent or parents, who is/are temporarily taken over by what is being put into him or her. When the parent stays stuck in this situation, entanglement and problems occur. If the parent can separate the child's projections from his or her own emotions, then a process of psychic digestion and transformation of the child's projections occurs. Helping parents to achieve a state of mind, where they can observe and separate their own feelings from those of their children, has extremely important consequences. It opens a channel of communication between children and parents. It empowers parents with a new understanding of their child's inner world and relationships and, most importantly, it gives the child the experience of being contained. This means that the child has a parent who can understand and withstand the projective identification from the child. The child eventually internalizes the containing parental function that forms a basis for healthy psychological development.

Most parents, who come to the clinic because of a problem child, need to keep the focus of their attention on the child, even though personal difficulties, marital problems, and inter-generational dysfunctions are often at the root of the actual symptom.

> A child who is a mixture of what the child really is and of how the child is seen through the lenses of parental projections and confusions with their own childhood is brought to the clinic. To externalise the problem in the child and in the relationship with the child can be a safety valve for those parents, who are too split and often feel too guilty, damaged or vulnerable to be able to want to look at themselves. [Pozzi, 1999, pp. 58–59]

I have found that achieving a modification in the relationship with the child and a relief of the symptoms is as much as one is allowed to do with some families. Permanent improvements can be achieved and also maintained even with short-term counselling. Occasionally, in the course of counselling or as a result of it, parents may decide to pursue individual or marital psychotherapy and may be referred further.

PART II
CLINICAL CASES

Introduction

In this section of the book, I describe a number of clinical situations in which under fives' counselling has been offered to families who are concerned about symptomatic behaviours in their children. In infancy and early childhood, symptomatic behaviours usually alert the therapist to family or parental dysfunction, to difficulties in attachment, to an unhappy relationship with the maternal figure or primary carer, or to more serious disorders or disabilities in the child. Unresolved issues in family life, individual frailties and an inborn predisposition in the child can produce disturbances and blockages in ordinary development, which are expressed through a variety of symptoms.

In some chapters, I examine a single case history in detail, such as "The little girl who could not sleep". In other chapters, I will group cases in more concise form under one topic, such as "Bereavement and loss". However, some case histories could have easily been included in a number of different topics, since the original source of dysfunction could have produced different symptoms. For example, we are familiar with the idea that separation anxieties are often at the root of weaning and sleeping problems, that maternal postnatal depression can lead to hyperactivity, aggressive behaviour, developmental delays or other difficulties. The cases included in the chapter on separation difficulties could have been included easily in the chapter on bereavement and loss. Therefore, my attempt to include a specific problem within a category is only indicative and effected for schematic purposes and it should not be taken in a fixed way.

One common factor in all the cases is a partial failure in the parent–child relationship. The failure is observed in the parental function of containing and transforming the emotions, the states of mind, and the needs expressed by the child openly or less openly by projection from the child into the parent. However, the result can be attributed to a lack in the container i.e. the parent/carer or in the contained i.e. the child. Bion proposed that the "disturbances commence with life itself" (Bion, 1967, p. 106) and that the origin of the disturbance is twofold. It can reside either in the inborn disposition of the child or in the mother or main carer. Both need to be dysfunctional to create a severe disturbance. When the two do not match, the child internalizes a parental figure that cannot receive the projective identification of distress, terror, and other feelings coming from the child. The child is left filled with confused, poisonous, meaningless, and nameless material and may present a variety of responses and symptoms that show lack of containment and integration.

I will explore two types of counselling in this section. The first one is the more traditional one where up to five sessions are offered to families, possibly followed by another set of five, if needed. By the end, a satisfactory understanding of the problem, the resolution of the symptom, and a modification of the parent–child interaction usually occur. The families who can use this type of brief intervention are the easiest to treat. They come to the clinic with what I have called a depressive predisposition of mind and do not present with a complex psychopathology. They are usually keen to keep within the bounds of five or ten sessions and bear in mind the time limit as treatment proceeds. Palacio-Espasa and Manzano (1993) describe the mothers who can use brief parent–child psychotherapy, as suffering mainly from a depressive conflict and presenting with a positive pre-transference towards the therapist.

The second type of counselling that I explore applies to more disturbed families for whom the initial five or ten sessions prove not to be enough. Further treatment is indicated and either the family treatment continues open-ended with the same therapist or other forms of therapy are suggested, such as individual therapy for the child or for the parents or marital therapy. Palacio-Espasa believes that a narcissistic, borderline or psychotic disturbance in the child, as well as a narcissistic or character disturbance in the mother, are present in those patients who have a negative pre-transference to the therapist. These patients do not benefit from short interventions. When long-term psychodynamic counselling is needed, the initial five or ten sessions become a form of assessment and a platform for further treatment (Miller, 2000). However, in my experience of working with this model, I have discovered that even families with long-standing difficulties or parental psychiatric disorders can benefit from brief psychodynamic intervention. If the therapist can tap into depressive moments in either one of the parents or in the child, a great deal can be achieved.

In the last two chapters I discuss variations on the traditional forms of under fives' counselling. The first is "Parents' Line", a form of telephone counselling that I have gradually developed in order to meet the needs of troubled parents and small children, before they are placed on the long clinic waiting list. The other chapter regards the consultation to a nursery school, in which the deprivation and neglect of the local population had filtered through the nursery school, teachers, and headmistress to the point that the school had become unmanageable.

I have chosen to discuss the different themes in a broadly developmental order, which provides the inner thread that strings together my ideas in this part of the book.

CHAPTER THREE

Post-natal maternal depression

Introduction

Post-natal depression (PND) or "postnatal distress" is not a rare event. In Western societies, it is estimated that, in the first two years following the birth of their baby, about half of those mothers suffer from some form of emotional disorder. Raphael-Leff writes that this emotional state can range from a mild form of "baby blues" to a more "organized and disturbing symptomatology and, in a minority of cases, to a post-partum psychosis" (Raphael-Leff, 2000, p. 61). However, more than half of the least severe form of post-natal depression remains undetected by general practitioners and health visitors (Kumar & Robson, 1984) and the distress accumulates and spreads into the relationship with the baby, as well as into marital and family life (Cooper & Murray, 1997). The effects of PND on the developing infant varies enormously, depending on the quality and quantity of maternal disturbance and whether the mother becomes intrusive or withdrawn. The sex of the baby also leads to different self-regulatory solutions: boys withdraw more easily while girls show more signs of sadness and depression (Sharp *et al.*, 1992; Tronick *et al.*, 1997). In the aetiology of childhood autism, psychosis, hyperactivity, social and cognitive disturbances, we easily find maternal depression as one of the components. (Cooper & Murray, 1997; Lebovici & McDougall, 1960; Tustin, 1990). However, in many cases of PND an inadequate diagnosis is made and treatment is not offered. Raphael-Leff, Lucas, Bourne and Lewis believe that psychodynamically-based therapy or counselling can help mothers, who are affected by post-natal depression and psychosis or perinatal loss, to understand and recover from it (Bourne & Lewis, 2000; Lucas, 2000; Raphael-Leff, 2000).

The king of the couch and the miscarried baby

Mother did not suffer from PND after the birth of John, the symptomatic child aged two and a half at the time of the referral, but after Polly's birth, who was then seven months old. She had been conceived very shortly after mother had had a miscarriage and no time to mourn. Lewis and Bourne (1989) have studied the deep effect of miscarriages and still births and found out that a period of mourning is essential in all cases of perinatal death. Mother had become aware of not having mourned that lost pregnancy and sought therapeutic input. However, John had become aggressive and spiteful before he was two, and at a time when mother had lost her baby. She was aware of having withdrawn her attention from John at that time and soon became pregnant again. John seemed to have become stuck at the "no" age and his infantile omnipotence was not dealt with. He spent the whole first session sitting on a chair, which he had placed on top of the settee i.e. higher up than mother and me and enjoyed himself with drinks and watching cars and lorries arriving in the streets. He looked like "the king of the couch", which we could also read as "the king of the parental bed", since neither parent was able to control him. At home he trashed the house, hit and kicked, while at nursery he could not tolerate other children. Mother's inability to defend herself and set any boundaries, was worsened by her husband's omnipotent attitude and the delicate family situation. It was a mixed marriage and she had to deal with some family opposition, as well as with her husband's different cultural beliefs about bringing up children. I think this lead to collusion between both father and son's omnipotent wishes and drives and ended with a lack of containment. The child was allowed to do everything in the name of his freedom. Mother appeared anxious, exhausted, and defeated and yet in love with her husband and keen to defend his position. The child was growing up unable to adapt to reality. Father came to the second and third session and tried to put me down with his superior and omnipotent demeanour and his defence of his son's behaviour, as if he was a crusader fighting for the Holy Grail. However, when asked what he thought about his son's freedom expressed in trashing the house over and over, he finally realized that something was not quite right. Boundaries could eventually be put in place, which caused "the great fall" of their child's omnipotence into rage and tantrums. Mother showed interest in looking at John's feelings and understanding them and she began to talk to him about his rage, tantrums, and jealousy. Father, although still appearing sceptical and provocative, converted gradually to a less idealistic and narcissistic view of his son and of himself. Mother's depression subsided and her sense of herself as a parent, who could have some power and affect her son, also began to be restored.

John's restless, meaningless and haphazard behaviour began to show some purpose, following "the great fall" into being an ordinary child, and he began to respond appropriately to the new limits set by his parents. The parents were pleased with the result and wanted to stop coming, having grasped some essential ideas about feelings and boundaries. However, a follow-up session was eventually arranged many months later as things had continued to improve and also mother was pregnant again.

"There's something wrong with my child"

This is a common statement we hear when mothers suffer from PND, but the child does not yet seem to show any obvious signs of disturbance. This of course depends on the age of the child, as we know that prolonged maternal depression has an effect on the emotional, social and cognitive development of the child (Cooper & Murray, 1997).

A fourteen-month-old infant called Harry, whose mother had a clear diagnosis of PND, was referred to our clinic by her G.P.

Neither the G.P. nor the paediatrician could find anything wrong with Harry. Mother had already suffered from PND after the birth of her first child Phil, who was three and a half at the time of the referral. Mother was nearly hospitalized then, as she was suicidal and wanted to free her child from her bad mothering, as she put it. This time she had felt better and could just manage by taking medication. As well as being very concerned about being a bad mother, she worried about both children suffering from all sorts of mental illnesses, from autism to psychosis and violence, despite the fact that they were rather ordinary children. My first impression was that Harry was quite restless and on the go all the time, which did not surprise me under the circumstances. Mother's self-doubting, negative, and depressed states of mind affected her view of her mothering. From a more objective point of view it did not appear to be as bad as she depicted: anxious but neither neglectful nor actively damaging. When Phil was conceived accidentally, mother did not want a baby yet. She told me that neither she nor her husband was ready to have a family. She was aware that her first child reminded her too much of her unhappy childhood experiences. Phil became "normal" only when he was two and mother had come out of her PND. She was partially aware of her distorted way of seeing her children and yet she could not stop it and, at moments, she almost believed that her feelings and belief of having very disturbed children were reality.

When I first met Phil, an intelligent and sensitive boy, I noticed that he behaved like his brother's guardian angel and never reacted even when the latter pushed him aside. He acted almost as an appendage to his mother and had unconsciously become connected to her fragile state. He had to curb any possible rivalrous feeling towards Harry, in order to protect his mother and to fill the gap of a busy and absent father. Father never came to these family sessions as he worked long hours away from home. I noticed that Phil let the toys with which he played, mainly dolls, slip out of his hands unintentionally and without aggression. He conveyed to me an experience of not being firmly held in the mind of his mother. He also spent long and slow-moving moments cutting small bits of paper, as if this activity allowed him to express some aggressive and cutting feelings in an acceptable way. It also conveyed to me a sense of fragmentation and feeling in pieces. Mother had already had some counselling during her first bout of PND and so she only skirted over her complicated family background and possible reasons for her depression. We could only try to concentrate on mother's view of Harry and on her massive projections, which had turned him into a "bad child" and which were impinging on his development. Harry's perpetual motion made me think of an uncontained child, who had to move to hold himself together, and who desperately attempted to infuse life into his mother. I also wondered whether he was shaking off his mother's projections by such restlessness. Maternal and mutual projections seemed particularly obvious on those mornings when Harry woke up in a grumpy mood, did not ask for cuddles but turned away from mother, as she reported. Mother felt rejected, hurt, and a bad mother. On the one hand, she could not understand why he was rejecting her and reacting in such a way; on the other hand, she felt extremely bad and responsible for anything he did, even breathing or moving. Then she withdrew from him and planned, in her fantasy, to abandon him, but soon felt ridden with guilt as her feelings of being a disgraceful mother increased. It was excruciating for me to witness her internal torture and the vicious circle in which she was trapped. Her children reminded her of her far-from-ideal childhood; hence she wanted them to be ideal children and her the ideal mother. This had not been possible since, in her mind, they had became awful and a constant reminder of her failure. I noticed that whatever thought and understanding I shared with her was easily accepted at first, but was soon turned into negativity and used by mother to blame herself. Also her tendency to see herself and her children as being bad and wrong soon contaminated her view of me. Despite trying to be extremely careful and gentle in what I said and how I spoke, she began to feel criticized, blamed, and accused by me of being a bad mother. It was at this point, i.e. after the second session, that a long gap of six weeks occurred as her mother's health deteriorated terminally and she went to be with her.

When she came back she was in a better state than I had feared: she was able to feel sad, cross, and also relieved about her mother's death and for having survived that much feared event. She could also begin to think of Harry as separate from herself. It had been interesting to see her going in and out of states of confusion between herself and him, due to her projective identification, which blurred their boundaries. Now she tried to separate her own depression from his grumpy state and, under my guidance, she began to observe and to control her flow of negativity over him. However, after her return to counselling for one session, she disappeared again and eventually returned for a final session, following my telephone contact with her. She was keen for that to be the last session. She reported that things had improved a lot: she was better, had stopped medication, without consultation with her G.P., and the children too were fine. Yet, she said she had not felt helped by this counselling and told me why. For example, when I had wondered whether she could take a step away from Harry and observe him, she knew that would be useful. However, she had not been able to do so as she had been too low in herself, had felt bad and turned my thoughts into a criticism of her. Also, the idea that Harry may have been active to help her when she was down, an idea she had found interesting at the time, now angered her and she did not want to return to see me. At this point, I felt I had been an insensitive, shameful, and bad therapist and felt a failure for not having tuned in adequately to her distress. It was hard to bear these hurtful feelings and I wanted to defend myself. However, things had also got better since I had become a failing therapist. I decided to acknowledge my regrets for having caused her such pain. However, I also reflected on the paradox that my "wrong approach" had somehow spurred her to feel better as a mother. I was now performing a containing and transforming function, because I did not become defensive, but accepted her criticism of me. As a result, she opened up a lot more and, for the rest of that session, she revisited her past depressions and also made reparatory plans for the near future, such as doing voluntary work. Harry who had come to this session, kept busy drawing and scribbling, playing and getting cuddles from mum. He appeared calmer than on previous occasions and we all parted amicably.

The transforming factor in this brief but interesting piece of work lay in the negative reaction and transference towards the therapist. Negativity and devaluation were soon projected onto the therapist who, by having borne mother's projections and persisted in encouraging her to return to counselling, performed that containing function which mother seemed to have lacked as a child. It was important that some mental digestion could take place in the last session when hurt and rejection were deposited into the therapist. The therapist did not retaliate, but highlighted how a primitive split between a good and a bad mother had allowed mother to reintegrate herself.

Manzano and Palacio-Espasa (1998) warn the therapist of possible counter-identification with the rejecting mother as this leads to premature termination of brief therapy. I think that such could have easily been the end of this piece of work, had I not got hold of my counter-identification with a rejecting object. However, I did telephone mother, even at the risk of being perceived as intrusive. Counselling was resumed and could terminate.

"He can only sleep when I'm not around"

Although this two-and-a-half-year-old boy was referred for a sleep disturbance and nightmares, it was really his mother's PND that had caused such a disturbance in him. Mother had suffered from PND after the birth of both her children, Carl and seven-month-old Jerry, and she was being seen for psychiatric support. Carl's ordinary bad dreams and difficulties were managed appropriately and contained when he was either with his grandparents or with dad, i.e. when his mother was not around.

By listening to mother's narrative and by observing her relationship with the boys, I witnessed the extent of her maternal projection of badness and wished-for ideal children onto them. She appeared demanding of them and impatient of their behaviour, which seemed to be age appropriate, albeit rather subdued. Both boys seemed to be an irritant for mother and not at all a pleasure. The irritation had begun with her first pregnancy, which had been fraught with medical problems and many threats of miscarriage. It also emerged that her depression was part of a more general clinical picture of sleep disturbances in herself and in her family. There was also a long-standing undiagnosed depression, which manifested itself openly with the pregnancies and the arrival of the boys. The marital relationship appeared highly unsatisfactory and her self-centred, breadwinning husband did not share any other family responsibility. Mother was filled with such negativity that it would have driven anybody away. Some improvement was achieved in five sessions of counselling, as Carl's sleep improved, but he became more openly jealous, disobedient, and cross during the day. This was not well tolerated by mother. In the sessions, the boys, who had been rather restless and hyperactive, calmed down noticeably and settled to playing. Maternal aggression and some marital grudges were discussed, but when we came to the last session, while father—who always attended the sessions—was pleased with the work done, mother complained about the lack of achievement in our work. I could sense that she was right, as there was so much in her that needed to be explored, but was outside our remit. She continued seeing her counsellor but, one year later, they were referred again. Jerry, who was now three and a half, was stubborn and had tantrums, not altogether unusual for his age. I only saw them once, but realized that not much had changed in their family dynamics: both parents were still very demanding of and intolerant with the children. The children were referred again later on, but I no longer saw them, as, by then, I felt defeated and hopeless.

Containment and transformation were not achieved in a satisfactory way in this case: the original sleep symptom had improved, but the basic disturbance in both mother and the couple persisted. The input from the psychiatric team, medication, and the short counselling with me had not been enough to contain such a pathological family nucleus. Raphael-Leff warns the therapist, who is engaged in treating maternal post-natal disturbances, of how difficult it is, "to bear in mind that the sudden onslaught of transferential rage or its corollary of guilt relates to reactivated original failures rather than current ones" (Raphael-Leff, 2000, p. 14). With hindsight I could see the onslaught that had occurred in those early sessions and I realized that mother's needs and the extent of her depression and negativity went beyond what I could offer her at the clinic and what she was prepared to work on in herself.

CHAPTER FOUR

Separation difficulties and parental input

Introduction

I n this chapter, I describe two families, the first one in greater detail than the second one. Both these cases have been published elsewhere in modified versions. The two families could have been easily included in the chapter on bereavement and loss, reflecting the fact that many problematic situations are rooted in a difficulty in negotiating depressive feelings and mourning.

The first case is about a little girl, the only child in the family, who was unable to separate from her mother and to start nursery school. Her mother was also stuck with issues of separation and could not contain her daughter's distress.

The second case is about a little boy who could not separate from his mother to go to nursery, and the mother who was unable to help him because she had not mourned the death of a previous baby.

Poppy is unwilling to go to nursery[1]
The referral
The Health Visitor had referred Poppy and her mother directly to

me, after having attended a discussion group for Health Visitors. She felt unable to go any further with this family, the Greens, as I shall call them. In her letter, the Health Visitor wrote that, already at the age of eight months, Poppy would become very upset when strangers looked at her, so that the developmental checks were difficult to complete. Poppy was three years and four months old at the time of the referral. She was so deeply distressed when left by her mother at the nursery that her mother had given up taking her there.

First encounter and initial impressions

One February, a woman in her thirties, quiet-looking and well-groomed, arrived at the Clinic in good time for their appointment, with a bouncing, chubby, three-year-old girl with curls and blue eyes, beautifully dressed in Laura Ashley lace and flowery clothes. There was something unusual in this couple; an atmosphere of "old times" was around. Poppy seemed to have taken shape out of an illustrated fairy tale book. She could have been a child princess. In the consulting-room, mother spoke, monotonously and at length, of the present difficulty in leaving Poppy at the nursery. She gave only a brief account of Poppy's early days, when I asked for it. Meanwhile, Poppy hopped, danced, ran, and pranced happily around the room.

The major problem in separating from her mother, both at the nursery and at a neighbour's house, was that Poppy was terrified of being left alone with children of her own age or older ones. In particular, she feared that the boys might bully her. Her mother reported that, even in a shop, when a boy went near Poppy, she began crying with no apparent provocation by the boy. Fear and anger were Poppy's main reaction to her mother's attempts to leave her. Mrs Green was aware that Poppy was a determined, bossy little girl, as well as psychologically frail and thus was unable to strike a proper balance of firmness and kindness. For a peaceful existence she would give in to Poppy's requests. She demonstrated this in the session, when Poppy wanted to take her shoes off, hop over the couch, or go under the blanket. Mrs Green told her not to do this, but without effect.

As a baby, Poppy wanted to be fed all the time. Mrs Green said that the feeding had felt like a never-ending experience. Poppy was breast-fed but used to have a bottle with water or orange juice as well, as she had been a very thirsty baby. When her mother decided to stop breast-feeding, feeling exhausted, Poppy took to the beaker quite easily.

No more was added about the past and Mrs Green wanted to move back to the present problem. It felt like the quick turning of a page in both the present session situation (not wanting to talk or remember about Poppy's babyhood) and in the past (suddenly withdrawing the breast).

Towards the end of the first meeting, Mrs Green told me briefly of having had a miscarriage about six months earlier. She was no longer trying to have a baby, as she was too preoccupied and busy with Poppy's problem. I suggested that we continued to explore the situation, offering five sessions to begin with and saying that we would review the situation after that. I emphasized that Mr Green, who had been invited in my letter to come to the first meeting but had not been able to, was welcome to come to the session.

The hypothesis that I had in my mind and that I was going to explore in the following session, was about the complex dynamic between Mrs Green and Poppy, with Mr Green in the background. Poppy was an intensely passionate child with strong feelings, since her early days, of attachment and possessiveness towards her mother. She seemed to have feared an intrusion into her "couple with mother" by other children, or even by her father. Mr Green worked long hours in another city and had left most of Poppy's care to his wife, thus allowing and encouraging such closeness to go on. On the one side, there was Poppy's hostility towards possible interference by other children, by the nursery environment, by any change of plans, by all sorts of things that would throw her into a state. On the other side, was her bossiness and control over her mother, which was likely to have been projected onto the children, who in her mind had turned into bad bullies. On her own part, Mrs Green, who came originally from another area of the country, had felt isolated and alone when she had come with her busy husband to the south of England. She believed that her relationship with Poppy was unique and was irreplaceable and that only she herself could calm Poppy down during her outbursts of fear, anger, and disturbance. In Mrs Green's eyes, the nursery teachers could not handle the problem as they were too busy with other children and could not attend to such a demanding child as Poppy. I wondered whether Mrs Green had held onto her belief that only *she* could appease Poppy, because she needed her as a baby and as a soother for her own isolation.

At the time of the loss of the much-wanted, but miscarried baby Poppy and her problem stood for a replacement baby and kept her mother company and provided comfort. This view was confirmed by the fact that Mrs Green appeared less concerned about the present problem than about the future. Both parents were concerned about the day Poppy would have to go to school alone. But also, if she had her mother with her, the children would tease her. At present Mrs Green was not sure she should persevere in taking Poppy to the nursery.

The depressed, monotonous, long-winded, and fairly insightful accounts left me thinking of unresolved loss.

Second session: the miscarriage

The second session was very interesting, and my embryonic hypothesis was confirmed. The first part of the session was again an outpouring, slow and lifeless, of facts and instances that had been narrated previously. Thinking was hard, and even breaking into the monotone of seemingly ungraspable sequences, became laborious for me.

Poppy sat on her mother's lap, sucking her thumb, looking at me in a worried and cautious way for some time. Eventually, I broached the issue of the miscarriage. Mrs Green began to say that she had been lucky, as this had happened when her mother was there visiting. Mrs Green thought that Poppy had neither been aware of the event itself, nor of any change, since her grandmother was around to help and Poppy had never been told of the expected baby.

Mrs Green had become very upset and overwhelmed in the session as she spoke and she could then say that she had been thinking a lot about the unborn baby during these days, as it should have been born in a couple of weeks. Interestingly, shortly after her mother began crying, Poppy bit her tongue while eating crisps. She cried and got consoled by being lifted onto her mother's lap. It seemed to me that seeking to identify herself with her mother in her distress, she had hurt her lips so that she could cry too. The reason for this identification seemed to be more to avoid separateness from her mother than to get attention. In fact, she had coped well so far with her mother and me talking; she had been very much part of it—rather than behaving as if feeling left out.

Mrs Green seemed anxious to believe that Poppy had not known about the pregnancy. At the point when I expressed my doubts whether she had really been unaware of the pregnancy, Poppy produced a startling piece of play. She curled up on the carpet, not far from her mother and me and sucked her thumb thoughtfully. After a short while, she lay on her back, legs wide apart and pulled the clothing off her tummy, which she touched and pressed down with her hands. She moved her tummy up and down with her hands resting on it, as though she were a pregnant woman in labour. I put all this into words; she looked at me and then shied away, hiding her face coyly and then lying flat on her tummy. Mrs Green said that Poppy had played in a similar way for the past three or four weeks while being bathed. Again, I thought of Poppy's identification with her mother, who should have been giving birth in the near future. Poppy seemed very tuned in with this idea.

Poppy should have started nursery in September to get used to being away from her mother before the birth of the baby five months later. Since there was to be no birth, however, Mrs Green said she did not mind having Poppy around at home. She seemed to accept that Poppy's acute distress at the moment of separating from her mother at the nursery was unbearable to herself, too, in view of the recent miscarriage. I spoke of the miscarriage that had produced not a new baby but a "baby" Poppy, still the only baby in the family. Mrs Green confirmed this and recounted how, since Christmas, Poppy had wanted to wear nappies. Poppy had seen a nativity play at the nursery she had been attending with her mother. I spoke of Poppy's wish to be her mother's only baby, a special Jesus-like baby. Although Mrs Green confirmed this, she added that Poppy had always resisted separation from her, not only since the miscarriage.

At this point it would have been interesting to get more information about Mrs Green's family history and her relationship with her mother. So far in the course of this short treatment, rare hints had been made to her relationship with her mother. She had mentioned feeling relieved when her mother and her sister, who had visited her, had eventually left; but at the same time she had appreciated her mother's presence at the time of the miscarriage. One wonders about the miscarriage of a much-wanted second baby, which had occurred during her mother's visit and about what had gone on between the two women.

It seemed to me that the unborn baby had not been mourned by Mrs Green, but had been replaced by either a regression to a baby state in Poppy, or a continuation of her non-separate baby state. The unmourned loss had probably reactivated past losses, which had not been dealt with, and left Mrs Green feeling depressed, deflated, tired, and unable to handle Poppy's difficulties about separating. A collusive dynamic between mother and child had set in, thus hindering the chances of moving on. Mrs Green could not have another baby and Poppy could not move out of being a baby.

The tyrant child

This attractive, princess-like child, terrified of children, of leaving her mother and of playing alone in the garden was, at the same time, a little tyrant. When her mother did not let her draw the curtain in one session, Poppy smacked her on her cheek. To go to the dentist, Mrs Green had to drive two hundred miles across the country, backwards and forwards, to take Poppy to the only friend—an elderly grand-mother-like person—with whom Poppy could be left happily. Poppy was said to have bitten her mother more than once. Mrs Green had endured such slavery to her child with passive resignation, frustration, and unhealthy tolerance. Already, however, after the first meeting, Mrs Green had reported that Poppy had been quieter and less boisterous during the week. She had felt more able to say and to carry through her "no!" to Poppy and had not allowed herself to be smacked any more. The focus of our work seemed to have shifted on to Mrs Green's capacity to control Poppy.

The issue of leaving Poppy at nursery had receded, and Mrs Green was beginning to postpone the problem of settling her in the nursery until September. I had noticed that Poppy's initial bouncing, which reminded me of a rubber-ball, had stopped and she could eventually respond to her mother's requests. It is hard to know what exactly had made the difference, whether it was the experience for both of them of being listened to and understood and being given the space for the projection of depression; or whether the mourning process was beginning to happen in Mrs Green. This had mobilized the part of herself that wanted to be able to control her relationship with Poppy.

Fourth session: the father appears

Mr Green came unexpectedly to the fourth session, at a time when Mrs Green had managed to be more authoritative with Poppy, both at home and in the sessions. It was as if she had re-owned the male or paternal function within herself and this was externalized by allowing her husband to come to the session. She had cancelled the previous session, which should have coincided with the birth of the lost baby, as I realized only later on.

I was dazzled by Mr Green's handsome appearance, but felt rather uncomfortable at first, as he sat, watched, and almost supervised the three of us at work. When I finally managed to involve him more, a conflict in the parents' way of handling Poppy emerged. Mr Green said that Mrs Green was too soft, while Mrs Green felt ashamed at her husband's harshness with Poppy, especially when they were in public places. Mr Green blamed his wife for reducing his authority; yet when she spoke at length and monotonously during this session, he listened rather passively, without intervening.

I was left wondering not only about Mrs Green's anxieties about men, her child's aggressiveness, the boys at the nursery who seemed to frighten Poppy in an uncontainable way, and her difficulty in conceiving even after she had been pregnant with Poppy, but also about Mr Green's possible discomfort. As a consequence, he appeared to have left Poppy's care to his wife and to spend longer and longer hours at work.

The nursery: a movement towards separation

At the beginning of the fifth session, Poppy looked at me wearily and anxiously as if scared of me. This was her usual way of reuniting with me. When I spoke of Poppy's anxieties, Mrs Green said, "Poppy wanted to come and see you today." I wondered whether Poppy had really felt this or whether she had been putting her mother's feelings into words. I had noticed at that point that Poppy had been copying her mother in pulling her own hair behind her ears, just as her mother had. Eventually Mrs Green agreed that she had been looking forward to the session. She had decided to send Poppy to a private nursery, which had fewer children and was less threatening. Poppy was to start after Easter.

In this session, some of the projections of wishes and anxieties seemed to have been withdrawn from Poppy back into Mrs Green, thus allowing me to think of their anxieties and phantasies as belonging to two separate, but interacting, people. Mrs Green was worried at leaving Poppy with her friend and her two children, as Poppy would scream for a whole hour. Poppy did not seem to be able to cope without her mother for such a long time. Mrs Green had given up attempting to separate. Poppy was likely to have perceived that her mother had given up because Poppy's fears, persecution, and anxieties were so intense and powerful as to be uncontainable even by adults. I expressed these thoughts to Mrs Green, who seemed to understand. She would "ask" Poppy if she wanted to go to Cherry Tree—the new, private nursery—rather than telling her that she was going to go after Easter. Mrs Green became aware that Poppy was treated either as a little baby, who could not be left alone for any length of time, or as a grown-up, who was asked to make decisions more appropriate for parents than for a child to make.

Mrs Green was always preparing alternative plans in case Poppy would not settle down at nursery. Her negative and hopeless way of talking about what might happen was again likely to become a self-fulfilling prophecy.

I became aware that Mrs Green's monotonous stream of words neither focused on anything particular, nor did it allow a pause for thinking. To pause would have meant to leave a gap, a space, and a separation, not just between Mrs Green and me, but also in her own mind. I struggled not to get engulfed by her and to continue to be a separate and thinking person.

The five sessions had come to an end, but the end of our work still seemed very distant. The small improvement did not seem to hold enough strength to be maintained or increased. I then proposed a few more meetings to help Poppy start in the new nursery.

Sixth session: the parents' fear of death

Mr Green came unexpectedly to the sixth session and sympathized with Poppy's wariness about me, because I was a stranger talking about her. I took it even further and I interpreted the transference to myself. Poppy felt this was like a kind of nursery, with me as a teacher who spoke of other children and of Poppy's fears of them and had other children coming to see me. The adults agreed and Poppy relaxed and was able to start playing. The parents' relationship was again the focus of the session: they either agreed with one another as if they were of one mind only, or else their opinion diverged a great deal.

The issue was the safety of their garden. Mrs Green seemed over-anxious about Poppy being alone in the garden, saying she always had to keep an eye on her from the kitchen window. Mr Green felt this to be unnecessary, although he, too, was worried about Poppy hurting herself out there and dying, as he put it. Apparently there was a dangerous river passing through the back of their garden. That worried Mrs Green, but not Mr Green, despite what he had just said. Even though the river seemed to be a real danger, nothing had been done about it. I linked the miscarriage with the fear that Poppy might die and suggested that we explored the miscarriage further. Meanwhile, Poppy expressed her feelings in play. One end of a long string was held tight in her mouth and she put the other end in various spots in the room. When I spoke about the string tying her to her mother wherever Poppy went, she made a bundle of it and threw it into the bin as if to confirm my point.

It seemed that the patents' anxieties were mobilized to the effect that separation, and being out of sight, were equated with dying. They could not trust that a good parental voice might have been internalized by Poppy and might sustain her when she was in the garden without her parents. It seemed, however, that not even a transitional object or space had been allowed to evolve in Poppy's mind, due to the parents' anxieties. The garden could have been a sort of transitional space, away from the mother, but not yet in the outside world, but seemed fraught with dangers and distant children. Poppy was able to play alone in the garden and had apparently never gone as far as the dangerous river. She had even watched the much-feared children from the protection of the gate. But Mr and Mrs Green still felt too frightened to let her be there outside.

The end of our sessions tended to cast an extra shadow of depression on Mrs Green, even when she had appeared, at times, to have brightened up and have been more alive in the course of a session.

Seventh session: inside and outside children

The seventh session occurred after a two-week gap for the Easter holiday. Mrs Green looked withdrawn and it was hard to get things going. It seemed that the absence of Mr Green was felt for the first time, especially because "he would have liked to have come today". The Greens had spent more time talking about Poppy and the issues of safety and so on, since coming to therapy. Mr Green, according to Mrs Green, had appreciated this way of thinking about the whole family and the work that we were doing in the sessions.

Mrs Green made a link between the loss of the baby and her dependency on Poppy. Had she had another baby to keep her busy, she would not have been so dependent on Poppy, she said. She had always had an ovulation problem and since the miscarriage she had not ovulated at all. Her anxiety about her possible inability to become pregnant again was high. She was aware of some psychological difficulties in her difficulty in conceiving and seemed to accept that she might never be able to conceive.

Poppy played some interesting sequences. She had put the doll people in a row inside a red washing-up bowl and placed the rubbish bin on top of it as if to close it. She had wrapped the string up around this box-like construction and one end of the string was inside it. She banged on the top part saying: "Mum, Mum". I thought of the babies inside the womb and of the cord connecting the inside to the outside. Later, she sat inside her own cardboard box and put the doll baby inside a thick round elastic band on the carpet and all sorts of animals outside the elastic band and surrounding the doll. I spoke of the baby Poppy being protected from the feared children (the animals) by her mother's womb (the elastic band and the garden gate). Poppy nodded to confirm my comments.

Her preoccupation with inside babies, her wishes to be the only "baby inside" and in her mother's life, the projections of her hostile feelings onto the other children, the animals in her play and her self-protective devices were expressed vividly and verbalized here.

Last session: good news and mother's jealousy is acknowledged

Our last meeting brought the news that Poppy had attended Cherry Tree Nursery three times. Things were going well. She had cried once at separating from her mother, who was now able to handle her warmly and could differentiate when Poppy was genuinely upset from when she was testing her mother out. At nursery, Poppy would not play at first. Mrs Green said Poppy needed time to feel safe and confident about the new environment. I said Poppy had been equally circumspect in all our sessions. Now Poppy was able to play with the children and enjoy it, although she was still wary of the older ones or bossy with the younger children. While Mrs Green had recounted this, Poppy had arranged the wild animals, the farm animals, the farmer, and the soldier round the doll baby. This time there was no protective elastic band or gate around the dolly-Poppy. I linked her play with the nursery situation. There she had been amongst the "tame" younger children and the more frightening "wild", older ones, just like the doll with the farm and the wild animals. They all stood together, with Poppy and with the parental figures of the nursery teachers. Poppy was listening to all this.

In the session it emerged that Mrs Green had felt quite unhappy when Poppy was at the nursery. She agreed that she needed to cling onto Poppy and to worry about her, in case she would not settle down, even when the teacher had commented on how well and happy Poppy had been. Mr Green, present at this session, suggested that his wife might be jealous. Mrs Green blushed and then quite honestly and openly confirmed she did feel jealous and left out if her daughter had a good time. "But isn't that natural?" she wondered? Mr Green said it would not help the child.

Mrs Green's infantile, rivalrous feelings had been aroused at a time when Poppy seemed more able to separate from her and to enjoy herself, while her mother was still struggling with a sense of emptiness and failure for not having had more babies. More mental space was available in the session to talk about her "infertility" and the circumstances that had allowed her to become pregnant for the second time. It had been during a holiday, when her husband had taken Poppy away from her for quite a bit of time and Mrs Green had felt quite supported and relaxed. The father's role in separating mother and child seemed to have been experienced as very positive, in rather concrete terms, as she had been able to conceive.

Our work stopped here, although I was aware of its limitation and of the desirability for more understanding, had there been a request for it.

Follow-up session

As we had planned, a follow-up session took place two months later, after they had returned from a holiday. The progress was reported to be steady and Poppy had felt more confident in playing with older children and even spending the night away from home. Yet, Mrs Green still seemed to be holding her back and she would not follow the nursery teacher's suggestion that Poppy was ready to start school in September. Mrs Green wanted Poppy to continue to settle in the nursery on four mornings a week, rather than two mornings, and wished Poppy to go to school after Christmas, when a close friend was also starting.

In this session I asked about the problem of her fertility; Mrs Green told me she had done all sorts of tests and they were planning to undertake in-vitro fertilization. Yet she was worried about becoming pregnant when Poppy started school. This was in case she could not handle a change of school, as well as her mother becoming pregnant. "It is never the right time" to have another baby and to let go of Poppy.

A follow-up questionnaire and letter were sent a year later. Mrs Green wrote back saying that Poppy was now looking forward to starting school in September and that she was more outgoing and happier in herself. She was going to parties and ballet classes and enjoyed them. She was, however, still anxious at being left alone with older children. No mention of the IVF plan was made.

Reflections

I will now consider a few facts and "coincidences" in Poppy's case history and refer to some relevant literature that will help throw some light on my work with this family.

I knew little about either the parents' family history or about Poppy's early childhood. Mrs Green's relationship with her mother and sister seemed characterized by difficulties in regulating closeness and distance. Mrs Green seemed to have needed to live far apart from her family. Her mother and sister were mentioned when they had once visited Mrs Green, and with reference to the relief experienced after they left. Yet, Mrs Green had appreciated her mother's help during the miscarriage.

I had learnt from the Health Visitor's referral letter that at the age of eight months, Poppy used to be upset when visitors just looked at her. This is a proper developmental response for a baby of that age, yet I wondered how her mother had handled that fear, since it went on for several years in a little modified form. She had, however, by the time I was seeing them, managed to separate as far as staying at a neighbour's alone. About nine months before the referral letter, Poppy, aged three, had refused to go to a neighbour's house to play. It was at the time when her mother had become pregnant. Mrs Green's belief that her child had never known or been aware of her pregnancy seemed to me to be a blind view, especially considering Poppy's acting in the sessions and at home following the miscarriage and even before they came to see me. On the contrary, Poppy seemed to be displaying a fine sensitivity.

The referral came to me at the beginning of February and I later learnt that the baby should have been born by the end of February. Mrs Green cancelled the session scheduled for that week. I now wondered whether the cancellation, which caused an "interruption of the therapeutic work", was similar to the interruption of the pregnancy and was being acted out in the relationship with me. Therapy did resume and, in the session following the missed one, a mini-mourning process took place as I have described. Mrs Green was able to cry and to talk about the failed pregnancy and her shaken hopes of being a mother for a second time, in view of her age and previous difficulties.

Lewis and Bourne suggested that the reaction to early miscarriages might be similar to a neonatal death, whatever the stage of pregnancy. "When ... a mother knows she has a baby inside ... she becomes psychologically pregnant and if the baby dies she has what is for her a stillbirth" (Lewis & Bourne, 1989, p. 939).

Freud wrote that, in the normal mourning process, "the withdrawal of the libido from [the] object and a displacement of it onto a new one, but something different," take place (Freud, 1917b, p. 249). This may be interpreted as meaning that in mourning a loss the task is to accept and acknowledge what has happened and to sort out the many mixed feelings, lost hopes, and expectations. In this way, the memory of the lost object is put into perspective, both allowing life to continue and enhancing it. Mrs Green seemed to have gone through a "double loss" at the same time: the loss of the baby-to-be and the loss of Poppy, had she gone to the nursery. It seemed to have been too much to bear and Mrs Green turned her investment from the lost baby to the existing child, Poppy, an already-born baby, seen as a substitute for the should-have-been baby. She turned her libido or life energy onto an object different from the baby inside, but treating the object Poppy, as if Poppy were the lost baby. She held onto Poppy and to the belief that only she herself could possibly have the time, inclination, and capacity to cope with Poppy's distress and anger at being left at nursery and to calm her down. I wondered whether she had compensated for her feelings of disappointment and failure to become a mother for the second time, by stressing how important and necessary she was for her first child. Because of her difficulties in negotiating the separation, the steps she had taken in leaving Poppy at the state nursery, not Cherry Tree, seemed to have been a recipe for failure, thus confirming her view of being irreplaceable. The work we had done on the lost baby paralleled the work on her low self-esteem as a parent and on the understanding of Poppy's feelings, displayed in her play. Freud considered the lowering of feelings of self-esteem to be one of the features of melancholia, which is absent in mourning (Freud, 1917b). Winnicott wrote: "If in an individual the depressive position has been achieved and fully established, then the reaction to loss is grief, or sadness. Where there is some degree of failure at the depressive position the result of loss is depression" (Winnicott, 1954, p. 275). Mrs Green was not aware of her depression, as far as I could tell. It was, however, very present in our sessions and took the form of monotonous, endless flows of words, as well as of great heaviness, which was projected onto me.

It seemed to me that Poppy had been affected by the miscarriage in two ways. Firstly, she was not "allowed" to go to nursery and to grow into a more separate child. Secondly, it is likely that she had been aware of her mother's failed pregnancy or, if not, she must have had phantasies of other babies inside her mother. The issue of other children and of being herself the only child seemed to have been in her mind and play for several months. After seeing the nativity baby she wanted to be the special Jesus-like baby. The death or absence of other children must have confirmed Poppy's thoughts and wishes to be the only and special baby—who could have power and possession of the mother—as well as her phantasy of having harmed the rival babies inside the mother and of envying her parents' procreative capacity. The extent of Poppy's distress and terror, *vis-à-vis* both other children and the "abandonment" by the mother, can be understood in terms of talion law, a retaliation by those vengeful babies and bossed mother. The reality of the great difficulty for Mrs Green in containing Poppy's feelings, increased their virulence and power. Mr Green was relatively "absent" at the time of the miscarriage, as well as at other times and was not a helpful participant in Poppy's upbringing. He seemed to blame his wife for Poppy's problems. It was only in the course of some sessions with me that some light was thrown on the parental dynamic, thus allowing both parents to modify some of their opposing views on Poppy's upbringing.

Limitation of the work with the Green family

As I have briefly mentioned, the parents' families were almost absent in this short therapy. It is obvious that the difficulty in obtaining more information, either about Poppy's babyhood or about her grandparents, was present in the sessions. Clearly the issue was not addressed enough. On reflection, it was as if anything other than Poppy's difficulty was like an intrusion, perhaps like a "separation" from the problem and a shift into the distant territory of family relationship and into the past. All sorts of gaps were left, both in my mind and in the outcome of the work. My impression was that Mrs Green was entrenched in her depressed state and equally resistant to thinking about it. At times, it had even been difficult to shift the attention from Poppy alone to the relationship between Poppy and her mother, Poppy and her father, or of the mother and father *vis-à-vis* Poppy.

In the third session, Mrs Green had come wearing a T-shirt with the words LIMITED RESOURCES printed in large letters on it. This seemed to be a warning to me about the extent of our work as well as about her feelings concerning herself. I often found myself introducing relevant issues, asking questions or interrupting the deadness of her flow of words. I did try to prevent thinking and understanding from being buried. Yet there was also a prohibition and a barrier to pursue certain issues further, especially if not directly related to Poppy. I, too, had come under the spell cast by Mrs Green. The focus of the intervention with the Greens was mainly the object relations that could be observed in the here and now of the sessions or in the present life of Mr and Mrs Green and Poppy. None of the "study of fantasies about and reconstruction of the past" (Balint *et al.*, 1972) was possible with the Green family.

The dead baby[2]

"He has always avoided looking at my eyes since being a baby at the breast", said Mrs Smith, the mother of two-and-a-half-year-old Peter. When I asked what he might have seen in her eyes, she replied: "Sadness as I always thought of Duncan." Her first child, born in another marriage, had died of a congenital disease before he was two years old.

In the family sessions, mother reported that, after Duncan's death, she had had a psychic experience in which she was leaving her body behind and "was going to die", in order to be with her first baby, whom she had loved so much. Intense separation anxieties and difficulties in mourning Duncan had greatly affected Mrs Smith's relationship with Peter. She became aware that she had never looked at Peter as Peter, but as if he were Duncan. Peter was referred to an Under Fives' Counselling Service of a provincial Child Family Clinic, because of nightmares and tantrums when he had to separate from mother to go to nursery. All this had started a couple of months before the birth of baby Lucy, who was seven months old at the time of the family's first visit to the clinic.

Peter showed clear signs of jealousy, both at home and with the children at the nursery. He was isolated, unable to play with them and, when mother collected him after a few hours, he would run away from her, hide and refuse to go home. He was described as always avoiding mother's eyes and preferring his blanket for solace rather than allowing mother to comfort him. He had a slightly better relationship with his father. In the session, he behaved as if he were in the nursery. He flopped by himself in a corner, then turned away avoiding mother's gaze and mine. I noticed the striking similarity between his dead-looking eyes and mother's depressed eyes. I was also told that he wanted to be called by his sister's name and to dress as a girl. The mother's response to Peter was of deep disappointment, hurt, jealousy, and rage, as he was not a "normal child" or a "perfect child".

Mrs Smith had not been able to mourn the death of her first baby or possibly the failure of her first marriage. She had turned to Peter, both as a replacement of Duncan and as her vessel for her feelings, expectations, projections, and denial of Duncan's death. Peter had turned away from her since the early days and had used a blanket as a total substitute for mother. He held on to it and dragged it along all the time in the absence of an object that received, contained, transformed, and returned the projections of the child to the child himself (Bion, 1962a). Mother's depression and baby Peter's depression went along hand in hand, unnoticed and in what seemed to me to be a symbiotic way, until separation at the nursery became a "must". At that point, Peter had not developed a sense of his own self or the inner goodness and strength that allow children to grow, to face separation from mother, and to deal with the arrival of new babies. He began to demand of mother a great deal and yet he rejected her and was angry with her as if he was aware of never having had an adequate maternal figure. A vicious circle had been set up when mother, who also was filled with anger and resentment towards Peter, consulted the Clinic for help.

It is apparent how mother's need to be helped over her bereavement and to be looked after had been acted out unconsciously in her relationship with her little child. He had become stuck at the point of becoming a separate individual and of becoming more independent from mother.

In the eight sessions Mr and Mrs Smith had, some with both children, some with Peter and not the baby, some with the parents alone, Mrs Smith was able to explore and to think of those painful issues, which she had always kept away from her husband in order to protect their marriage. She could understand and withdraw her projections from Peter and begin to mourn the loss of her first baby. She was then able "to see" Peter as Peter, for the first time ever. She had previously mirrored herself in her child's eyes and mind rather than the other way round, i.e. to be there for her baby to see himself in mother's eyes. Lovely sparkles, smiles, and a link with the world began to appear in both mother and son's eyes and their dead and switched-off look went. The mutual rejection decreased, physical closeness began as mother reported and as it was seen in sessions. Father visited the new land of his wife and child's experience and proved to be very supportive, thoughtful, and grateful.

Notes

1. This chapter was published, in a modified version, with the title "It is never the right time: how to help a mother separate from her young child" in *Psychoanalytic Psychotherapy*, 1993, Vol. 7, No. 2: 135–147.
2. This is a modified part of the chapter entitled "Early problems in mother–child separation as a basis for narcissistic disturbance" in *Narcissistic Wounds Clinical Perspectives*, edited by Cooper, J. and Maxwell, N., published by Whurr Publishers Ltd, 1995.

CHAPTER FIVE

Eating problems

Introduction

As I was collecting my thoughts to write about this topic, I realized that I have encountered two main categories of under fives with eating problems. In the first group, children present with general developmental delays including problems in the area of feeding. These children are unable to move from taking in liquidized, mushy foods to eating lumpy, solid, and crunchy foods. They seem to have great difficulty with their ordinary aggression, which they seem to experience in their phantasy as having a devouring and destroying effect on their feeding mother. I have observed this type of eating problem in children who have been exposed to depressed or very preoccupied and un-attuned mothers. I have written about this group in the chapter on parental guidance with severely developmentally delayed children.

The second group include those children who have mastered the skills of chewing, biting, tearing, and swallowing food, but for various reasons, have to stop eating and to take control over what they eat and how or when they eat. In this way, they take control of their feeding object or reject her effort to feed them. Gianna

Williams, in her recent book on eating disorders, has explored in depth the "no-entry system of defences" i.e. the conflictual relationship with the feeding object and the denied dependency on it. It is mostly due to unbearably persecutory and painful events, which usually date back to the early months and years of the patient's life (Williams, 1997). Jeanne Magagna also, has written extensively on eating disorders (Magagna, 1994).

I have noticed that the psychological disposition of families with children with eating problems often resembles the anorectic type, in that they are very controlling of the counselling. They almost have tightly shut lips, which do not let much therapeutic feeding enter, a no-entry type of defence. It is also interesting to observe that when improvement in the eating symptoms and family dynamic occurs, it is despite a degree of denial in the parents that counselling had made any difference. The family and child that I will discuss in detail, indeed presented difficulties in being fed psychologically, but still benefited slowly from counselling and could somehow acknowledge the help that they received.

Henry Rey in *Universals of Psychoanalysis in the Treatment of Psychotic and Borderline States* (Rey, 1994), explored how greed, anxieties, and confusion about eating, being fat, and having babies seem to be at the root of eating disorders, such as anorexia. The following case, of Francis, confirms Rey's thinking with regard to the patient's inner world. The patient's parents also seemed to be caught up within themselves, with one another, and with their son. They were inclined to project their conflicts into him and also were unable to deal with his projections into them. The family showed a possible early origin of the eating disorder and how an appropriate, early intervention, that reaches unconscious layers of the child's and the parents' mind, can ameliorate the situation and possibly prevent serious, pathological outcomes in adolescence.

The anorectic greedy boy and the squabbling parents

Francis, aged four and a half, was referred to the child and family consultation clinic by his G.P. for poor eating and poor dietary intake. The problem had persisted despite the family having seen a paediatrician at the local growth and nutrition clinic. They had also attended the eating disorder clinic at a leading children's hospital, but to no avail. At that time Francis's weight was very low, on the 3rd percentile, while his height was on the 50th percentile. He had been prescribed iron medication for iron deficiency anaemia. I had a telephone conversation with mother, prior to our first session and established the urgency of the situation.

At our first session, I gathered the history of Francis's difficulty and the many methods that had been attempted to deal with it, as well as general details of his developmental and emotional milestones. Mother attributed his eating problem to an attitude of control, which had originated at the age of five months, when he had to be spoon-fed antibiotics by force to treat a ureteric reflux.

An initial physical problem can often lead on to an entrenched psychological difficulty and to the formation of a defensive system based on splitting, projection, and control.

In the first session, Francis displayed his internal world quite openly, as if he knew why he had come to see me, even though no prior explanation had been given to him or to his younger sister Mary. He drew a picture of a fat boy with a long, peeing, willy. Next to it there was their cat sitting on father's lap and Francis grabbed him and sat him on his lap. Then he feared father's anger as a daddy crocodile appeared and wanted to eat angry Francis, who did not want to eat. Meanwhile mother was at work and had a fat tummy, as baby Mary was inside her, I was told.

In his fragmented phantasy we already have a number of elements, which will form a more complete picture, and an explanation of Francis's difficulties and confusion. I thought he was the boy with the long willy, who was free to be greedy and eat a lot. He felt left out and jealous of mum's baby in her tummy and he wanted to steal dad's cat standing for either dad's penis or a baby. He resorted to not eating as a way to take control of the painful scenario of jealousy and exclusion. He projected the anger onto his father who, in phantasy, had become a threatening presence. I also learnt that father easily lost his patience with Francis, thus confirming Francis's phantasy that dad was an angry and threatening figure. I thought Francis had a phantasy that eating meant growing a baby in his fat tummy and this was fraught with anxieties, confusion, and conflicts. I used a direct way of talking with Francis, as one can do with a child of such young age, while I spoke in more generalized terms with his parents. "Children of this age have phantasies of having babies themselves, and this can be a way to counterbalance feelings of jealousy and exclusion by the grown ups." I shared with them some of my thinking about Francis's inner world, as they seemed receptive and interested in these ideas. Francis, too, went along beautifully with my understanding. At the end of the session, I proposed to have four more sessions. They were pleased and decided to try to be firmer and also to stay calm with Francis at home.

In the following session, mother's defiance against the children's hospital eating programme, which she had tried to follow only half-heartedly, emerged. The programme required that the parents gave Francis the food he liked most, only as a reward after he had eaten some other food. Mother had soon given into him and fed him only what he liked. Somehow she could not follow the eating programme. I realized I had to tread carefully in my work with her in particular, and I became aware of her warning me that she would not easily do or take in what I might offer or suggest. I was already sensing that she was not easy to feed, metaphorically speaking.

In the session, father played with Francis at being "the boss" and not letting him climb up and behind the settee. Father said he wanted to practice managing his authority with Francis without losing his temper, something he found difficult at home. Mother recollected Francis's babyhood and the difficulties following weaning. He had fed well at the breast for six months, but had refused solids well into the second year of his life. In the first year, he had also been a poor sleeper and this, combined with his weaning difficulty, gave me a picture of unmetabolized and uncontained separation anxieties in this mother–infant dyad. In the session Francis became contrary and controlling with mother and she became cross and hooked into an authority battle with him. Later on he drew a baby in a pram—himself—he said. Baby Francis had a wide-open mouth and wanted a pear. I said: "A pear for baby Francis that is like mummy's good milk." He continued to draw bits scattered all over the pram and said: "food". At that point Mary asked mum to draw her a pram on that same paper. Francis did not protest, but made the crocodile bite and eat mum's blouse, then dad's, and mine. I spoke of Francis's wish to want all the pear/breast for himself and when Mary came along and took it away from him, the angry crocodile/Francis bit mum, dad, and me. He could be very cross with dad, when the latter did not let him be the boss, and then the angry crocodile/Francis bit dad, too. However, because of such feelings he was no longer sure of his parents' love for him and kept asking them if they loved him.

This scenario, so typical of an individual psychotherapy session, can be easily displayed with the real parents and siblings, as well as in symbolic play activities in under fives' counselling. Under favourable circumstances, the scenario can be verbalized by the therapist and taken in by the parents. Francis was deeply engrossed and free in his associative production of play; however, he was inclined to take over entirely and not to allow a dialogue between his parents and me.

In the third session, it was reported that eating had continued to improve with regard to the quantity, but not to the variety of food, which was still the same. We explored more about the parents' families of origin. Father had a brother who was a monster, according to him, but not to father's mother, who thought it was father who was a monster. She had had to give in to him all the time for peaceful living. No negotiation had apparently been possible, when he was a little boy. It seemed that father was stuck with rivalrous and competitive feelings towards his brother, feelings which were now projectively identified into Francis. The latter stood for a rivalrous brother in father's eyes and was—momentarily—not seen as his son. Father could not behave as a father towards his son, but rather as a brother, and either gave in to him or dominated him cruelly. Mother had a younger brother whom she bossed about but also played with. She seemed to relate to her husband as she did with her brother, i.e. in a competitive and superior way. I could observe this in the session, but it did not seem appropriate for me to comment on this, as yet. She wanted him to do things her way and no negotiation was possible. Francis was caught up in this sibling-type relationship between his parents. Mother also remembered being shy, thin, weak, and bossed about by her own strong mother, when she was little. Francis's mother finally revealed having had eating difficulties as a child. She had not said so when I had asked very explicitly in the first session and I wondered whether there was an issue of control in having withheld this important information. She remembered having been forced to eat her food, even after a fly had fallen into her dish and her mother just took it out. Mother seemed to fluctuate between identifying with her own angry and forceful mother, when she got cross with Francis, and with the shy and weak child, when she gave into him. She had not found a third way of being. The parents were now keen to disagree with me and I felt, at times, this was just for the sake of disagreeing. For example, they rejected the previously accepted idea that Francis may have felt jealous when his sister was born and this had added to his earlier difficulty with eating. I felt stuck at this point and was worried about the long summer break coming up.

However, after the holiday, they returned to the fourth session saying that Francis had eaten more types of food and things had been better. Both parents were very needy of my attention and time for themselves and did not want to talk about Francis. Then they agreed, by smiling, with my transference interpretation, that they had felt hidden resentment towards me, looking relaxed and suntanned, while they had been struggling to do their best with their two children. Father and mother were still cross with each other and father was still losing his temper with Francis and feeling guilty for failing, despite having tried. Mother, on her part, had been able to be firmer with Francis without getting angry with him. This had given her an obvious sense of superiority over her husband as well as pleasure at helping Francis, who had eaten well.

In the fifth session, the progress in eating had continued, apart from a brief relapse due to Francis starting nursery after the summer holiday. It finally emerged that mother had taken Francis's not eating as a personal rejection, as she said: "He would not eat dinner for me!" I thought he projected his feelings of rejection, which had re-emerged with the return to nursery. I wondered aloud whether he was feeling rejected as he now had longer hours at nursery and away from mother and whether he was getting rid of such feelings by not eating Mum's food and thereby hurting her. They listened. She also reported having been less anxious about his food intake, apparently since she had spoken to me on the telephone before the first session. Father was still struggling with losing his temper, when he had to stand as the authority figure with Francis. I observed him playing with both children and easily becoming angry with Francis, if he did not comply with his requests. Mother could not intervene to help, as father easily felt put down by her and her tone of voice, which indeed conveyed feelings of competitiveness and resentment on her part. We had planned to have five sessions altogether and then review the situation. As I sensed that unresolved, marital issues were becoming predominant, I suggested that we met another time without the children, to which they agreed.

They did come to the sixth session, but after a number of cancellations and with the children, as they had forgotten our arrangement to come by themselves. When I mentioned this, they seemed surprised and minimized their marital difficulties. Stability in Francis's eating was reported, even though the types of food he ate still did not satisfy his parents. I still perceived parental antagonism towards me and it felt as if they did what they expected me to tell them not to do. In reality, I had never given them any specific prescription about eating, unlike the children's hospital. When I asked if *they* had been any different with Francis, father confessed that he still lost his temper, while mother had continued not to worry about his eating. In this session, Francis appeared fragile and vulnerable as never before. He burst into tears, and became almost hysterical, when he could not cut the sellotape. He wanted to stick sellotape arms to a picture of himself. Mum helped him and this calmed him down. However, he got into a panic later on, as mum had cut too much sellotape. "Too much, too much!", he shouted in terror. I commented on his fear about "too much sellotape, too much food", i.e. his fear of being greedy. His parents nodded and Francis relaxed. His unconscious greed could not be expressed openly as it caused him too much terror and anxiety. Since the progress had been maintained they were ready to end today and to have a review after some months.

I have not mentioned Mary much during these sessions: on the whole she was rather active in playing, drawing, copying her brother's activities quite a lot, and wanting attention and involvement from the parents. I made occasional comments to her, although Francis was definitely taking most of our thinking time and space. I also have to say that someone else had monitored Francis's weight at our clinic and there was no cause for concern.

A long gap followed before we met for a follow-up session many months later. However, I had telephoned the family a few times, while trying to arrange and rearrange the review session and I had learnt that things had continued well with regard to eating. Even the types of food Francis had started eating had slowly increased and mother reflected on the long way they had moved on, since a year earlier.

In that review session, the family had somehow grown up: the atmosphere and relationships were noticeably different. Both parents were in charge of the children in a calm and appropriate way. They were less competitive with each other and mother let father take over the care of the children without her old worries. Father said that he was now able to manage Francis without losing his temper. Francis ate most food with appetite and only rarely had tantrums, which were short-lived. He looked and behaved as if he had moved into latency. He chatted with me about school, his teachers, and friends in a friendly and open manner, as he had never done before in sessions or at home, the parents told me. He also played more with his sister. He looked well settled in himself and in his environment.

This review session dispersed my concern and earlier thoughts that Francis may have needed individual psychotherapy, if he was to move on the developmental path. It seemed that the seven sessions and a few telephone calls during the twelve months had functioned as a slow feeding, which had been taken in by Francis and his family and had fed them all, very much at their own pace. Father was able to say that our talking had sparked off some ideas, which they could put into practice. Mother was more reluctant to acknowledge the input from the counselling and she preferred to attribute the big leap forward to our initial telephone call and to the firm boundaries in the new school environment. Perhaps an element of greed and control in her internal world devalued the good work we did and which she had only rarely been able to recognize in the sessions.

CHAPTER SIX

The little girl who could not sleep, or psychic bolts[1]

"In Veritate Libertas Vitae"

One can read the above slogan, which is very appropriate to the theme of freedom, on an old pamphlet of the Lincoln Centre and Institute for Psychotherapy. The slogan means that the freedom of life lies in truth. This chapter is on the concept of psychological freedom and my understanding of it, as a psychotherapist working with children and families. I took inspiration for the title of this book from the work with the family I describe in this chapter.

The theme of freedom is seen here from a psychological point of view and, in particular, from the vertex of the internal world of the individual, rather than from a political, social, cultural or moral point of view. Yet, I am aware of the difficulty in separating these closely interrelated dimensions. The movement towards individual, internal freedom is an attitude, which hopefully leads to free choices in life, rather than perpetuating models of psychological slavery, pathology, deprivation, and abuse.

In an article in the *International Journal of Psychoanalysis* on human freedom and its transmission, Neville Symington writes: "It is central to Bion's thinking that the expression of freedom lies in a person's activity of thinking his own thoughts. The person who is able to think his own thoughts is free" (Symington, 1990, p. 96). I would like to add that such a capacity, to think one's own thoughts, is very often impaired by all sorts of conditioning and that even when it exists within the individual, it is important that it is also expressed in appropriate actions. All this is possible only when the individual can understand and contain his or her anxieties and unconscious conflicts. It seems to me that by being aware of and taking responsibility for such conflicts, the individual becomes free and able to act his own thoughts.

A family, consisting of the two parents in their late twenties or early thirties, a four-year-old girl and a baby of four months, was referred to me. They had asked for an urgent appointment at the child guidance clinic. The problem, as it emerged in the first consultation, had been afflicting them for over three years. Their little girl had been unable to sleep since she was one. She had refused to go to sleep at night and after endless, tearful, and exhausting battles with her parents, she would either end up in their bed or make one of them sleep next to her in her bedroom, thus preventing them from having much needed rest.

The families of small children with sleep problems usually come to clinics with great urgency. The parents, having sought advice from various sources, reach a point at which they almost explode with exasperation as Dilys Daws, child psychotherapist, shows so poignantly in her book *Through the Night* (Daws, 1989).

From my first contact in the waiting room with the whole Smith family, they struck me with a sense of their undifferentiated union, as they all sat squeezed next to one another. Susan, the referred patient, was squashed between the two parents, while dad held Bob in his arms. In the therapy room, they sat in a similar uncomfortable way and I expected that sooner or later someone would slip off the small couch.

In this first session, the young couple gave me a considered and detailed account of the problem. Susan had refused to sleep alone in her bedroom for three years. She would cry hopelessly at night, at times in the grip of some terrifying fears and at other times with great rage at having to be separated from her parents. They had either been gentle and persuasive and spent some time with Susan in her bedroom or had been angry with her. Nothing would calm her down and they eventually ended up having her in their bed or falling asleep next to her in her bedroom. It had all started at the age of one, following a sudden outburst of projectile vomiting and acute earache, that had struck Susan in the middle of the night. The doctor on night duty had been contacted, but had not thought the case to be urgent enough to justify a visit. The Smiths had brought Susan into their bed and from that night on, she had not moved out. Subsequent to her illness, she had started to vomit in the evenings. It was projectile vomiting that had gone all over the room to the extent that, after a few months, the Smiths had had to re-carpet Susan's room. They thought she was manipulating them, so as not to be left alone to sleep, but they still had never been able to make her sleep alone in her bedroom. The feelings of terror communicated by this distraught little girl were too intense and powerful for the parents, too, to process. The violence of Susan's oedipal rage emerged one evening when—in Mr Smith's account—Susan had told him: "Get the gun and kill mummy."—Mummy had tried for the thousandth time to take her back to her room.

I commented on Susan's jealousy and the impossibility of her letting her parents be in bed together at night and Susan's unbearable feeling of exclusion from their bedroom. I was also struck by Susan's fear of being left alone with such intense, murderous feelings and the fear of death, which one-year-old Susan must have felt that night together with her great pain. The Smiths received my ideas, which were meant to widen the understanding of Susan's distress, with passive acceptance, as if already known to them. They said, with a good deal of insight, that Susan had been an excellent contraceptive. Mrs Smith had been unable to become pregnant again for a number of years, despite their wish to have another baby. In the end they had attended a very prestigious clinic in the country to have Mrs Smith's supposed infertility looked into.

During our first session, I realized that the great quantity of information I had been told and my insightful comments, had both been simple intellectual exercises. Their accounts had been conveyed in a detached manner. The Smiths were calm and flat and did not communicate the impact of the night battles described to me. The emotional violence of the events seemed to be absent. Susan was the one into whom such feelings had been projected by her parents. She was been looked upon as the cause of any discomfort and the source of the most unthinkable and unacceptable feelings. Mr and Mrs Smith had told me these facts in a tone that conveyed detached hopelessness. "Thank you very much, we know all this already, but there is really nothing to do," they seemed to say.

The second session took place a fortnight later, rather than a week, because Susan had not felt too well on the day they were supposed to come to the clinic. Even then a similar account was repeated with an increasing sense of passivity and failure on behalf of the parents. My comments did not appear to touch any emotional chord. It was as if they were unconsciously trying to make me feel the failure they were feeling, via the mechanism of projective identification. When I suggested that this might be the case, they replied negatively. I felt a sense of paralysis, impotence, exasperation, and professional failure. It seemed that we could speak of nothing else except this sleep problem, which was showing no improvement.

Sometimes, when a child is referred for a specific problem in the area of sleeping, feeding or phobias, the symptom is so charged with meaning that it becomes impossible to explore other areas of the development of that child and of the family relationships. The child and the symptom somehow become identified and nothing else exists. This element of obsessionality and exasperation may paralyse the therapist's capacity to think and to explore the situation further. Being aware of such a phenomenon and feeling exasperated by my incapacity to penetrate into this family unit, I asked if they had had any bereavement in the family. My unconscious "choice" for this question, rather unusual in the circumstances, was linked with the sense of death and of undigested violence that was present in this family. This had been subsequently pointed out to me in a discussion with colleagues in the Under Fives' Workshop at the Tavistock Clinic. On one side there was Susan's murderous wish to kill her mother and to be able to be with father in bed. On the other side there were unexpressed, hostile feelings in the parents towards Susan. Moreover, both the terror of dying in the one-year-old baby, in the grip of the acute pain of earache and projectile vomiting, and the parents' anxiety and aloneness *vis-à-vis* such violent physical manifestations, had contributed to making the situation almost explosive. It was a situation that could otherwise have been rather ordinary in itself.

Following my question on family bereavements, I was told of the death of an uncle. A curious and fairly common phenomenon in psychoanalytic psychotherapy then occurred. Despite my wish to listen to Mrs Smith's account of these new facts, my attention kept wandering and was almost pushed away from the story. Meanwhile, Susan had begun whining and wanting her parents' attention with increasing insistence until she managed to interrupt her mother's account. At this point, I realized that I was facing something new and I had a flash of insight. In the here and now of the session, a new situation had occurred in which Susan, with her sleep problem, was not the focus of attention. Susan, unable to bear exclusion, had managed to interrupt her mother and to bring the attention back onto herself. My distraction seemed to have reflected this fact. In my countertransference, I had picked up that something was not quite right and that there was discomfort when the little girl was not at the centre of the psychic life of the family. I verbalized this process, which we had all observed in the course of the session. The parents were struck and touched at an emotional level, possibly for the first time since we had begun meeting. We had reached an important point, which had been previously discussed, but only at an intellectual level. It had not brought about any change, as it had not involved the Smiths emotionally.

Mr and Mrs Smith mentioned a number of circumstances in which Susan had shown her intolerance at being deposed from the centre of attention. She could not allow people to form couples, independent of her, nor could she permit them to engage in their own interests, even when it only meant two people having a conversation. This would be felt as excluding to her. At this point some marital disagreement emerged. Mrs Smith was feeling alone and isolated at home and she had little help from her husband, who worked until late. The arrival of the second baby had only worsened things. Yet the two parents hardly ever confronted one another openly, nor had they tackled the issues within the couple. Instead they saw Susan as the cause of their tensions. The second session ended at this point and the marital discomfort, which I could sense, was deliberately avoided in the following sessions.

The following week they telephoned the clinic to cancel the appointment, as Mr Smith was away for work. They did not come the following week either. I felt that they were losing interest in the work we were doing, despite their having told me that this type of exploration had interested them. My wish to give up was strong, but I then decided to ring and offer them another appointment. Mrs Smith answered the phone sounding very distant, as though having missed two appointments had had no importance at all, but, at the same time, she talked as though we had met the previous day.

They came for their third appointment without showing any bad feeling about the two missed sessions. We had to use a different room and although they told me, almost with an air of triumph, that the problem was still there, the atmosphere in the session had changed. For the first time, Susan sat by herself at the small table with the toys. She used the animals and the plastic containers. A sense of individuality and separateness reigned amongst them all. Even Bob, their little baby, who up to this session had been like an amorphous lump in his mother's arms, looked more alert, alive, and interested in his surroundings. This time he was in his pram. There was more psychological space and freedom to think, as well as more active emotional participation on the part of the parents.

They told me how difficult they found it when Susan cried hopelessly in the night before going to sleep. They felt that they would be being cruel parents, had they insisted in leaving her sobbing her heart out alone at night. Hence, partly to assuage their own feelings and partly for peaceful living, they ended up giving in to her demands. I could feel that a diffuse sense of guilt was around in both Mr and Mrs Smith and Susan during this session. They reported that Susan had told her nursery friend of having woken up in *her* bed hearing her parents preparing breakfast in the kitchen downstairs. This lie brought to our attention Susan's unhappiness and guilt in still occupying her parents' bed. Following this session, Susan told her parents that she wanted to sleep in her own bedroom, but she only managed it for four hours.

In the next session, partial improvement was reported, together with an unhappy event that had occurred at Susan's nursery. Susan and a girlfriend had excluded a third little girl from their playing and said to her: "We don't like you!" The nursery teacher had told them off and Susan had been very upset. "She had been confronted for the first time by an authority figure," said mother smiling and admitting that neither herself nor her husband had ever been able to exercise a firm authority with Susan.

It emerged that Mrs Smith was trying to modify her childhood experience of a weak and ill father and a strict and authoritarian mother. Mrs Smith, in her attempt to be an understanding and kind mother to Susan, had ended up by being tyrannized and dominated by her daughter. Mr Smith had had a happy childhood. His parents were kind and there had been no problems with discipline or restrictions, as according to him "the children knew their limits well". He wanted to perpetuate similar happiness in his present family. I believe that the interactions between the couple and between their families of origin were more complex, but there was no willingness in the Smiths to explore this further. It could be observed that the parental authority had either collapsed or was lacking, hence reality could not be faced. The lack of parental authority seemed to have been caused by unresolved unconscious dynamics and conflicts belonging to the Smiths' past. They had tried to modify such dynamics at a conscious level but the unconscious imprisonment was too powerful (Byng-Hall, 1986).

The Smiths were aware of their weakness and wondered how they could be firmer. Their friends had had a similar problem and had let their little boy cry in his bolted bedroom, for three evenings. The Smiths did not feel like doing the same. Their difficulty was in finding a middle way, but their alternatives oscillated between two extremes: to bear with Susan in their bedroom night after night or to bolt her up in her room. We explored the possibility that I suggested, of leaving her alone in her bed for a few minutes and to visit frequently. They doubted whether it would work.

In the course of the session, they had turned to Susan several times "asking" her whether she wanted to be left alone for a few minutes, rather than "telling" her that they would do so that night. I was under the impression that they kept asking her for permission to do things, i.e. to be parents, rather than informing her on what she had to do. The role of parent/child was being reversed. An apparently liberal upbringing had lead to tyranny. I pointed out to them how they were relating to Susan and I spoke of the need for "psychological bolts" in their minds and not so much on Susan's door. This would allow internal boundaries to be set and would then create separate spaces between them and Susan, as well as allowing the blossoming of a solid parental authority.

The following week they came to the session saying: "Success,

success!" Susan had gone to bed at eight o'clock and had slept through the night since our last session. She was now a different child, happier and more alive during the day.

Later on, a temporary regression occurred on one occasion, when father agreed to take Susan alone to the local fair on a week night, rather than waiting to go on the weekend with the whole family. The old difficulties had re-emerged and the Smiths had rung me. The review session that we had arranged to have after two months was brought forward. After this session things settled more permanently.

Comments

Mr and Mrs Smith, initially tyrannized by their first child and unable to sustain a position of authority, had gradually become able to establish firmness and authority. This had implied the freedom to think their own thoughts and ideas and to practise them in the rearing of their daughter. Such ideas had been previously imprisoned by unconscious conflicts, which had prevented them from being put into practice.

In the course of the sessions, a number of factors had facilitated the establishment of the sense of freedom. Firstly, there was the relationship with the therapist, who listened and understood the unconscious anxieties, processed them at a psychological level and then either verbalized them to the parents or used them to help the parents in an indirect way. The containing function, as Bion called it, is based on the mother's "reverie". The mother shows the infant her capacity to love by reverie and her mental state is open to the reception of the infant's projections. Through what Bion called "alpha function", the mother transforms the projections of states that are unthinkable for the infant, into thinkable forms and returns them to the infant in a form that is now acceptable, thus feeding the psyche of the infant (Bion, 1962b). The function of the therapist is similar to that of the mother, insofar as the projections are received, contained and transformed via reverie. This maternal function implies a real or symbolic presence of the father, the male element that separates and differentiates the mother–baby dyad and that sets limits and boundaries.

In the case of the Smith family, an important moment of containment and reverie had occurred not only during the sessions but also between sessions. The flexibility of the therapist, in offering more appointments than those originally agreed, proved to be useful. However, the therapist had to avoid falling into a boundary-less situation, since this would have recreated a model of tyranny similar to the one experienced by the Smiths. The firmness expressed in offering to see them again and not abandoning the task of facing the sleep problem, had been an example of real life experience for the Smiths and not just theoretical advice. The sense of discouragement, impotence, rejection, failure, rage, and, last but not least, the wish to give up that I had experienced, had been contained and not acted out by abandoning this family. The Smiths had been too familiar with giving in to and abandoning hope in the struggles that they had had for many years with their daughter. The feelings, experienced by me, had made me realize that what was happening in the relationship between the therapist and the family was a repetition of what was going on between the Smiths and their daughter. It was important that my therapeutic authority and freedom was disentangled from the very intense paralysis, rejection, and aggression, which had been projected onto me and had almost destroyed my therapeutic function.

Mrs Smith had wondered what had happened in herself that had made it possible to move out of being a passive victim of her child. She had been able to differentiate herself from the child and to embrace a more adult position and to face the anxieties and terrors of separation, so intense and powerful just before going to sleep. She reported having realized, in the course of the sessions, that they used to "ask" Susan permission for her to go to bed alone, rather than to "tell" her to do so. She said that this had been very important in throwing light on the situation.

Change in one's own way of thinking and acting is brought about by the actual experience of an emotional knowledge of a situation. I refer again to Symington who, in interpreting Bion's thinking, distinguishes between two sorts of knowledge: the intellectual knowledge that can be learnt and the emotional one that has to be lived through. The first one does not provide freedom from anxieties and conflicts, while the second puts the person in touch with anxieties and conflicts, which become known personally. It is only the direct and emotional awareness, felt deeply inside, which leads to an internal change in the direction of freedom. It was the emotional awareness that occurred in the here and now of the sessions, as well as the digestion of the experience in between sessions, that had unblocked the situation with the Smiths.

A paradox occurs when we approach this issue from the point of view of psychological freedom. This was only possible when "mental bolts", well-set boundaries and limits, were firmly established. The word "mental bolts" seems excessively strong, but it is exactly what was needed with the Smiths, who had been so unseparated and undifferentiated when they first came to the clinic. Mrs Smith, supported by her husband in their shared task, had decided to leave Susan alone for few minutes and then to visit her at regular intervals. She had transformed the idea of using the door bolt, into the idea of the mental bolt, thus giving space to the paternal function that separates a too-close mother–child unit. Mother had felt more able to be a separate and free adult, who could expect certain responses from her child. Susan had felt that her anxieties were contained and that she could eventually have a quiet and restful sleep.

The paradox consists in the fact that human freedom can only blossom in a climate of boundaries and limits, psychological and concrete, precise but flexible, which provide the child with safety and security. We can observe this in the growing child, in the student who wants to learn, in the patient who asks for help with psychic pain and in the citizen who lives in society.

In conclusion, the Smiths were very caring, concerned, and kind parents who wanted the best for their children and went to the extent they did to find a helpful solution to their problem. They did not bolt Susan in her bedroom. Yet the subtle form of emotional abuse that we could detect in this family, lay in the lack of boundaries and separateness between the parents and the child. This led to a situation where Susan would end up in bed with her parents, thus being exposed to an eroticized and highly seductive situation. It had fostered her phantasy and wishes to be with her father, as well as to control the parental intercourse. Her phantasy had become reality. I was very impressed with the Smiths for their efforts in seeking help year after year, until they finally found an answer to their difficulties.

Note

1. This chapter is part of the paper published, in a modified version, in Italian as: "Dalle catene del conflitto psichico alla liberta'" in: *Psychologos International Review of Psychology*, Vol. 0: 5–15.

CHAPTER SEVEN

Soiling[1]

Introduction

Soiling is usually a symptom of psychological difficulties, anxieties, and conflicts in the child and in the relationship with his parental figures. It is often present in cases of sexual abuse. Some soiling children may have achieved mastery over their bowels, but regress to a developmental stage previously acquired. Other children may not have managed proper bowel control, as one can read in the following case with Rosy. However, in both groups of children, we observe determined and often seemingly deliberate action, aimed at the retaining or overflowing of their bowels.

The soiling symptom can present either a mixture or a prevalence of oedipal or pre-oedipal issues, as Forth (1992) and Barrows (1996) argue in their writing about the soiling children they saw in individual psychotherapy. A four-year-old girl, described by Forth, had experienced traumatic losses within her family relationship and had turned to her own body products as a precious comfort and also as a way to hold on to her object and to control her feelings of anger and sadness about her losses. At a very primitive level, she may have also feared losing bits of her body, had she let go of her faeces.

Barrows focused more on oedipal issues in the soiling children he treated. They seemed to have lacked the experience of a robust parental couple, while living in the illusional phantasy of being like a parent, for example in being able to have babies and also of having omnipotent control over one parent to the exclusion of the other one. Both an oedipal and a pre-oedipal scenario emerged in my work with Rosy's family.

Rosy

Rosy's family was referred by the health visitor for an intractable problem of bowel training and soiling in their three-year-old girl. Rosy was functioning well in all other areas of her development. I saw them, in different combinations of family sessions, for two sets of five sessions, which were agreed and formally "contracted" with the parents. The treatment lasted about three months. Three follow-up sessions took place in the following year and a half.

I focus mainly on the first three sessions when issues emerged which are related to my method of working. The rest of the treatment, its development and outcome, will only be summarized.

First session: getting to know the family

Prior to this session, mother had phoned me a couple of times to find out more about the sessions, what they would consist of, and whether they had to bring toys for Rosy. I was able to respond briefly and in a matter of fact manner to her questions, but was struck by her anxious keenness. It betrayed her need to take charge of the unknown venture of coming to the clinic.

I noticed, when we first met in the waiting room, the parents' low-key appearance in contrast to Rosy's attractive presence. In the session, they wanted to know what I had been told by their health visitor, again betraying anxieties and a need to control. I summarized the little information I had been given and suggested they told me first-hand about Rosy and their concern. Rosy used the toilet only occasionally. Mostly, she would withhold her faeces till they were hard and hurt her. Alternatively, she let it out in bits in her pants. Because of the pain involving in passing faeces, Rosy used to request mother's presence every time she felt the need to go to the toilet, often many times a day. It was like "poohing on demand", with mother there all the time. In a very controlled and unemotional way, the parents told me that they did not want to have children at first. Later, mother, who had been a career woman, changed her mind and they decided to have one child. She had a number of miscarriages before being able to give birth to Rosy. Quickly they moved on to tell me that Rosy had never been properly toilet-trained. When she was two years old and mother was told it was the appropriate time to start toilet training, father was in and out of hospital. He had collapsing lungs and finally underwent two big operations. I noticed both the absence of emotion while mother reported this and a somewhat harsh attitude in both her and her husband. They were not, it seemed, allowing themselves to feel anxiety, stress or worry, either now in the session as they recalled those times, or in the past. They rebuked my idea that it must have been a difficult time for them all, including Rosy.

A conflict in mother soon appeared. As she felt herself to be a controlling personality, she could not strike a balance with Rosy and she was either too permissive or too bossy. Although she resented having constantly to follow Rosy to the toilet, she could not stop it, as she sympathized with her child's pain and distress. Father expressed his exasperation that family life was revolving entirely around this issue and no space was left for anything else. He was occasionally away for work for a few days in a row. Mother was often resentful with him for not sharing enough of the toilet burden with her—changing pants many times a day. When I began to reflect on the idea that Rosy's problem seemed to embody a rather complex situation and that she may have found her own way to deal with feelings of pain and frustration that she may not have been able to let out more directly, I was met by an equally complex response. Mother seemed anxious and interested, while father was, on the whole, sceptical. However, he somehow wanted to know more, to have an answer to their questions. Rosy had been moving from father to mother and back to father to have some attention from them: she had no interest in the toys provided. Also, at crucial points in the session, Rosy started to moan in a crescendo of physical discomfort and pain. She asked to go to the toilet. One of these moments was when I suggested that Rosy may have felt cross and upset when, as a little girl who was learning to use the potty, her dad went away to hospital. My mentioning this had almost an immediate response in Rosy. She held her tummy, bent forward and her face crumpled with pain; she had to go to the toilet, she screamed. Mother got up immediately and took her, to return after many minutes, looking frustrated and lost. Rosy had *not* gone to the toilet. This became for me an indication of the emotional constipation going on in Rosy and in her parents. As soon as there was a chance to think and talk about feelings in the session, the body took over: the tummy hurt and the bottom felt like bursting. This happened at least four times in that session. As I had been asked my view about the problem so directly, I ventured again the idea, now with obvious evidence, that talking about daddy in hospital and Rosy's feeling about it, had been followed so quickly by a strong reaction in Rosy's bowels. Hoping to make it more acceptable to the reluctant father, I continued to generalize. "In my experience of children with these difficulties," I said, "soiling problems are linked with feelings and both can get stuck."

Father looked blank and then increasingly rejected this idea. He said my ideas were too complicated and asked me incredulously to explain myself again. I felt a fool. I felt I was up against a brick wall and I then tried to address Rosy. I said, in a surprised tone of voice, that Rosy had kept her lips tightly shut from the beginning. "Was she trying to keep her words and feelings shut up inside her as she was fed up with us talking about this pooh-pooh business? Was she doing the same with her pooh tucked tightly in her bottom?" Rosy listened and drew a brown and black chocolate cake.

Mother wanted some practical advice to use at home, so together we worked out a weaning programme. She would gradually reduce the time she spent in the toilet with Rosy, would leave her for a while and return a few minutes later. The end of the hour was approaching, but I felt the parents' dissatisfaction. They made more demands and did not seem to want to go. I usually allow between an hour and an hour-and-a-half for these first family sessions and let the parents know, but I did not tell them in this case, so caught up was I in the turmoil of the session. However, when this time had gone, they still seemed reluctant to go and the wall of non-contact and dissatisfaction had grown thicker. They agreed to return, despite father's reluctance and doubting attitude. I was left feeling battered.

Comments

With hindsight and having considered my countertransference, I realized that the process of the session had been more important than either my ideas expressed to the parents and to Rosy, or their pseudo-curiosity and interest. I had felt pushed forward to tell them what I thought, to describe my way of working—"We are intelligent people and want to know what's involved in these sessions", father had said. I made some interpretative comments in the session and yet I was constantly pushed back and made to withdraw, in silence, mainly by father's doubting, questioning, and rejection of what I said. Initially, I had to undergo the same destiny as a faecal lump: pushed forwards then pulled backwards. This process was to be expressed by Rosy in a very graphic way in the next session.

Second session: an assault on the therapist

Rosy's parents were very cross with me and critical when they returned the following week. Why did I not tell them what I was doing and what I was aiming at in that meeting? Why did I have no structure and keep them so long? They did not understand me, I did not communicate with them and mother had felt criticized by me. I quickly examined myself and my crimes in my mind, to see where I had gone wrong, what they were projecting and how to make sense of all this. However, they also reported some improvement in Rosy, who had used the toilet twice, successfully and only once soiled her pants. "But it was big, soft and didn't hurt," mother said. The childminder, too, had noticed that Rosy had cried in a different way: sad and not uptight and angry as usual.

I noted that Rosy was more separate from mother in this session and played more independently using the toys. She hid the ball in a big, open cupboard-shelf and she, too, hid inside and sat on the ball. She looked at me mischievously, letting the ball peep through from under her bottom, then pushing it back again. She repeated this play a few times: we were all watching her silently. I was still trying to recover from the ongoing onslaught and tentatively ventured into engaging directly with her. I said that perhaps that ball was like her pooh, coming in and out of the bottom and she was taking control of that pooh-ball. She then asked her mother about kangaroos and baby joeys in their mother's pouch. Her mum did not reply, as at that moment she must have been talking to her husband or myself. Rosy banged the two kangaroos noisily on the chair to express her anger, I suggested, at not being spoken to. At a later point a painful interaction between mother and Rosy occurred, when, out of the blue, Rosy hit her mother's face and arm with a cloth, as she sat on her lap. Then she banged mother's chest. Mother lost her temper and pushed Rosy away roughly and angrily. Rosy looked rejected and hurt. I asked mother how she had felt in that short interaction with Rosy and her obvious reply was: "Angry and fed-up as she hurt me." I then wondered aloud whether Rosy's actions had made mum feel something that Rosy had often felt, when trying to go to the loo, as we had also seen here in the session last week. I continued to say that perhaps Rosy was trying to push her feelings into her mother so that both of them were feeling angry, hurt, and in physical pain. I was addressing both of them and their feelings. Mother listened with some curiosity, while father remained sceptical in the background.

Working on parental projections

To begin with I worked again with the negative transference and had to allow the parents to control me, to cross-question me, what I said, and how I said things. I had to accept my total defeat and mirror back the bad feelings and experience they had had with me the previous week. I had to be given unconscious permission to go on and to gain some therapeutic alliance with the three of them, if any work was to be continued. It was Rosy who was very helpful when she played with the ball and engaged me to talk freely with her about the meaning of that play. She was the one who allowed me access to her mind. I tried to reach mother by working on her feelings towards Rosy when Rosy hurt her and this helped Mum to have some curiosity about their relationship and to link it with Rosy's pain. Mother's feelings towards her daughter's pain, when Rosy was unable to go to the toilet, were mixed up with her inner crying infant who, as I learnt later on, had not been heard by her own mother. Therefore mother was giving Rosy unlimited time and could not contain and limit Rosy's demands, in the attempt to be helpful to her. The issue of separateness and yet inter-relatedness between mother and child was also spoken about. They both had feelings that were being bounced off from one into the other and *vice versa*. Unfortunately, father continued to be unavailable and sat in the background, watching us struggle.

Third session: the projections are withdrawn

They returned two weeks later, as agreed, and the parents looked rather relaxed and different from the previous time. They reported more progress on "the pooh-pooh front". Rosy had used the toilet many times at home and at her grandparents' house, although she had regressed lately. Mother spoke a lot about her own effort to talk to Rosy about Rosy's feelings, as well as being firmer in the toilet-weaning programme and with setting limits in general. We spoke about "who is in control" at home; about Rosy's needs to be cuddled, to cling on to mum, to kiss, and lick her mum's cheeks. Meanwhile, from the beginning of the session, Rosy engaged freely with the toys. She played with the ball as before, protesting when mum told me of a pooh-on-the-floor "accident". She stuck out her tongue at me a few times, cried, soiled her pants, and then went to the toilet. In this session, mother cried a lot as she felt exasperated, exhausted, disappointed, and let down by her child's disobedience and defiance. She felt she had failed as a mother. She cried in despair. Father confessed to me: "It's my fault for not being around enough and not supporting my wife by taking Rosy off her." I had to hold the hope in this session and remind them of the noticeable progress already achieved, as well as acknowledge their hard work and the pain involved in it all.

Comments

In this session, the bombardment of projections and blame had stopped. Enough containment and transformation had occurred and the therapeutic process could take place. Both parents had become more able to look at themselves and to stop "shitting/evacuating" on the therapist, to use a language relevant to the presenting problem. The parental inadequacy emerged, as well as unmet infantile needs of containment, boundaries, and separateness in Rosy.

Parental guilt had also become apparent. Guilt was now

overwhelming mother, while it had so far paralysed father, who had opted for withdrawal. I became aware, in a graphic and almost surprising way, that the range of feelings that I had experienced so far, failure, exhaustion, exasperation, bewilderment, despair, guilt, and blame, were now being felt and expressed by both parents.

It was interesting that, not only was I now thinking with the parents, but also they had been reached through the child when she started to play and my attention was then free enough to go to her. It had almost been like an oasis in the midst of a desert land and a key to access the parents. Previously, Rosy had to hold things (faeces/feelings) inside her, as she was in the middle of parents who were either spilling out or withdrawing, but not able to be there for her and to perform reverie and alpha function (Bion, 1962b).

The treatment

The parental conflict soon emerged more fully. They had different boundaries with Rosy. Father's boundaries were stricter, while mother's were fuzzy. They competed in the care of Rosy, when father was around, and he belittled and criticized his wife. She, for her part, accused him of being unemotional and cut-off.

I realized that they had dumped all these feelings on me in the first session and they had taken them back by the third session, hopefully to look at them. They had always been aware of their difficulties and had sought help as a couple in the past.

Rosy's toilet problem was steadily getting better, usually with relapses at times of stress, for example, when Rosy moved to nursery and had to leave her beloved childminder. A picture of a baby, who played with her faeces, liked them and held on to them in her nappy or in her bottom as a comfort also emerged. A baby who did not have enough of mother to help her and who also became her mother's consolation when mother cried at home. Aspects of unmetabolized mutual sadism, cruelty, hatred, and rejection in their relationship appeared in the therapy. As a result they could not separate adequately. Mother tended to baby Rosy, but then also rejected her badly. I felt that the parents needed some sessions on their own to explore these feelings, without exposing Rosy to what now clearly belonged to the adults.

This posed an ethical question. How and when does the therapist draw the limits on the parents' sadism and abuse of the child in the session, in view of the fact that the session is usually a re-enactment of the sadism that is likely to occur also at home? I had noticed that Rosy would poke mother's pendant into mother's chest until it hurt and mother either reacted violently and pushed Rosy away or let her hurt her excessively, remaining almost unaware of the pain. This was not a consistent way of handling Rosy's admitted sadism and need to project her pain into her mother. "I like it when Mummy is in pain", she had said in a session. Her mother's response was one of shock, anger, and retaliation or masochistic endurance. Her full hatred for her daughter, her husband, and originally her mother burst out in a session with mother alone. In a flood of tears and distress, she told me that she had lost her father soon after she was born. Her mother was breast-feeding her and she could not visit him in hospital. She held her baby daughter responsible for not being able to be with her husband; this she told her daughter later in life. Her own mother had never been able to mourn her husband's death, so Rosy's mother had somehow lost her mother as well as her father. When she had Rosy, she did not know how to play, to cuddle or to relate to her. She had not had an internal good mother with whom to identify. She had tried to do her best, but felt resentful of her baby's demands. The difficulties in their relationship had been noticed by the childminder who looked after Rosy. She had discussed her concerns with social services who had in turn contacted us. I decided not to say anything as the family was well engaged in treatment.

Mother did not know when and how to strike a proper balance in letting Rosy be a baby and helping her to grow up. Her guilt and sense of failure had now been put into perspective in my mind and I could share with her the links existing between her childhood experience and her difficulties with Rosy.

Her envy of her older sister, who had had both parents in her first few years of life, had kept mother in an isolated position within the family. During these counselling sessions, mother reconnected with her sister. She also envied her friend, the mother of a child of Rosy's age, who was able to chat with her and to attend to her own child at the same time. I realized that some of my paralysis and cautiousness in the first session was linked with this envy for me, as a luckier sister or friend in the transference. However, I did not interpret this, as mother had become well engaged and open with me. She had appreciated some of my thoughts and used them with Rosy at home. She compared her experience of this counselling with some "useless" counselling she had had years before. She concluded that she had not been ready at that time. Her need for me and the wait in between sessions had become intolerable and she began to ring me between sessions, in great distress. One weekend when her husband was away at work, she called the Samaritans in despair.

We explored the issue of more help for herself and I recommended intensive psychotherapy, which she was able to start locally. In addition, both parents had wanted more help for themselves as a couple, so we met a few more times before a final session with the whole family.

Father had "lost" his father to the army in the Far East when he was five years old. He dealt with this, he said, by cutting off emotionally and getting on with the positive aspects of life. Instead, he had developed a chronic cold, his lungs collapsed and his silent presence in the sessions was often accompanied by sniffing and sneezing. His heart was dead, but his body cried, I thought. I tried to put that idea to him gently and lightly, but he rebuked me contemptuously. However, the following week his cold had gone. Had he magically been cured or was he holding it back for fear of my funny ideas?

We had also been able to keep space for Rosy, in our minds, in these sessions; to think of more meanings of the "pooh-pooh problem" and how mother could continue helping her by talking openly of her feelings. Mother's therapeutic intervention with Rosy at home had continued and a good exchange of communication and feelings was taking place between the two of them. Rosy continued to improve.

In the last session with Rosy, there were still issues of control and mother's uncertainty and worries regarding appropriate developmental needs, play activities, and behaviours in her daughter. Rosy made a big mess with black plasticine as she played on the table. Then baby bear and tiger, which protected baby bear from night monsters, came along. It seemed to me that things had now been set in motion for Rosy, who was feeling more helped by good figures. Her progress needed only to be monitored, since mother was about to start psychotherapy.

Review session

About three months later, we met for a review before the summer holiday. Father did not come. Rosy's soiling had relapsed badly recently, after a steady improvement. At home, Rosy admitted to mother that she soiled because mother did not like her. Mother had felt sad and disappointed about this and somehow got hooked back into relationship difficulties with Rosy. It appeared that Rosy used soiling again as a weapon against mother. Mother cried in the session and she was also distressed at seeing me again, then having to part. In the session, I related mother's sadness to her earlier difficulty in bonding with Rosy as a baby. I added that Rosy might, in addition, have previously projected her dislike of mother.

Rosy was still demanding of mother's attention and love and could not play alone for any length of time, mother reported. In my view, this insecurity was partly due to Rosy's weak internalization of mother as a good and sustaining figure. Mother, in the grip of old guilt, passively accepted Rosy hitting her chest painfully in the session. This probably did not help Rosy with her guilt about hurting mum. A clear balance between separation, rejection, and need for closeness was still hard to strike. I felt somewhat hopeless and tired about this never-ending, exhausting, and repetitive process.

We decided that I would monitor Rosy's progress and we would meet occasionally. The whole family came back in September with very good news. The soiling was now 95% cured. Rosy was now saying goodbye to her faeces, even if they had already disappeared down the loo. Rosy listened and spoke to me more in this session. She drew a picture of herself with one ear (usually Rosy omitted the ears in her pictures at home, she and mother told me). Then Rosy drew and told me a story of herself, mother, and another girl on a boat trip. Father was not with them. The issue of father's minimal presence and involvement in Rosy's life was spoken about a lot in this session. However, he had tried to become more involved with Rosy and mother had managed to stand back and let them get on together. I also noticed this in this session.

Things had moved a bit with mother's own mother, and old family ghosts were being dug out and faced, together with the older sister. Father insisted that this should be the last session and mother reluctantly had to accept this. She parted slowly and sadly. I verbalized for Rosy that she had said goodbye to her pooh and now to her time here with me.

Letters

Mother kept me posted on two occasions; once by letter and the second time by answering, at length, a routine questionnaire the clinic sends out sometime after the end of therapy. Rosy's problem had resolved and mother's therapy was going well, helping her and indirectly the whole family. It also helped the relationship with her reluctant husband. She was grateful for the help she had from me and listed the ways I had helped her, one of which was that I had been like a catalyst to their intricate family life. In the questionnaire, she had expressed regret for not having received any reply from me. I had, in fact, replied, but the letter had gone astray, so a copy was sent to her again. She replied by asking for a final session alone with me, as she had felt bothered by something I had written in that letter. We met again a year after our last family session. As well as clarifying some outstanding issues, the session was used to think more about Rosy's jealousy of the parental couple and wish to control and spoil it. Thinking of mother's own family scenario gave her some clues as to how to deal with Rosy. She said she was now leaving me, feeling that our work was concluded properly and again she was very appreciative of the work done.

Conclusion

The example of brief psychodynamic counselling with the whole family highlights the circle of mutual projections of the child on the parents and *vice versa*, as well as the response of the child to the lack of reverie and containment and further response of the parents. This dynamic is re-enacted in the sessions and in the transference with the therapist. Understanding of the current dynamic relationships and links with the parents' own childhood experiences were made. Containment, through mental digestion, transformation (Bion, 1962a), and silent or verbalized interpretations, took place so that the parents and the child achieved some insight. The parental feelings towards the child, seen as a tool to understand the child's world and feelings and to achieve separateness from the child, were addressed and explored. Adequate decisions could be made and changes in the family relationships eventually occurred, together with the improvement of the symptom in the child.

Note

1. This chapter is modified from part of the paper "Psychodynamic counselling with under-5's and their families: clinical and technical issues". *Journal of Child Psychotherapy*, 1999, Vol. 25 No. 1: 51–70.

CHAPTER EIGHT

Gender identity

In my working experience in Child and Family Consultation Clinics, I have not come across many under fives referred for issues of gender identity. I have encountered the problem in male twins, referred because the parents had noticed and were worried about one of the twins showing excessive feminine traits and interests. Being a twin constitutes a situation of risk and vulnerability. What is meant for one baby has to be shared by two babies from the very beginning of life in the womb. We are often given accounts of one of the twins being weaker, more vulnerable, ill, and slower in developing than the other twin.

I will consider the issue of gender identity in a twin boy, who was four years old when he was referred to the clinic. The presenting problem was that Ron had played with dolls since early life and had shown an attraction for feminine clothes, which he himself wanted to wear. The whole family was invited and attended the first session, following which four more sessions were offered, but only the parents came. They were anxious about exposing the twins to, and possibly influencing them adversely, by us talking openly in front of them.

Ron was described as unhappy and having tantrums, as well as being easily bothered by mess. He only drew female figures and was fascinated by long hair. His parents let him wear a female hat with plaits, even indoors and all day long. The parents were particularly concerned about his almost obsessive interest in dolls and lack of boy-type activities, in view of a relative having recently declared himself to be homosexual. They were very anxious to learn more facts about homosexuality and appeared to need reassurance about their son's behaviour. Ron's parents feared a genetic component to their son's interest and were filled with anxieties and questions. With regard to the early history, I was told that both the pregnancy and the birth had been difficult, complicated, and risky. A Caesarean section had to be performed, near to term, to avoid further complication, a common outcome in twin pregnancies. Mother and twins had been unsettled for the first two years and they travelled backwards and forwards from her country of origin to have family support. Mother had maintained a strong attachment to her family and country. Ron's symptoms apparently began not long before starting playgroup. Both twins presented clingy behaviour, which required mother to stay with them for many weeks before they settled. However, while the other twin was able to settle in a gender appropriate way, by playing boy's activities with boys, Ron became friendly only with the girls and joined them in playing with dolls.

In the first session, he appeared rather clingy to his doll, was interested in the doll's house, and put all the dolls together in a heap. Soon he turned to mother, placed himself on her lap and clung around her neck. She accepted this rather passively. His brother played more independently with bricks and drew pictures by himself.

After the session, my thinking began to take shape around the issue of separation. I wondered whether Ron had developed such an interest in female attributes, play, and companionship as a way to hold on to mother and to almost become like mum, with long hair. Parting from her had been unbearable for him and possibly unthinkable for mum. Freud, in *Mourning and Melancholia* (Freud, 1917b), wrote that when the process of mourning fails, the person, rather than separating and letting go of the object, takes it inside and clings onto it, almost by becoming like the object itself or like aspects of it.

My hypothesis took more shape in the following sessions, when I heard that mother had felt overwhelmed by having to bring up the boys away from her family's support. She had not built enough of a support network in this country and had travelled backwards and forwards to and from her country. She expressed anxieties at being criticized and being looked on as a bad mother. Ron was described as a dreamy child who did not demand much of her attention, initially. She, therefore, left him to his own devices while she concentrated on the other twin, who was described as being forthcoming and relating more to her. She felt gratified by him smiling at her and reassured in what appeared to be her self-doubts about being a good mother, especially to twins. Once Ron awoke from his dreamy state, he became demanding, clingy, and had tantrums to which she responded by "having tantrums too" and by shouting at him in exasperation, as she had told me. I think he then responded by inhibiting his more robust and aggressive mode of being, turning to dolls, stroking their long hair, and drawing only female figures in order to reassure himself.

Coates and Moore (1998) describe a similar outcome in Colin, aged three and a half. He presented signs of gender-identity disorder as a result of a traumatic relationship with his mother, who had not worked through an earlier termination of pregnancy. The inter-generational aspect of Ron's difficulty was located in his mother's difficulty in working through the loss of her country and family of origin. She could not perform the container–contained function described by Bion, as she had not managed the separation from her own parental figures and somehow she took to over-indulging on Ron's hypersensitivity and feminine aspects, probably as a compensation for her lost relationships. The recent news of the family's young homosexual relative complicated the issue some-what. It was not easy to shift their attitude of needing information. It was particularly present in mother, although father more readily attempted to look at the family dynamics and at their child's feelings. Mother showed her resistance by insisting that she knew it all already, and thus rejected the ideas and suggestions proposed in our sessions, despite her conscious, desperate wish to learn about her child. Father was able to mobilize a more robust side and helped her in weaning Ron from her, by proposing an alternative parental model, which had been lacking until then. He was more involved and did more activities with Ron, rather than just indulging in his wish to be only with his mother. In the four sessions, changes were reported. Ron had given up his obsession with dolls almost entirely, the tantrums decreased and he looked generally happier and showed an interest in his brother's play.

The family cancelled the last session because of father's working commitments. It became difficult to meet again, but the parents decided not to come back and, on the telephone, they expressed criticism of our work, because I had not given them factual information on gender disorders. I was left thinking that a re-enactment of a difficulty in separating had taken place in relation to myself. I had turned into a bad figure and was not given the chance to work on these issues thoroughly. However, I learnt in a telephone conversation that Ron's progress had been maintained and that he now joined his brother in boys' play activities.

Mother's own personal difficulties were rather entrenched and she would have benefited from individual psychotherapeutic work. Her feelings of guilt, anger, and blame had become mobilized in our somewhat tumultuous piece of counselling, but could not be dealt with satisfactorily.

Comments

In his study of the atypical gender-identity organization, Di Ceglie supports the view that separation anxiety may play an important role in its development. He suggests that boys who develop atypical gender identities seem "to experience separation from the mother or any other attachment figure as a psychological catastrophe, and they fear psychic disintegration and chaos" (Di Ceglie, 1998, p. 19). Psychic survival may be achieved, he continues, by "disavowing some aspects of reality, and in particular, the male body" (*ibid.*, p. 20). I believe that a containing maternal or primary-carer figure had neither been available, nor been internalized properly by Ron, whose growth and separation had consequently been impeded. Prompt intervention at an early age is always recommendable, as then the situation can be more easily rectified with appropriate help.

An atypical gender-identity organization was possibly prevented in the case of Becky, whose mother had approached a child psychotherapist for help. Becky was aged four years when her beloved father suddenly left the marital home and initiated a bitter separation from mother. Becky had been a well-adjusted child, much loved by both her parents. She began to play-act male roles, such as the tough guy, the cowboy, and the policeman, as her way of identifying with the sex of her lost parent. It was the strong, tough, and winning aspect of the paternal figure that she was trying to reclaim in her identifications. Gradually through the psychodynamic counselling offered to her and mother together, Becky was able to get in touch with a feminine part, as well as with feelings of loss, sadness, and anger for both her father and mother. Becky introduced female roles in her play and resumed her feminine identification. Her gender identity was back on track and her development continued unperturbed.

CHAPTER NINE

Bereavement and loss

Introduction

A number of case histories could have been included under the title of bereavement and loss. It is a huge subject in our practice and clinics. I have chosen three situations that represent relatively common events, yet are quite different. They all focus on how the death of a close family member has affected the young child and other family members.

The question of how death affects children, whether it is the child's own death (Judd, 1989) or the death of a parent or of a sibling (Bowlby, 1980; Furman, 1974; Kubler-Ross, 1970, 1983), has interested clinicians, psychologists, and researchers for many years. It seems generally accepted that, under favourable circumstances, the stages of mourning that a child goes through are not dissimilar to those of adults. Stages of shock and numbness, denial, search, anger, guilt, bargain, despair, and acceptance are recognized as being part of healthy mourning (Parkes, 1972; Pincus, 1976). Children, from the age of two, have been observed going through similar phases of intense feelings and longing, although they follow different progressions and patterns (Smith, 1995). Since the child is dependent on the adult for his survival and welfare, the attitudes to death of the surviving parent or closest carer are of paramount importance to the child's mourning process. This can be facilitated or impeded, as the following vignette quoted by Bowlby shows: "... a small boy whose mother chided him for not shedding tears over his father's death [...], 'How can I cry', he retorted 'when I have never seen your tears?'" (Bowlby, 1980, p. 272).

It is also generally recognized that the best way to help children with the death of a parent or a close family member is by being honest and truthful, and by sharing with the child some of the grief and pain of the loss. Gustav lost his mother when he was not yet four years old. His father had difficulties himself in mourning due to his own childhood experiences of unprocessed losses and separations.

A child has to have developed a secure attachment to a maternal figure (Bowlby, 1980), or internalized a good object (Klein, 1952a) to be able to hold on to it in his mind and feelings, even when that person is absent or dies. The child, with the help of the surviving parent, will then be able to feel the loss, sadness, and range of feelings regarding the beloved, dead person and also the fear of his own death. This is considered to be a psychologically favourable condition.

In 1971, the Robertsons studied the emotional effect of a prolonged separation from their mother on children below the age of two. They observed that a supportive and thoughtful environment can reduce a state of pain, loss, and distress in the child. It is more difficult to study, but we can try to imagine the impact of the death of a parent on a one-year-old child. No doubt this has a long-lasting influence on the child, just as any change of main caretaker effects that early age.

The death of mother in the eyes of a four-year-old boy

Gustav lost his mother when he was nearly four-years-old and his father approached the clinic almost immediately, asking for help as he felt his son was not grieving the death of his mother. She had only died the week before. Mother and son had already parted several months prior to her death, as she had returned to her country of origin for medical treatment. However, they had kept in frequent contact by telephone. Father himself had some difficulties in mourning his wife, as their relationship had been complicated and shadowed by her illness, since early on in their marriage. Father's strict and militaristic upbringing had made it hard for him to be open to his feelings. He expected Gustav to cry almost "on demand", yet he did not have the emotional tools to facilitate his son's grieving. In this respect, father was quite wise in asking for help so soon after his wife's death and showed his wish to do the best for his bereaved child. Gustav had grown up with an ill mother, who nevertheless had taken good care of him when she was still at home. His first and most natural reaction on hearing about mum's death was to become particularly clingy to the surviving father, for fear that he too could disappear. We began to explore this in the first session, which took place just over two weeks from her death.

In that session Gustav drew his mum and dad close to each other and with no feet but with big arms and hands. He also drew himself with no feet or hands. On the top of the drawing there was a big eye with flowers. This drawing seemed to represent the loss of a part of the body, as well as the funeral flowers. Father said: "Mother's eye high up in the sky and looking down at Gustav." This he had already told his son at home. We can see how this little boy was preoccupied with his mother and how the stories and explanations he had been given were mixed up in his mind. Father did not believe in heaven or hell, but found it easier to conjure up that belief in the hope of rendering death less crude for his child, as he told me in the session.

In the ten sessions that followed, father told me many facts about his own childhood, life, and marriage and about Gustav's first years of life. Gustav gradually began to go through some of the phases which resemble those of mourning adults (Kubler-Ross, 1970; Parkes, 1972; Pincus, 1976). He felt a sense of shock, disbelief, and denial, which made him cling to father or use the toy telephone in the sessions to talk to his mother, just like he had done during the last few months of her illness abroad. He wanted to talk to her but could not hear anything on the other end of the 'phone. Gradually, he came to realize that she could no longer speak to him. In one of these sessions, he lay on the settee on his tummy making sinister, deep growling noises, which made me think of an ill and dying person. He seemed to be identified with his ill and dying mother and perhaps wanted to go with her. Bouts of anger and tantrums also began to appear and were a healthy sign for such a well-behaved and self-controlled child. These tantrums appeared when he had to give up things, like the drawings in the session when he was asked to leave them behind. These drawings seemed to have represented his mother, and leaving them behind was like losing her. He also began to fall down while running around and playing at school. The old picture of a strong, prim, and proper son of a soldier gave way to the picture of a dishevelled, tearful boy with cuts and scratches on his legs. A feeling of being left, dropped by an absent mother, was beginning to get hold of Gustav, as well as the experience of falling out of a false-self, the pseudo-mature boy his father had always encouraged him to be.

Easter was approaching. It was about three months since mother's death and the promise that she would come home and hide a basket of Easter eggs, as she had done in past years, could not become reality that year. In a session, Gustav made three baskets with eggs using plasticine. One basket was for dad, one for Gustav and ... he hesitated to say for whom he had made the third basket. Then he eventually said, "Dad's girlfriend." Both father and I expected him to say it was for mum. We verbalized this thought, as it seemed to me that Gustav was trying to protect his father from the idea of a dead mother. Gustav nodded. He remembered mother's playful habit and good surprise, which would not happen this year. At home Gustav had begun to show signs of anger and hatred, for example, when father had bought him the wrong Easter egg. Father was able to link such an intense emotional reaction, inappropriate for such trivial issue, to the loss of mother. The egg was not like the one mother had bought him and it reminded Gustav of her not being there. He was also beginning to talk about his dead mother on a rational level, but was still working through his omnipotent wishes, phantasies, and rages. He prayed to God to make her better and also wished to fly to heaven in a spaceship to take his healed mother back home to earth. He often played hide-and-seek with a plastic egg he had brought from home and made it disappear then re-appear in the sessions. Small children often master separation in this way (Freud, 1920) and his play brought Gustav some relief, possibly as he hoped that his mother would appear again, just like the egg, under his wish fulfilment. In reality, the telephone contacts had stopped and the idea of death was becoming more and more of a reality for him, especially when in a session he telephoned mother in heaven, but no one answered the telephone.

I will now focus on some details of the last four sessions as they are rather telling of this boy's struggle to come to terms with death. Father used to start sessions by saying, "Nothing, nothing at all has happened", referring to the mourning process of his son in the gap between sessions. He expected some miraculous event to occur rather than a slow working through. However, he kept the continuity with the previous sessions and, during the week, he would try to talk with Gustav about what we had spoken of in the session, thus continuing a dialogue with his son when appropriate. For example, he once reported this to me: "As you have said, Gustav believes that he can get mother back by praying to God, who will make her better." In the seventh session, father and son sat very close to each other and my impression was that Gustav was trying very hard to interest and entertain his father, by talking about willies and girlfriends. He eventually made a plasticine heart for his depressed-looking dad. In a role-reversal, he tried desperately to enliven him by taking the place of the grown-up in this bereft and lonely father–son couple. This was moving indeed and very sad to witness. Gustav had begun to count down our sessions and at the end of each session he would remind us all of how many sessions were left. By then I had offered them a second set of five sessions. He had become rather involved in our work and I wondered whether seeing me, a female therapist, to "talk about mother" was a way for him to stay connected with a memory and a picture of mother and also to have another maternal figure. I held him and his dad at this painful time. I had no doubt that father was struggling with the loss of his wife and other past losses and, together with his son, they were both engaged in a mourning process and also helping each other as they spoke to me, or played in the sessions.

In the eighth session, father appeared to be more alive and pleased as he had found an audiotape of stories, which his wife had recorded for Gustav to listen to. In this way, both had got her voice back, could feel sad, shed some tears, and be together at such painful time. However, Gustav asked to see mum, not just to hear her voice and wanted to touch and go inside the tape-machine and, appropriately for his age, hoped to see and find mother alive there. Father proposed to put together a photo album with pictures of mother. More memories of her were recovered in the session. Her illness emerged, as well as a picture of a child who had desperately tried to cure her by giving her sweets, but had also pushed himself physically on her in a desperate attempt to reach her, when she had began to switch off from him. Father too got in touch with feelings of loss as he remembered their life together and Gustav's birth, which had occurred already under the Damocles' sword of mother's cancer. Father had cried the previous week, as he had bathed his son, seen the changes in his body and thought that neither mother nor son could share together the joys of him growing up. I felt that he was also mourning something about his past, perhaps the loss of his own mother when, aged five years, he was sent to a boarding school after fleeing their country of origin. He was also sad and tearful in the session and Gustav wiped his tears gently and consoled him. It was indeed a moving session and I was left filled with sadness, as they went looking a little relieved and grateful.

In the last two sessions, Gustav gradually distanced himself from me, while father recollected his childhood memories as they fled their country to come to England, where he lost his father to the war and mother, not long later, when he was sent to boarding school. I understood why he had had to harden himself up and develop a number of defences to survive those wrenches. The wrench from these sessions too was felt and carried mainly by myself, as Gustav became more depressed and angry and father denied his obvious attachment to our work and to me. He only admitted, in a somewhat rational way, that coming to the clinic had brought some changes in his son and given him some links. Parting was slow and heavy.

Five months later, I saw them again for a planned review session after the summer. It appeared that Gustav had been unconsciously working through the loss of mother and getting ready "for a new mummy", as he said. Father seemed stuck in his depressive and negative frame of mind. He could not recognize how helpful the links he had made for Gustav had been. For example, father linked his son's excessively distressed reaction while baking cakes with their au pair girl, to the fact that he had baked cakes with mother a year earlier for the last time. Gustav had had interesting dreams, which were reported in the session. They showed the mental work he had been doing on his mother's death. In the first dream, mother was there and Gustav went to get her. She turned into a green flower and said "Too late". He woke up in tears. In the second, there was a girl holding jewels and precious necklaces and Gustav stole them from her. In the third dream, he was pulling mother by one arm, while black monsters were pulling her by the other one. Her arm broke. In real life, he had been pretending to steal things from a shop, but then returned them before leaving the shop. Father said he had been going through a repair phase and had fixed things, which he also did in this session. It seems that the loss of his precious mother was experienced by Gustav as the theft of a goodness that had been taken away from him. His longing to have her back was dealt with by stealing precious objects, which could represent mother. The underlying anxiety was that of breaking and damaging her in this process of taking her away from the monster/father or black monster/death, in this oedipal struggle, which ended up in a real defeat and loss when she died. Gustav was struggling with issues and anxieties about his relationship with mother and father, the oedipal rivalry and his fear of having damaged his mother irreparably in his struggle to have her, or in his anger for her illness.

Somehow he remained a vulnerable child, who lacked a stable female figure to balance the complex relationship with his father. He could have benefited from individual psychotherapy, had his father chosen that option then.

The under fives' counselling fostered the beginning of a mourning process in father, but more so in the child. It gave Gustav space to begin to explore the feelings, phantasies, and implications of losing mother at such a young age and gave father the opportunity to link the loss of his wife with losses that, as a little boy, he had not been able to mourn properly. He identified fleetingly with both the bereaved child and mother, when he cried in noticing his son growing up, something mother could not enjoy. Years later, I heard that individual psychotherapy for Gustav had been sought by his father.

The dead twin

In the following example of under fives' counselling, the focus of the work is mainly on the parents of the surviving twin and on how the death of the other twin had affected the whole family. Bourne and Lewis, child psychiatrists and psychoanalysts, who have an interest in neonatal death, discuss the effects of miscarriages and neonatal deaths on all the family members (Lewis & Bourne, 1989). The case I am going to consider is more complex as one twin's death was decided by the parents at the twentieth week's gestation, due to the foetus's congenital abnormalities.

Ross, as I will call the surviving twin, was one year old when his father visited the family doctor in despair. He had become quite fearful of losing his temper and hitting his son. The latter was born with some physical problems, which had been attended to with good results. Mother said that she had been able to mourn the death of Ross's identical twin, because of her experience as a carer with disabled children. This had alerted her to how poor a quality of life the disabled children had, despite everyone's best input. Father had not mourned the death and reported having wished for both twins to be sacrificed *in utero*, since Ross's head had showed some abnormalities on the scan. Father did not want to risk having a damaged child, nor could he trust the medical tests entirely. He had never bonded with Ross and often shouted at him, while he had a very good relationship with his four-year-old, eldest son. Father could not make sense of the strong passions he felt for Ross, in view of the settled and stable life and background he had had as a child. His wife had even asked him to leave the family, if he could not change his aggressive and unpleasant behaviour towards their one-year-old toddler, as well as his unsupportive attitude towards her.

In the first session, Ross entertained himself with toys and involved his parents from time to time, whilst they were speaking to me. He appeared rather active and unable to settle with anything and I wondered aloud, whether he was still looking for, or missing the physical presence of the twin with whom he had shared the womb for twenty weeks. It became apparent that his parents handled him differently at home. His mother was able to set healthy limits and boundaries, while his father overindulged Ross out of guilt for his own aggressive feelings. Little emerged about mother's early life, but something rather crucial about father's childhood was raised. He was the only son of a couple who wanted three children, but his mother could not have any other children after father's birth.

Birth was clearly charged, at a very profound level, for this man. He was feeling guilty about the phantasies that, as a child, he had damaged his mother and, later in life, that he had wanted the death of both twins. He had become the spoilt, only child of his parents and the "king of the castle" of that altogether happy household. Father was aware that he had repeated that happy childhood experience (Byng-Hall, 1995), when he had become a father for the first time to his son, Matthew. However, problems loomed during his wife's second, and very difficult, pregnancy. During this time, father had already distanced himself from his wife, especially when one twin had to be sacrificed.

My hypothesis was that he was dealing with a rivalrous situation with Ross, who confronted him with feelings he had never had a chance to experience deeply when he was a child himself. Ross stood in father's unconscious mind, for the second sibling that father had never had. Father was struck with "enlightenment" by this idea and mother also confirmed that Ross and her husband together were like two toddlers fighting. As well as being faced—at a child level—with the new situation of having a sibling, he also had to be a father to two children, without having had the model of parents with two children. He did not have a parental model to identify with when his second child was born, nor an infantile experience of being a little boy with a baby sibling. It was really encouraging to witness the impact of this understanding on Ross's father. The situation improved dramatically as he "knew emotionally" (Symington, 1990) what had gone wrong.

The second and last session occurred four weeks later and the progress reported had been maintained. Ross appeared calmer and generally more settled in the session, during which he and his brother played together. Also at home, he had been more settled and responded well to father's appropriate handling.

This piece of work shows the validity and efficacy of short intervention at a time of family need and distress. The family, father in particular, was emotionally ready to accept the interpretation about unconscious, unresolved, sibling rivalry. This interpretation had a mutative effect and prevented a possible family breakdown. It had unblocked family life, which had become stuck, and brought about psychic change in the whole unit.

However, some questions remained unanswered about the

couple's dynamics. In particular I was concerned as to whether there had been mutual splitting and projection with regard to mourning and whether mother's rationalization about the sacrificed twin was based on projecting her guilt and anger onto her husband. One also wonders about the link between Ross's ongoing constipation and the absence or disappearance of his twin. Since Ross was an infant, mother had had to remove his faeces manually, an enormous intrusion, similar to the intrusion into the womb to remove the malformed baby.

Cot-death in a family with a three-year-old sibling

This family went through the cot death of their four-month-old baby girl, when their older girl was just over three years old. They were seen urgently for bereavement counselling.

Emma had become clingy and obsessed with babies dying and her mother had felt ill equipped to deal with her questions and loss. Father, mother and Emma came to the first session. The atmosphere was of palpable anger, resentment, and blame, pushed from one parent to the other. Emma either entertained herself by playing or tried to distract her parents from arguing or to cheer them up. Mother had not been able to begin to mourn her baby's death, but had attempted suicide a couple of weeks earlier. She still spoke of her wish to die and I felt she was using it as a threat against her husband. He, on his part, had cried for some days after the baby's death and was already ready to start life again. He was going out to pubs with friends and wanted to enjoy himself again. He could neither understand his wife, nor accept and support her in her distress. However, it emerged that their disharmony had preceded the cot death. They wondered aloud whether they stayed together only for Emma's sake. In the session, the only possible intervention was to elicit an account of facts and feelings experienced by them both and to verbalize their mutual anger and resentment. I also gave them permission to go through the complicated process of, and feelings about mourning, at their different paces and without holding it against the other spouse. Mother could begin to explore her distress, as she had been very possessive and almost jealous of her baby, who had been in an intensive care unit for four weeks.

When she returned home, she had never left her alone, but despite this she still "slipped out" of her care and died. Hardly any emotional space was available for Emma in this first session.

Only mother and child returned to the second session. Father had already informed us that, due to his new job, he could not take more time off. Emma had become the centre of our thinking and attention and we could explore her behaviour and feelings, which seemed quite appropriate for a bereaved child of her age. She had become very clingy and wanted to be carried by mum all the time. "Like a baby, perhaps like baby Mel (the dead baby)," I said and she nodded. She also wanted to go back to sleeping in her parents' bed, which they did not mind, so it did not create a problem. I commented on her worries at being left alone at night in case she too died. She nodded and mother seemed to be able to understand this worry. Emma had also been carrying around her dead sister's teddy bear and kept looking for Mel in cupboards and rooms. This appeared a little strange to mum, who was again quick in grasping the need both to hold on to a teddy which stood for, or reminded Emma of, her dead baby sister and to look for the lost object, the baby sister. Searching for the dead person is part of healthy mourning for both children and adults. It is one of the stages before an acceptance of the finality of the loss can take place. At nursery, Emma kept telling children whose baby siblings were still alive, that their babies too would die. This was disconcerting to mother, but we tried to understand it and eventually it seemed clear that it was rooted in the envy of those children, who still had their baby siblings. It would have also made Emma be like other children. She started to hold babies very tightly and this could be seen as either a wish to squeeze them to death or to test that they would not die and to make sure they stayed alive. She responded positively to the latter option, again by nodding. In this session, Emma too was given permission to mourn the death of her baby sister in a way most appropriate to her age. Her feelings were verbalized by me and understood well by mother. As these behaviours, which were odd and inexplicable for mother, unfolded, understanding was gained and, from the perspective of a bereaved small child, they could begin to be seen as normal.

The third session was cancelled as Emma had chicken pox. The last time I heard about them was a month later when I telephoned to make another appointment. Things had got better, as Emma had worked through her obsession with dead babies and mother had come out of her depression and was able to look forward to life again. She was pregnant again and she said she knew it was not a replacement baby, but a new and different creature growing in her womb. She had been, and still was, attending group therapy and this was proving to be helpful.

In this very short and effective counselling, the catalyst to change had been the chance "to talk to someone who was not so directly involved", as mother reported on our last telephone communication. She and her husband had been too caught up with blame, anger, and competition to be able to talk to each other. It was the recognition and the naming of these feelings and of the spouses' different times and ways of mourning that helped them to work through it. Emma seemed to be the one who, in a graphic way, could go through the normal phases of mourning and also help her parents. I wondered whether she was the "useful child" who brought them to the clinic, and had been able to express her grieving feelings for them too.

CHAPTER TEN

Learning disabilities

Introduction

When children with severe disabilities, such as autism, Down's syndrome, congenital or hereditary syndromes or mental handicaps, are referred to the clinic, the help that under fives' counselling can offer is limited. It does not aim at modifying such severe conditions, but to help both parents and children to live together in a more tolerable and even satisfactory way, despite the disability. Sinason's concepts, of "opportunist, secondary handicap" and the "stupid smile" (Sinason, 1988, 1992), are useful tools to understand patients with handicaps and to help parents, who are confused, lost, frightened, and guilty, to see better and not to create a secondary handicap.

The "secondary handicap" consists of a psychological problem that is superimposed by families and carers on the original, primary handicap. For example, parents justify not setting limits and not allowing their handicapped child to become independent by arguing that they do not want to upset them. The "secondary handicap" can cause far greater distress and destruction than the original handicap, but it is this that can be treated, differently from the primary handicap, which may be ameliorated only in some cases. The "stupid smile" is a defensive, false smile, which many handicapped people show. For example, it may be used on meeting a new person, in order to be liked and to deny that they are different and may be shocking to look at. It is a mask that attempts to deny differences and feelings of unhappiness, envy, and the awareness of being unwanted by society. The "stupid smile" is a form of "secondary handicap". To be aware that the child with a handicap is still a human being with feelings and reactions, and to begin to understand his or her apparently inexplicable behaviour, can be a first step towards integration and a happier relationship with that child.

He cannot understand because he is not normal

Ralph, five years old, was referred to me by his paediatrician for very aggressive behaviour. I saw him with mother and father only four times, but such brief counselling allowed his parents to see him as a child with ordinary reactions and emotions. He had a moderate learning difficulty, that could be observed in the context of parents who also had difficulties with thinking. Moreover, maternal grandmother had taken a drug during her pregnancy, which had affected the foetus, Ralph's mother, badly. She thought this had also caused her child's difficulties. In our sessions, the parents described family situations in which Ralph was left out of either parent's attention and became violent towards them. The task I decided to take on was to address the feelings of exclusion, jealousy, and anger of both the child and his parents. However, Ralph stared at me as if he expected to be attacked when I spoke to him, perhaps as a punishment for his aggression at home. His mother also insisted that he could not understand, because "he was not normal." His unusual and slow gait, as well as his handicapped look were indeed noticeable and I could not detect whether and how much he understood me. He replied, "yes", to all I said in a somewhat mechanical and fearful manner. A painful account by mother followed, where she had been treated as "stupid", incompetent, and unaware of herself and her body phenomena, when she went into labour. I realized that "stupidity" and "abnormality" were being passed down from the generation of the parents to the generation of their son.

In this first session, which was attended only by mother and son, I was irritated as I witnessed Ralph being cast in the role of the "stupid one." I was clearly identified with him in my original reaction of irritation and I used this awareness to comment on mother's anger towards both her own mother and the doctors, who had put her down so badly during her pregnancy with Ralph. I also expressed my view that the "abnormal" child, as she referred to Ralph, still had feelings and responded to human interactions like ordinary children do. If anything, he was indeed able to have very intense feelings, as he had demonstrated at home. In this session he looked at me murderously, then drew pictures of his mum and dad with big eyes and looking very handicapped.

Dad came to the next three sessions and both parents could gradually see that Ralph felt rejected and angry with them when he returned home from his weekly respite care. He behaved badly, smeared faeces all over the house, kicked his mother ferociously or set one parent against the other, after having behaved like an angel at the respite carer's home. The parents began to talk to him about this anger and things improved in that area.

However, he still had difficulties in going back to sleep when he woke up in the middle of the night, because mother would give him special attention, thus encouraging his habit. Ralph seemed to feel the oedipal rivalry with father particularly intensely when he was away at weekends and mother seemed to enjoy his wish to be alone with her at night during the week.

Both parents gave examples of Ralph actively playing the role of the "stupid child" to get what he wanted. Mostly this seemed to be to draw his mother's attention away from father. In the session, he demonstrated this by talking to mum and dad like an ordinary five year old, while acting "stupidly" with me by agreeing with all I said in a mechanical way and with no conviction. He also glued his fixed gaze onto my face, which seemed to be his way to get my attention back to him and away from his parents.

Mother seemed keen to talk to Ralph about his feelings and she could see the benefits of it. In this respect, a shift had occurred in the parents' relationship with, and understanding of, Ralph. However, an area that could not be shifted was that of parental guilt and it brought the counselling to an end. The parents felt too guilty for sending Ralph for respite care at weekends and could not be reconciled with my understanding and acceptance that they needed a break, if they were to continue to care for him during the week.

The family came only one more time, but I was not able to change their perception. Their guilt about respite seemed too much for them to think about. I wondered whether they felt guilty for having produced a child with learning disabilities and for excluding him from their life at weekends, while they also identified with his experience of exclusion.

Other professionals considered this family to be extremely hard to help. I felt we had done as much as was possible and we had hit a spot of concrete thinking, which could not be shifted. The parents felt too responsible for Ralph's unhappy and angry feelings, when he was sent to respite at weekends. This conflict lead to the interruption of counselling prematurely and with hindsight, I felt I had somehow been caught up with my "stupidity", as I had not addressed their guilt soon enough.

A Down's syndrome girl obsessed with mother's death

Janet was approaching puberty when she was referred for refusing to eat, and having become obsessed with thoughts of her adoptive mother's death. I include her in this book on under fives, because her psychological age was that of a five-year-old girl. She had been adopted at the age of six months. Janet had always been clingy and found separation from her adoptive mother very hard. However this had worsened since adoptive mother had developed a life-threatening condition, followed by an operation and a sudden relapse. Mother had had to deal with the real possibility of her death, her fears, and an unsupportive, overwhelmed husband (who chose never to talk about this issue) and also with Janet. Janet reminded everybody, in an obsessive way, of this Damocles' sword hanging over their heads. Her parents used to get annoyed and fed up with her. Janet's protest had taken the form of refusal to eat.

I saw this family together with a colleague and we decided to offer five counselling sessions to begin with. Feelings and fears were very much at the surface for both mother and Janet. They were both overwhelmed and caught up with the fear and the real possibility of mother's death. The counselling provided a structured space, where floods of feelings, fears, anxieties, and conflicts were expressed, accepted, contained, and linked by us to other family events, which were not necessarily related to the presenting problem. The family had been very open about the fact that Janet's natural mother had given her for adoption, because of her Down's syndrome. Janet was able to tell us, in an intellectual way, how cross she had felt about it. I suggested that she might feel that she was like the alien she had spoken of in the context of a book and that her natural mother had given her up for that reason. Janet appeared deeply touched emotionally, but went on to tell us of the teasing and scapegoating to which she was being subjected at her special school. In the next sessions, mother reported some improvements in Janet's difficulties. Janet could feel and talk of her angry and negative feelings for her natural mother and her good feelings towards her adoptive mother, who had rescued her, through adoption, from an abandoning mother. However, her adoptive mother had also become the bad, abandoning mother, when she became ill and had to go to hospital and might still leave her if she died of her incurable illness. I could verbalize this conflict, which was projected onto us. My colleague became the nice lady, while I was the not-so-nice one. Janet showed these feelings when she drew a picture of herself and gave it to my colleague, while turning away from me and ignoring me when I spoke to her. Janet felt relief at being understood in this way but also became more connected with the painful feelings of her life situation.

She refused to come to the fourth session, as we "made her sad", mother reported. Mother had given in to her easily, partly because of the well-established improvement and partly because the sessions were emotionally very intense for her and had brought up a painful emotional awareness in mother.

Mother agreed to return for a final goodbye session, which we finally managed some months later. Janet had continued to do well. She ate properly, looked like an adolescent and was free of earlier anxieties about death and separation. The anniversary of mother's illness and operation had gone by without producing old obsessions and anxieties. In the last session, Janet drew and spoke about sex and the boy she liked. She seemed to have been able to go on developing emotionally and socially, although mother appeared more stuck with deep anxieties about her health and lack of marital support. Father had only come to the first session, as he admitted that it was too much for him. Mother turned down the possibility of further help for herself.

In this brief counselling, it emerged that adoptive mother and daughter were caught up with issues of separation, rejection, and death, all of which had the strong reality-based component of mother's severe illness. We were able to help the young girl to become unstuck and more separate from her mother, at a time when unresolved infantile losses and grievances had stopped her from growing up. However, mother was unwilling to continue exploring her own anxieties, a choice we fully understood and respected.

From chaos and depression to new life with a four-year-old boy with a rare congenital syndrome

Jerry, aged four and a half, was referred to the clinic by his paediatrician, due to his extremely aggressive behaviour. He had a rare congenital syndrome, which made him bigger than children of his age and particularly strong. He was unable to speak properly and was likely never to develop proper language. His parents were concerned about their difficulties in managing him now and feared for the future, when his physical growth and strength would be beyond the ordinary. The older sister had taken to copying his behaviour and, together with the whole family, had been severely affected by the birth of this disabled child. I saw them for a total of twelve sessions spread over one year and saw many changes in this time, including a final marital separation and a family stability not known beforehand.

I had to gain the parents' trust and convince mother that I had experience in mental handicap and understood the implications of having a child like Jerry. I did have to admit that I did not know about this particular syndrome. The early history was recounted with despair, depression, hopelessness, and a certain amount of anger towards the professionals, who had not been able to pick up any signs of an abnormal pregnancy until the last few weeks, "when it was too late", sighed father. However, since they were all deeply attached to this loveable, survivor child, it was almost impossible, especially for father and daughter, to look at their ambivalent feelings towards him. Father told me he had been very disturbed by the birth and had reacted in an unbalanced way, later becoming passively resigned. It had been a huge strain for them all to have Jerry, who was initially in a premature baby unit and then struggled to stay alive. A high percentage of similarly affected babies die in the first few weeks of life. Mother, on her part, had been very much alone in dealing with the burden, as her husband was psychologically "gone", despite later having managed to bond well with Jerry. Both parents had been helped by medication, and by marital counselling to stay together. However, by the time they came to the clinic, their relationship was very strained. Boundaries were almost non-existent and the sister had taken over a huge parental role with Jerry, as I could observe in the sessions. Jerry was out of control and in control of his defeated, depressed, and hopeless parents. Chaos was described as governing this family.

Mother was an articulate and insightful person, who had had counselling previously in her life. She was keen to talk, to understand Jerry's "jumbled-up brain", as she called it and to get some help. Her guilt, for both having produced a damaged baby and having ambivalent feelings towards him, did not prevent her from being open and somehow spurred her on in our work. Sadly, father was much more entrenched in his unrecognized guilt and despondent denial and was unable to see Jerry as separate from himself. He saw my understanding of Jerry's feelings and predicament as a critical attack on Jerry. For example, when I described Jerry as feeling cross, father disagreed and protested that Jerry was not evil or bad or mad. During one of the first sessions he walked out and never returned, despite mother's and my attempts to have him back at least once. Mother had been receptive to the ideas of boundaries for Jerry and of "secondary handicap" (Sinason, 1992) that could be reduced by taking charge of both children. Despite her tendency to give in to depression, she gradually became stronger and Jerry began showing signs of improvement as he responded to new limits and boundaries. Mother stopped hitting Jerry and then feeling guilty. She began taking back a firm and fair parental authority.

Jerry was a loveable child, keen to engage me in sessions by talking to me. He was happy to play with water, to draw nice pictures, and to interact with his sister or his mother at appropriate times and not with attention-seeking anxiety. He was described as a sensitive boy and intuitive of people's feelings and this could be seen in our sessions. His language improved in the course of the year I saw him, with help from speech therapy. His sleep problems and unruly eating habits eventually subsided as mother's capacity to set boundaries increased. This gave a sense of security and safety to both children. Mother's initial guilt at having to say "no" to Jerry was somehow linked with her guilt for his handicap and earlier suffering as a baby. Father felt unable to set limits for Jerry and continued to indulge him and his own depression, as I heard from mother. Eventually the parents split up, once mother felt strong enough to stop mothering her husband and began setting much-needed boundaries to his abusive relationship with her.

The little girl was sadly very identified with her father in her silent anger and despondency and once her parents split up she refused to come to sessions. Jerry's progress continued and the sessions petered out as mother cancelled or forgot to come. Then we planned a final review session.

Even in short or non-intensive counselling, I insist on having a formalized last session. Last sessions always bring up interesting, painful aspects of saying good-bye and this is still part of the therapeutic work. In our last session, Jerry, who had learnt where I kept my appointment diary, pointed at it for a next appointment, despite having being told that it was the last session. He had become very attached to the sessions and to myself and seemed helped by them. Ending was difficult for mother, who had a huge, temporary regression as she denied that coming had helped at all. She insisted that I could not know what it was like to have a child like Jerry, an issue we had discussed and analysed endlessly in the past.

This painful piece of work with the family helped to establish a communication of feelings and thoughts that had not been possible before, due to the traumatic shock, the stress, the guilt, the burden, and the ambivalence of having a baby born with a severe handicap. Honest communication was achieved and was based on the acquired strength to look at the difficulties of the family. However, the work also led to a restructuring of the family in a way that had never been faced properly. Father, after a huge crisis when he had to leave his family, managed to take more responsibility. He started a new life and still maintained his involvement with the children and eventually had a friendly relationship with his ex-wife.

An important aspect of my work with this family was my capacity to share the stress, pain, and guilt of them having a handicapped child. Also I pursued a connection between the thinking and the emotional sides of the family members and of Jerry, which had not been previously given much credit. The parents came to realize that Jerry, despite his handicap, had been a baby who had had to struggle for his life and go through the terrors and sensations of edging towards death, just like all babies who have to struggle with life and death. Jerry had developed a thick skin as a defensive survival measure, which needed to be understood and given proper limits in a firm and compassionate way. This was achieved in counselling and improved this family's life altogether.

Conclusion

Communication with children with severe disabilities or congenital illnesses is usually rather problematic for at least two reasons. One is, as I have mentioned, the false belief that these children do not have feelings and reactions like other children. They are therefore treated very differently or indulged, out of guilt, by their parents and carers. Secondly, their reactions and emotional life can be particularly intense, obscure, and incomprehensible to those around them. The two factors reinforce each other and strengthen the sense that stupidity is not just within the handicapped child with his stupid smile, as Sinason wrote, but is also reflected in the system. Adults cannot understand, and so feel stupid and de-skilled *vis-à-vis* the disabled child. It is at this juncture that the contribution of psychodynamic thinking can help the impasse and the lack of communication. It can change the spirit of family life, despite the unchangeable physical condition or primary handicap in the child.

CHAPTER ELEVEN

The borderline child and the establishment of internal reins

Introduction

I found myself in a quandary, once again, in thinking of cases to include in this chapter. Alistair, the boy I discuss, could have easily been included in the chapter on hyperactivity. Equally, children presented in other chapters, such as Pilar in the chapter on hyperactivity or Craig in the chapter on parental guidance, could be diagnosed as borderline children. The difficulty in categorizing borderline children is shared amongst clinicians, who find that many features of the borderline group are similar to those of a range of psychological disorders in childhood. Lubbe writes that the current profile of borderline children is "loaded down as it is with descriptions of conduct disturbance, attention deficit, impulsivity and emotional disregulation" (Lubbe, 2000, p. 6). In his review of the literature on borderline personality disorders, he quotes authors who have outlined some diagnostic features in this type of childhood disorder. He mentions a "rapid shift between psychotic-like and neurotic levels of reality testing; a lack of 'signal anxiety' (Freud, 1926) and a proneness to states of panic dominated by overwhelming concern of body dissolution, annihilation and abandonment" (Lubbe,

2000, p. 41). We also find idiosyncratic thinking and disruption of thought processes, impairment in relationships, and a difficulty in distinguishing self from others. There is a lack of impulse control, of the capacity to modulate destructive tendencies and to contain intense feelings. These characteristics are generally thought to define borderline personality in children.

In the work with very young children and their parents, we witness the origin of non-thinking and of the distortion of thinking as well as the lack of transformation of body states into mind states. Impulsive children, who seem to act out of the blue with no apparent reason to justify their behaviour, "directly translate their wishes into actions" (Lubbe, 2000, p. 48). These children show a low level of tolerance of frustration and "experience little sense of guilt and responsibility" (*ibid.*). They believe that things and their actions just happen, rather than stemming from their choices and from themselves in relation with others.

Alistair and his mother provide a clear example of a "reactive duo" rather than of a "thinking duo". During psychodynamic counselling they showed a progressive change from mindlessness and impulsivity to thinking and mentalization.

Alistair's story

Alistair had been difficult since birth, when he could neither latch onto the nipple nor feed properly. He could not relax or sleep through the night and he had always been very active. He was almost three years old when he was referred to the clinic after seeing a paediatrician and a dietician with no lasting improvement. The family was very keen to be seen, since both parents were at the end of their tethers and feared that Alistair was suffering from hyperactivity. Following a telephone consultation, I offered to see them in the near future, before Alistair was due to start nursery school, as mother was unsure whether he would settle there.

In the first session, I gathered the history of the problem, observed the family interactions and made rare comments. It seemed that they wanted to be mainly heard on this occasion, unlike other families, who may want to engage sooner in an exchange with the therapist. Father was rather laid-back and keen to let me know that Alistair had ruined the parental relationship and not the other way round, as I might have thought. Mother appeared overpowering, both physically and psychologically and almost like an elastic band, in that she reacted to any movement or action of both her children. My impression was that no separateness was present between herself, Alistair, and the older girl. The girl soon revealed herself to be mostly her brother's guardian, acting as a parent towards him and only occasionally as a sibling, when she ganged up with Alistair against mother. She was the good child, praised for her deeds and the drawings she did in the session, while Alistair was the bad, aggressive child, who was inclined to pick up chairs and other big objects suddenly and to throw them around dangerously. He knew how to get his parents' attention only by negative and destructive actions and behaviour. In the five sessions offered, I noticed that he could not tolerate being left out of anything, whether it was a conversation or a play activity. He would throw toys or destroy his sister's drawings, not as an immediate reaction to a frustration or a scolding for his misbehaviour, but rather out of the blue as a sudden reaction. When he did so, he looked almost mad and as if he were driven by an inner push. Also, when mother prohibited him to play, say with plasticine, she almost pounced on him and he cowered, withdrawing to being a baby, sucking his thumb or dummy and eventually crawling to mother and curling up on her lap. We came to realize that this infantile behaviour stirred up mother's guilt and other feelings. She turned from the angry and disapproving mother into the soothing and controlling mother in a short space of time that did not allow any understanding of what had happened. It seemed that Alistair, terrified by his mother's strong reaction, split off his anger and withdrew to a safe, baby state, so that mother returned again to being his protector. It was a very interesting sequence to observe and I shared my thinking with the parents, who were keen to know and prompted me to tell them my thoughts. Mother was able to confirm that she had always had a quick fuse and was aware that she tended to pounce on both children. She did not know how to be different, but I felt that she also seemed too quick in taking on my view. In that first session, she was not aware of feeling persecuted or criticized by my comments, but after she left these feelings festered in her mind. When the family returned for their next session, mother had the courage to tell me that she had felt criticized, on the one hand, but she also knew that I had struck a chord in her. It emerged that I had momentarily become her over-critical mother in the transference. She made this link herself in the session. Later on, I also anticipated the possibility that she might feel pounced on by me when I made further comments. However, a working alliance was created, following the interpretation of this negative transference and the alliance continued steadily till the end of the counselling.

Both parents developed trust in their therapist and were keen to reflect on and practice what we came to understand. Alistair had found a way to provoke huge rage in his parents. While it did not take much to make mother angry, his apparently self-contained, detached father was often drawn to smack him at home. The main work we did in the sessions was on the mother–child relationship. However, I shared with them my impression that father seemed to have given up taking an active role with Alistair. He responded positively by agreeing and reflecting on the necessity for more active involvement on his part. Eventually mother was able to stand back and observe her interaction with Alistair before she did or said anything. Changes in Alistair's behaviour became apparent, followed later by changes in the marital relationship and in the whole family atmosphere.

Alistair had been a difficult baby since birth and mother had not found a way to help him settle, but had been caught up in a fast dance of actions and reactions, unable to think and to separate from him. She almost had to latch on to either of the two children and to intervene in their most minute interactions and play as if she, too, could not tolerate being left out. She was almost like a hyperactive child herself, wanting to be forever included. She became aware of how hard it was for her to have two children in mind or two of anything, including thoughts. She was almost in an adhesive state of mind and her attention was totally absorbed on only one thing at a time. It seemed that Alistair felt lost any time mother was busy and not thinking about him. He showed this in his play with a little boy doll, which was often dropped or fell into holes and gaps. He clearly represented his sense of falling inside his mum's mental gaps and distractions and of not feeling held firmly in her mind.

We discussed Alistair's fearful reactions and his very different ways of being, when mother used to react to him so impulsively. On the one hand, he regressed and thus regained his mother's protection and love. On the other hand, he developed a tough, aggressive, uncontrollably angry side when he acted defiantly and seemingly did not bother about anything. His sense of false power was also increased by his mother's threat that she would lose her temper, if he did not behave. The capacity to contain Alistair's projections was still undeveloped in mother at that point. Father had become rather concerned by the fifth session, as he was aware that despite Alistair having settled in the new nursery, they still had difficulties with him at home. Another five sessions were offered, although it only took two more sessions for a major improvement to occur at home. Alistair's ever-lasting sleep problems were resolved and he had become less destructive. In the sessions, he was able to play for some time by himself and to show an interest in the toys. We noticed that he gave up his regressive and aggressive reactions when faced with a "no", a limitation or a frustration. Once, his sister sat on the chair he had sat on earlier in that session. We three adults looked at each other, expecting an eruption and an attack on her. However, he listened to his mother explaining about the chair now being used by his sister and he moved to play with something else. Mother and father had taken to talking to him and explaining his feelings at home, such as his jealousy for his sister. They stopped fostering baby reactions in him unconsciously. The "dummy fairy" had also visited their home and taken his dummy away, after adequate preparation. He had accepted that he was a big boy and could dispense with it. The aggression towards his mother and the tantrums were the last to go and he was greatly helped in letting them go, by mother's admirable efforts in self-control, in containing him and in her generally calmer attitude. When things were still on edge, it was enough for mum and dad to say to Alistair that they would have to use his reins to go shopping with him, for him to calm down, to accept their limits and to decide that a big boy did not need reins. He was internalizing the parental reins, a capacity to accept limits, and this made him feel much safer internally, to the point that, as I have mentioned, even going to sleep was no longer fraught with anxieties and fears.

In the last two sessions, progress was consolidated and old ground was covered. In Alistair's play the animals were now inside the shed, which was their home and the little boy, that had fallen off the cliffs so many times, had a string around him and could be rescued by granddad. He was a different boy and it was a pleasure to see him being praised by mother and father and looking pleased, relaxed, and able to play and enjoy interacting with them.

Conclusion

Things had gone wrong for Alistair and his family since the very beginning. Mother and child had not managed the ordinary developmental phases and Alistair's severe disturbances had even affected the marital relationship. Understanding, guidance, and containment of the parental feelings and reactions, as well as knowledge of the child's inner world of phantasies, fears and anxieties, were provided and shared with the family members. Gradual changes and transformations occurred in the mother–child relationship and also in the marital relationship, due to the availability of the parents to look at and to question their ways of being. Mother, in particular, was able to accept herself and her difficulties and shifted her attitude in an admirable way. She was very motivated to change and to see how she could be different, without feeling excessively persecuted. She was in what can be described as a depressive state of mind. It was useful that the nine sessions were spread out monthly, to give the family time to assimilate and practice changes while they were still being seen at the clinic. The family, as I was told by mother in a telephone conversation some months after the end of therapy, felt ordinarily happy and enjoyed times together with Alistair, who had become well integrated in all areas of his life.

CHAPTER TWELVE

Hyperactivity and Ritalin[1]

Introduction

I have written about this topic elsewhere and this is a revised, shorter version of that paper (Pozzi, 2000). I will discuss some of the current thinking about hyperactivity and Ritalin, before considering clinical situations.

In 1957, the psychiatrist Tom Main conducted research into the use of sedatives in hospital for patients suffering from mental disorders. His finding was that sedatives were used to soothe the feelings of frustration, aggression, guilt, and despair of therapists, doctors, and nurses, rather than for the sake of the patients. When the nurses who had taken part in Main's research project became aware of their negative, as well as positive, feelings about their jobs and their difficult patients, the use of sedatives dropped almost to zero (Main, 1957).

In my experience, in child and family psychiatric clinics, I have observed that Ritalin is often prescribed to soothe the parents' anxieties, conflicts, and exasperation at particular times of their life, irrespective of the accuracy of the diagnosis, the needs of their children, the long-term side effects of the drug, or the possibility of the child benefiting from psychological therapies. Some clinicians use the drug together with other forms of therapy, like behaviour therapy or individual psychotherapy for the child and/or family, as a satisfactory and often necessary solution to the "whirlwinds" (Orford, 1998) inhabiting and taking over the life of children and families (Taylor, 1991, 1994). The combination of pharmacological and psychological therapies is useful and necessary in severe cases of child and adult psychiatric disorders (Jackson & Williams, 1994; Fromm-Reichmann, 1959).

The speed at which the diagnosis of attention deficit hyperactivity disorder (ADHD) is made and the diffusion of Ritalin to treat it, is a worrying trend, particularly while there is still a lack of knowledge about both the diagnosis of ADHD (McGuinness, 1989; Taylor, 1991, 1994) and the side effects of Ritalin (Breggin, 1998; Taylor, 1994). Moreover Ritalin is too often prescribed to children below the age of six years, despite there being no license to treat children of such a young age.

Furman believes that the psychiatric diagnostic criteria of ADHD correspond to the old hyperkinetic syndrome, that was succeeded by the diagnosis of minimal brain damage (Furman, 1996). Taylor, a leading authority in the study and research on ADHD in England, writes that the "inheritance of attention deficit is not known" and that "no evidence of structural damage in the brain of children with hyperactivity has yet appeared" (Taylor, 1994, pp. 294–295). A detailed history and family assessment is necessary to understand the possible origins and causes of ADHD and to plan an adequate therapeutic intervention (Stiefel, 1997; Taylor, 1994).

Ritalin, the psychostimulant drug methylphenidate, belongs to the amphetamine group. In adults, it acts as a psychostimulant and causes severe addiction while, for unknown reasons, it has a sedative effect in children. The physical side effects may range from nausea to weight loss, sleep problems, tics, growth suppression, and heart disease and, rarely, to autism (Breggin, 1998; Taylor, 1994). However, the psychological side effects of long-term treatment are just beginning to be investigated. McGuinness reports a number of follow-up studies of children with ADHD medicated with Ritalin. They present a lowering in self-esteem and suppressed creativity. "... the children come to view the drug as a crutch and feel helpless in controlling their own behaviour without it" (McGuinness, 1989,

p. 180). Moreover, I have often seen that parents renounce any awareness that family events, parental tensions, attachment difficulties, traumatic events or similar problems affect their children. If, on the one hand the psychiatric diagnosis may relieve an unbearable guilt in the parents, it may on the other hand, absolve them from any responsibility and awareness of some of the possible causes at the root of this problem.

The most satisfactory psychological model for understanding ADHD encompasses neuropsychology and brain development, along with attachment and object relation theories. The hyperactive behaviour is considered to be a defence against intolerable affects which belong to the child's early stages of development, when a maternal figure or substitute, has not been adequately present to perform a shock-absorbing function of mediating and transforming unbearable affects and events for the infant. (Bion, 1963; Tustin, 1989, personal communication; Winnicott, 1960).

A brief example follows here of a three-and-a-half-year-old boy, who spent the first year of life in a state of utter neglect and physical and emotional abuse, before he was fostered by a member of his extended family.

The boy showed a marked hyperactive behaviour in the only session I had with him and his foster mother. It was an extremely graphic example of how the hyperactive behaviour can be present instead of unbearable feelings and *vice versa*. This boy flitted about from the moment they entered the consulting room and ignored any attempt his foster mother or I made to talk and interact with him. He was also very demanding of adult attention and could not be left unattended for long. I decided to ask foster mother to sit him on her lap and hold him there, while we were trying to talk to him. She did so with great difficulty, despite being a big lady. As he resisted it I told her to hold him firmly, while trying to soothe him and saying that he was very scared, but mummy was not going to hurt him. Eventually, and one can speculate on what triggered this change, his mood changed and he collapsed into a desperate and lonely cry. He screamed: "No ... no ... mummy no ... mummy no..." He looked around as if he was looking perhaps for his real mummy, and held onto her neck and shoulders tightly, as if feeling safe. But this lasted only a few seconds. Then he tried to wriggle away and a similar sequence occurred. When, eventually foster mother let go of him, he switched off totally from the intense emotional turmoil and turned to moving around the room, as if nothing had happened.

This painful, but enlightening, sequence somehow confirmed the hypothesis that this little boy had not had an experience of an emotionally available maternal figure to manage his early infantile states and help him transform and integrate his raw emotions. We know that his maternal figure exposed him to traumatic experiences. He had to use his own body to discharge anxieties, as the Freudians would say (Shill, 2000) or to make use of his strong muscular structure as a second-skin type of defence, according to the Kleinians (Bick, 1968).

In the next section, I will present therapeutic interventions with two families with hyperactive boys and how they turned to Ritalin at specific moments in the course of counselling.

Stewart

Stewart, aged three years and eight months, was referred by the health visitor for a variety of reasons. He had language difficulties, was unable to participate in group activities at playgroup, was attention seeking and unaware of dangers, and was very aggressive. I met Stewart and his parents three times before the summer holiday with an agreement to initially have five sessions of under fives' counselling. In the sessions, we aimed to explore the present difficulties in the broader context of family relationships, early history, and inter-generational links. The three sessions took place at an interval of two-and-a-half weeks, as we mutually agreed.

In these few sessions, a strong transference was soon forged between the family and myself, mother in particular. Stewart had been a wanted and planned baby, but the pregnancy had been risky and mother had been in and out of hospital. There was a chance that the baby would develop a rare disease. Despite this, the birth and the first thirteen months of Stewart's life had been an ideal time for mother and baby and he gave his parents great pleasure. However, subsequently Stewart developed aggressive and very determined behaviours and turned into an uncontained and rough toddler. In therapy, the picture soon emerged of a vulnerable, scared, and overanxious mother, who was unable to set boundaries and to stop the sudden, and apparently inexplicable, physical attacks of her son. Father seemed to support his wife with an unconditional understanding of her struggle and yet was unable to intervene appropriately to unlock her difficulties with Stewart. On the one hand, he was proud about his tough little son, as he himself had been the victim of children bullying him when he was a small child. On the other hand, he risked losing his temper with Stewart, thus repeating a familiar experience of his childhood, when he became labelled as having temper tantrums.

Stewart slept for the first half of the first session and on waking up he was grumpy, cross with dad, overtly possessive of mother's lap, and jealous if she and father spoke to each other. He portrayed the picture of a younger child in the grip of unbridled passions. Later sessions became the arena of his violent attacks on mother's chest and lap, as well as of his defiant and superior attitude to father as soon as he was confronted with limits, requests or lack of attention for very short moments. As part of our work in the sessions the parents wanted to practice setting limits, compromising, and talking to Stewart about his anger, possessiveness, and jealousy. They also reported some progress and changes at home, in both their way of relating to him and in Stewart's behaviour. However, he also continued, albeit not so frequently, to show mum up in public places and to behave in an uncontrollable way. Mother was very tired and also feared, as she said, the approaching summer holiday and my absence for a month. She had already made an unusually strong positive transference to me in such a short time, despite the long gap between sessions. She feared being left alone with Stewart and missed seeing me, she said. They had already wanted to find a label for Stewart's behaviour and wondered whether he suffered from ADHD. They had consulted the local paediatrician, who confirmed their idea and asked them to fill in the Conners questionnaire.

When we met again four weeks later, the emotional tone of the family was completely different: I would say, sedated. Mother announced that Stewart was now on Ritalin, that he had been a demon in those weeks and she had contacted various local and national groups for advice, including the autistic society. The paediatrician had prescribed Ritalin and this had allowed mother to manage her child and to begin to have a better relationship with him.

My feeling was that I had lost both this family and the work done to understand Stewart and the emotional difficulties experienced by them, since they had moved into the pharmacological arena. My feeling that they had turned to another approach during a gap, too long to bear, undoubtedly reflected mother's feeling let down by me and by other supportive figures, as she reported openly. Father had not been too keen to start Stewart on Ritalin, but had no other solution to offer to his collapsing spouse. He felt I might criticize him for having accepted the drug treatment for his son and admitted feeling guilty when I suggested that the drug had filled up the absence of a supportive network, in particular our sessions. However, an interest in continuing this psychological work re-emerged as we resumed the sessions. It became clear to me and needed to be explored with them, that Ritalin had calmed mother's anxieties and helped her to regain strength in facing Stewart. But it was still unclear why she could not manage this child. His challenging and tiresome behaviour had partially decreased due to the effect of Ritalin on both mother, who changed her ways, and on Stewart. We could say that Ritalin has helped this family to break a circle of negativity, helplessness, and parental projections into the child. However, had we had longer time to explore the difficulties, before the crucial break and had mother been able to explore her frailties with me or with an individual therapist, young Stewart would have been spared taking this drug with all its unknown consequences.

The revelation of abuse

It was not until the approach of the next holiday that mother finally opened herself up. Meanwhile a general progress had continued in all areas of Stewart's life, including his likeability at playgroup. Relapses had also occurred and scared mother, but on the whole the parents felt helped by the input from innumerable sources, including Ritalin. I was always struck by the fragmentation of the many people and agencies called upon to help this family and a child who, in my view, was not suffering from any severe mental or emotional problem. It was not until mother revealed her childhood abuse that I could make more sense of what had gone on *vis-à-vis* Stewart. She was still having difficulties in setting limits and had a tendency to lose her temper. In the last session before Christmas, she began expressing her self-doubts about being a parent. Her doubts were exacerbated by the fact that parents at Stewart's nursery school occasionally complained about his behaviour. As a little girl, mother had been overindulged and preferred to her other siblings by an older uncle, to whom she had grown close. He had abused her sexually for many years till she finally was able to break the silence. Later on, she was abused again by a figure in authority in a professional field. Her account was confused, complex, and painful, despite the previous counselling she had received. It seemed to me that unhealed wounds opened up again at a time of becoming a mother to a male child. In her relationship with Stewart, mother overindulged him by being very permissive, not setting boundaries, thus identifying with her childhood abuser who had given her something special. However, she also lost her temper easily and reacted to Stewart's aggression quickly as he also stood for the abuser who forced himself on her violently, as I had the chance to see in the sessions. She felt powerless and ineffective, like she had felt with her abusers, when Stewart grew into a mobile, inquisitive and active toddler. Her identification with the adults of her childhood and the projections on her actual child prevented her from keeping a grip on her present role as a mother with a small child.

All this seemed to be the key to understanding what lay behind the various diagnoses put upon Stewart: Asperger's syndrome, pragmatic semantic disorder, ADHD, and the prescription of Ritalin. In my view Stewart's behaviour did not call for such diagnosis but was rather a reaction to his mother's difficulties with him. I wondered whether Ritalin was experienced by mother as another "sweet" that soothed both her deep hurts, or the unruly child/ "abuser" she could not control. Father also seemed to be caught up in this complex web and in various conflicts. He wanted to be kind to his wife and not increase her pain and difficulties, so he accepted the drug as a way to help her. However he was also feeling doubtful and guilty. The ending of this piece of work was complicated, patchy and interrupted, but mother managed to return to see me once and eventually decided to take up individual counselling again.

Pilar

Pilar was two years and ten months when he was referred to the Child and Family Psychiatric Clinic by the speech therapist and on his parents' instigation, because of speech and language difficulty, poor concentration and attention. The clinical picture presented by both the parents and my close observation of Pilar—so I will call this little boy—was much more serious than Stewart's. Pilar appeared rather merged with mother and presented psychotic–autistic traits. He was unmanageable at home and at nursery, as he was either in a world of his own most of the time or exercised omnipotent control over anybody coming near to him and making any request of him. Mother had been suffering from an undiagnosed chronic depression. Difficulties in becoming pregnant had increased her depression. Pilar was diagnosed as suffering from ADHD, then Asperger's at two subsequent times during the two years I saw him together with his parents. Twice the parents were offered treatment with Ritalin for Pilar, whilst I was seeing them and both times they held it off. The first time was shortly after we had begun family counselling and it was not difficult for them to give therapy a chance. Ritalin was offered a second time, again as a way of alleviating the parents' difficulties and the child's symptoms at a time when the family was going through a crisis in their personal life, and also in relation to therapy. I shall mainly focus on this second occasion, after drawing a picture of the work done and the progress achieved up to this point.

First fourteen months of therapy leading up to the second summer holiday

The parents' main concern in bringing up their child from when he was very young was to make him fit in with their requirements and expectations of being a good boy.

The early history had not been reported with interest by either mother or father, who only remembered and mentioned that Pilar had been a voracious feeder never satisfied by the amount of milk he was fed and that he had cried a lot. The main area of discussion, which was welcome by the parents for many months, was how to cope with him at the present time in their life. They often wanted advice, not understanding. Pilar's internal world seemed dominated by chaos and persecutory figures attacking, rejecting, and teasing him. Hence he spent most of the time trying to fend off those internal terrors, which he also projected outside. He threw things around, controlled the adults by ignoring them, not speaking, and making strange repetitive noises/words. He avoided eye contact, spun around, and was always on the move. The sessions were an arena of either battles between father, in particular, and child, or of defeats, where exhausted adults succumbed this very active and domineering child.

After five initial sessions of under fives' counselling, which were followed by another five sessions, ongoing treatment was offered and took place at intervals of two to three weeks, according to need. The family developed a strong attachment to the therapist and went through a number of changes. Improvement also occurred in Pilar's development. We came to understand—and that contributed to changes in the parents and in Pilar—that turning off the water tap in the therapy room, stood for the turning off the milk supply when he was a baby. This seemed to have been experienced as a traumatic event, which had left Pilar in a state of despair and loneliness, and subject to prolonged and agonizing crying. He re-experienced this in sessions and it was followed by a flight into perpetual movement, by a tendency to stick to his mother's body, and by having defiant battles with his father. Hopelessness and helplessness were the main features in the parents, even in father, who eventually let us know what was behind his cultural belief in male dominance. He felt lost and defeated by his son and humiliated *vis-à-vis* his wife, since she seemed to have a better grip on Pilar.

The parents learnt and practised a different way of holding and handling Pilar by being firm, less punitive, and by addressing—although in a rather mechanical way—some of the feelings we had explored in the sessions. Pilar's language improved, but did not lose entirely, some echolalic aspects. His tolerance of separateness also improved and he related a little more to people, although at times still maintaining his control over them. However, a recurrent pattern in this family was that any progress was inevitably followed by negativity and regression. A sense that things were never right became another feature of our strenuous work.

Turning to Ritalin during the long summer break

This break occurred after fourteen months of regular sessions and proved to be a difficult time, as a maternal aunt died unexpectedly.

This event threw mother into depression and Pilar was totally forgotten, while family members gathered from abroad. The parents stopped talking to each other, which they had begun to do during treatment. Pilar found new tricks to get their attention back by tormenting them with the continuous noises he made with his mouth and tongue. Having seen the paediatrician some time before returning to therapy, they considered giving Pilar Ritalin out of despair and helplessness. Therapy was resumed and as they reported the summer events, I decided to make a direct transference interpretation—a technique used only very occasionally in my work with this family. I said that therapy had died during the summer, just like their aunt had died, and they had thought of turning to the drug, instead of therapy, because of their unexpressed anger and a feeling of being let down by me. Father responded by giving me one of his "knowing looks", which meant that I had touched a point. Mother continued to want to give Ritalin to Pilar. However, she soon accepted her husband's idea to wait and see if things improved since they had returned to therapy. They both expressed having missed therapy and its help, regretting that "things always happen when you are away", said father. They both seemed surprised at having lost so much ground during the summer. This was a hopeful awareness. Soon Pilar and the parents' communication with him improved considerably. The option of Ritalin was disregarded for the time being and even later on, when the devastating and traumatic diagnosis of Asperger's syndrome was made, it was again rejected.

Discussion

These two cases are self-explanatory: in both of them the parents turned to either using or thinking of using Ritalin, during a long summer break. In Stewart's circumstances, I do not think the main reason for taking up the offer of using the drug was that the break came too soon in therapy, although this may have contributed to it. It was rather mother's vulnerability and her proneness to being easily invaded and taken over, which was at the root of Stewart's problem. Ritalin, as I have indicated, became necessary to sedate the three-and-a-half-year-old boy, who was seen by mother as an adult abuser of her past, from whom she could not defend herself. At the same time the child became the victim, not only of her projection of adult power and violence, but also of her unmodified anger, when she was at the end of her tether. It seemed that the family did not want a closer and more frequent involvement with the therapy, but diluted their needs by taking up several forms of therapeutic support. This provided an easy opportunity for this family to keep turning a blind eye to the problem and also helped shield mum from possible excessive guilt and depression. The whole onus to change was put upon the child who, by taking Ritalin, also became his mother's saviour.

The second family was more determined to sort out their difficulties with Pilar and—father in particular—could use his tenacity and stubborn disposition, as he himself admitted, for the therapeutic work. Thus, they achieved good-enough results. However, they ran the serious risk of turning to Ritalin as a substitute for their lost good object, i.e. therapy, during that long and difficult summer break. This was indeed a family for whom mourning was rather hard to work through and their tendency was either to be depressed (mother) or omnipotent (father and son). However the family resilience contributed to their strength and their wish to continue therapy, to fend off the drug-substitute, all to their benefit and merit.

Note

1. This chapter is a revised version of the paper "Ritalin for whom? Understanding the need for Ritalin in psychodynamic counselling with families of under-5's" in: *The Journal of Child Psychotherapy*, 2000, Vol. 26, No. 1: 25–43. Published by Taylor & Francis Ltd, http://www.tandf.co.uk

CHAPTER THIRTEEN

Mental illness in the family

Introduction

The family I write about here was described in a paper in the *Journal of Child Psychotherapy* (Pozzi, 1999). They had caused some concern to the local services due to mother's disturbance, for which she was known to the local Adult Mental Health Service. Her daughter, the only child in this family, had been only mildly affected by her mother's illness due to her father's presence and care, which had provided her with relative stability. However, this child and her parents had experienced prolonged difficulties, which could be resolved fairly satisfactorily by the under fives' counselling offered and did not necessitate a psychotherapy treatment for the child alone.

Bonny[1]

The health visitor referred this family because of four-year-old Bonny's uncontrollable behaviour. She was not responding to the usual behavioural modification techniques suggested to, and implemented by, the parents. In a telephone conversation with the health visitor, I had learnt that father was rather worried about mother's inability to cope with Bonny, that the parents were not working together and that mother had had violent outbursts, but she had never hit Bonny. When I telephoned the family, father told me that the nursery teacher, as well as his wife, had difficulties in coping with Bonny. He believed that Bonny was a hyperactive child. I had the impression that he was very preoccupied by both an uncontrollable and challenging child, who had disturbed sleep and was leading younger children into trouble at school, and by his wife who was just pregnant and unable to cope with Bonny. I could detect urgency and almost panic in his voice. Therefore, I decided to prioritize this family and to offer an early appointment with my social worker colleague and myself. The latter had wanted to join me in an under fives' family work to learn about the approach used: we had already co-worked with families creatively, complementing each other's different approaches.

In the first session, the parents poured out a litany of complaints about Bonny, her bad behaviour and violent fights with her mother over trivial things. A declaration of hatred of Bonny on mother's part, as well as guilt, did not surprise either my colleague or myself. Father sounded shameful and desperately wanted some help, but what and how? Both of them were extremely tense, uptight, almost frightened and mother was on edge all the time as if ready to burst into tears or, more likely, to explode into a rage. Suspicion and anxieties floated around and father looked very weary and worried about his silent, almost sulking wife. It was a very fragile and potentially explosive situation. Bonny sat on the settee in a rather self-controlled way and listened attentively to all that was being recounted. Only towards the end did she relax and move to play with the toys on the nearby child's table. We learnt that, following intense negativity on mother's side about having children, they had later tried desperately for a baby and felt hopeless when it did not happen. Eventually Bonny was conceived and born but it was "at the wrong time". Mother was no longer ready to have a baby, they said. The pregnancy, delivery, and first two weeks of life went smoothly. However, Bonny began crying and cried non-stop for four years. She was bottle-fed without ambivalence on mother's part, but she had diarrhoea, stomach ache, and sleep difficulties with no apparent physical cause. No one was there to help. The GP and the health visitor found nothing wrong with Bonny, but blamed mother for her attitude and for being neurotic. Hopelessness, despair, and rage were thick in the air. I put into words their negative and hopeless feelings about any possibility of help from any professional, including us at the clinic. The parents nodded. I was able to say how difficult and unbearable it must have been for both the mother, who had felt unsupported and rejected, for the distressed and crying baby, and for the father, who had done his best but felt unsure of what else to do. I was sharing with them in a sympathetic way what—I imagined—it must have been like for them all. I also suggested that baby Bonny, who must have felt frightened, helpless, and lost, had later become the powerful "boss in charge" in order to manage her feelings. I could intuit some vague curiosity in father, but a wall of negativism, rejection, and despair in mother, as I spoke. It seemed that she still needed space for herself, for her distressing experience and rage, before she could think of Bonny. The end of that first session approached and they agreed verbally to another four exploratory sessions. We were left feeling rather disconcerted, powerless, and very doubtful whether they would actually make it back to the second session, such was the strength of their negative projections.

Negative transference and projections

The first sessions in working with families of under fives are often very intense and difficult for the therapist, as well as for the family. Raw, unthinkable, undigested, and chaotic experiences, which have affected the family for many months and years, are brought out and violently or subtly projected onto the therapist. Also, and this is different to individual sessions with patients, it is the range of experiences of the various members of the family which can bombard the therapist. These experiences result from the many relationships involved: mother–child, mother–father, father–mother, father–child, child–mother, child–father etc., to mention only a few and to speak only about the present generation. We learn from family therapists (Byng-Hall, 1995) that parents bring their own relationships with their parents into their present family scripts.

Working in the negative transference and being able to bear the negative projections from the family members and if necessary verbalize them, can be the only key to open the door to hope. This happened with the family described in this chapter and many others in this book. My colleague and myself were not frightened of mother's potential outbursts of rage in the session, or of the general mistrust of professionals. We had somehow to absorb an emotional atmosphere without doing much else. Also we had to be careful that, in taking up their negative experience with their health visitor and GP, we were not colluding with them against professional colleagues. It was the mother's perception and experience of those carers which we were addressing.

In my work, I have noticed that one of the two parents is usually more available and receptive to the therapeutic thinking than the other one. They occasionally swap this role in the course of treatment. Father, in this first case, "stood" for the link with reality. Mother talked to me indirectly and via her husband. I commented on the fact that Bonny and mother appeared to be in a power struggle and father reinterpreted this to mother. I sensed that father understood what I meant, when I said that mother had felt criticized and blamed by her health visitor and her GP, while I think that mother believed that I agreed with her that those people were bad and unhelpful. Father was able to stand back and think while mother was caught up in believing her thoughts and feelings. It soon became clear to me in the session, that one needed to be particularly skilled and trained to understand the internal world of such a disturbed woman, who, beneath her attacking explosiveness, seemed to be deeply lost, fragile, and in pieces.

Working with a colleague can be interesting and my colleague social worker, who was an observer to begin with, became more involved in later sessions, complementing me with her questions and comments. She also reflected mother's position and changes when the latter became more directly involved with us. My colleague was already familiar with some of my thinking: she could follow comments like the ones on negative transference without flinching.

Second session

This happened, as agreed, five weeks later and after the Christmas holiday, despite our uncertainty and scepticism. The family arrived quite early as if they could not wait and were keen to be back. Things had got worse since the first visit to the clinic, according to father. Mother felt just the same: nothing had changed; nothing *could* change was her implication. However, a new picture of the family dynamic appeared. Father had always been soft and laid-back with Bonny: if she hit him he would take it in a playful way. His wife had always been the one to discipline Bonny and would get very cross when Bonny hit her. However, following the first session, father had become firmer with Bonny who, on her part, had also become difficult with him. He now shared his wife's problems, he sighed. Also, mother had decided to set different boundaries with Bonny and was able to stick to them, probably feeling supported by her husband's new attitude. She only gave Bonny one drink at bedtime and did not let her daughter hit or bite her any longer. Bonny eventually accepted this.

They could tell us more of their family life. An oedipal constellation had reigned in this family up to our first session. Father and Bonny had been the playful couple, excluding the "bad mother". Mother had felt jealous and resentful of the good time her husband and Bonny could have together, as she revealed in the session, while she had always been left with the disciplining role and in a tug-of-war with the child. We were also told that Bonny could not tolerate mother and father sitting next to each other and I pointed out that she demonstrated this in the session by sitting between them. She was very jealous if mother and father had a cuddle or a kiss in front of her. I verbalized this scenario to the three of them by addressing them separately and also by sympathizing with their individual predicaments. Bonny was too jealous to bear being left out of the parental couple, hence she either tried to split them apart or she would make a couple with her father. In the latter case, mother would become the disciplinarian, jealous, "bad witch" left out of the playful toddler-couple. In this way, I said, Bonny got rid of her unbearable feelings and it was mum who became the jealous, naughty, left-out one. They seemed able to relate to this description and Bonny moved to the toy table for the first time and played with a crocodile, which bit the plasticine. More examples of this oedipal scenario were mentioned and also re-played in the session.

Parental feelings

Helping parents to understand that their feelings towards their child may have also to do with their child's feelings towards them, can be a useful tool in this work. This is more so if between mother and father there is what I call a depressive and reparatory disposition towards the child; that is, a wish to look at the parental input into the problem. This disposition was obvious in father, who felt guilty for having coupled up with his daughter and against his wife. He wanted to make things better and began to take it upon himself to change. In this way he became our ally in the therapeutic work, which became possible thanks to his input and availability. His wife was, to begin with, too dominated by a paranoid–schizoid state of mind to be able to think, and she had found a culprit in Bonny. When they first came to the clinic her guilt was intolerable and she felt so persecuted, blamed, and criticized by people that she then blamed them in return. In her view those people were "the bad parents".

Coming to a child and family clinic tends to stir up feelings of guilt and self-blame. "Am I a bad mother?" "Am I a bad father?" "Have I failed my child?" Often families do not make it, as it feels too bad. They split and project the guilt and they blame others. At other times, families come when they begin to have a glimpse of hope that something can be done to help with their problems.

I find that, as well as verbalizing this guilt when appropriate, working on the parental feelings (similar or different ones in the two parents) can alleviate their guilt and open up their trust in the therapist. I take seriously the idea that the child—at times even a two year old—can become the "monster" or "the boss" in the family and that the adult parents are reduced to feeling frightened or bossed about by their two- or three-year-old children. Their potency, authority, and control have been projected into the child. I usually share this idea with surprise and puzzlement and this often helps parents to think about how this came about.

The parents found it almost humorous that Bonny was running the family show. I reminded them and Bonny of how she must have felt as a baby when she cried non-stop, in pain, fearful, and alone. Now, I said, she had found a funny sort of way to make them feel as she used to feel then or even now at times: rejected, excluded, and bossed. This thinking can usually empower the parents, after an initial reaction of surprise, and give them a sense of separateness from their child's feelings. Bonny was also listening attentively and she must have felt understood and freed, as she changed in the session. She, too, contributed to the change in the family dynamic. It seemed that things had been contained in this session (Bion, 1962a).

Third session

Three weeks later, a "miracle" had occurred: "Bonny is a different child," the parents reported, father excitedly and mother joylessly as usual. "Bonny is much more settled at night and gets up to go to the loo by herself. She is more obedient and no longer argues with mother." Bonny smiled as her parents spoke positively of her.

More about the families of origin was revealed in this session. Father's father was rather laid-back, favoured him over his older brother and had left his wife to discipline the boys and be "the tough one". Father himself was an unruly and wild child, who—he told us—"liked fires a bit too much". When he became a father, he identified with his own father in being soft and leaving his wife to be the authoritarian figure, as his mother had been in his childhood. Mother's father, on the contrary, had been abusive and violent to his passive and resigned wife and had no interest in his children, she reported, apart from hitting them. When she became a mother, she was still somewhat identified with a harsh father, who was full of hatred. Bonny's parents were both interested in talking about their past. Father was repeating his family script (a laid-back father) and mother had tried to modify her past by being less cruel with Bonny than she felt her father had been with her. However, they had felt caught up in a spiral of jealousy and in some repetition of their past.

Interestingly, the one who was being left out of our sessions and minds was the new baby who was due in five months' time. Bonny had been interested in the toys and drawings for most of this session. However, when the expected baby was mentioned, Bonny, who had also slipped out of our minds as we gathered the parents' histories, was back with us, showing a drawing of worms. She drew a dead worm, a bad worm, and a hissing worm, she told us. "Worms, you mean babies?", I asked and Bonny nodded. Yes, she knew and used to talk a lot about mother expecting a baby and her belly getting fatter and soon exploding, she said in the session. Her parents felt that she had accepted the idea of the baby.

They had achieved as much as they wanted from these sessions: a different child and a better capacity to be parents. They were therefore ready to say goodbye today.

In my experience of working with families who come to the clinic because of the problem child, most parents need to keep the child as the focus of their attention, even though personal difficulties, couple problems and inter-generational dysfunction are often at the core of the problem. A child, who is a mixture of what the child really is and of how the child is seen through the lenses of parental projections and confusions with their own childhood, is brought to the clinic. To externalize the problem in the child and in the relationship with the child, can be a safety valve for those parents who are too split and often feel too guilty, damaged or vulnerable to be able or to want to look at themselves. When this family succeeded in shifting the oedipal triangulation and in resolving Bonny's symptoms, they felt ready to leave. However, as I felt that the issue of the new baby had slipped away and Bonny's explosive wish towards her mother's belly had been unnoticed until the end, I suggested that another session nearer to the birth might be advisable, to explore things further and consolidate the good progress. They agreed.

I was also still struggling to understand the reason why they had come to the clinic at this time in their life, in view of the fact that they had struggled for years with an unhappy child, a grumpy mother, and a helpless father. Perhaps the new pregnancy had thrown up more worries than could be coped with, and than we had so far addressed.

The last session

Two months later father and Bonny came together, without mother. She could not attend as the session time was too near to a hospital appointment. The pregnancy had been very difficult, father reported, due to serious gynaecological problems, which had occurred prior to the present pregnancy. Bonny had continued to be a different child. She had been very helpful to mother and sang songs to the baby in the womb. However, her anxieties and phantasies about the damage caused to her mother, to her grandfather, who had died the year before, and to a previous baby, who had never been born, popped up almost like an explosion in this session. Father had been very much in touch with Bonny's feelings and fears and had been able to talk to her openly. I was very impressed by his insight into her world. At home he had put into words for her, that she had feared having made mum ill by being naughty and, for the same reason, she felt she had sent grandpa away. Bonny had agreed. In the session she volunteered that, as well as loving the new baby, she also hated him and this was linked with having felt responsible for the death of the previous baby-to-be. This deep unconscious stuff had apparently been on the surface at home and father had been able to be both an interpreter of such fears, as well as a good container by putting things into perspective for Bonny. He reassured her that people died for other reasons than for her naughtiness. It seemed that much fluidity in thinking and talking about Bonny's world, fears, and feelings was now possible without putting her any longer in the seat of the naughty child. I acknowledged the improvement and the capacity on his part to help Bonny and suggested a final session with his wife to celebrate the birth of the baby and say goodbye. He agreed, but they did not come back. However, father popped into the clinic once, following our letter. The baby boy was born and well and so was his wife, he informed us. However, Bonny had caused them some concern due to her jealousy and they were thinking of coming back.

My wish to formalize the end of this piece of work in the last session with this "new family" was not granted and, for a long time, I wondered how things had been with the four of them. Was I the one left out and excluded by them all? I also wondered whether father wanted to keep a door open to the clinic in case of need, when he said that they were thinking of "coming back". To me that would have hopefully been the "going away session": an ending with our blessing and satisfaction.

Note

1. This chapter is a revised reprint from the paper "Psychodynamic counselling with under-5's and their families: clinical and technical issues", *Journal of Child Psychotherapy*, 1999, Vol. 25, No. 1: 51–70. Published by Taylor & Francis Ltd, http://www.tandf.co.uk

CHAPTER FOURTEEN

The use of under fives' counselling as parental guidance with severely developmentally delayed children

The writing of this chapter was inspired by a very creative and exciting piece of work with a family, whom I will refer to as the Somers and their four-year-old boy, Craig. The work with these parents was particularly interesting, because it guided them to help Craig to catch up on the developmental stages of the first two years of his life, which he had missed out on due to major events.

Mother had suffered from severe PND for which she had been treated. This restricted her life immensely, as well as her capacity to relate to her newborn baby, the only child in this family. Craig was born with a hereditary genital deformity, which had required a number of operations during his first three years of life. We can see that he had a very traumatic start in life that resulted in a generalized developmental delay. His feeding, sleeping, toilet training, language development, and socialization were almost at the level of an infant. At the time of their referral by the health visitor, the family was receiving help and support from a number of agencies, including PND counselling for mother. The health visitor had previously discussed this child and family with me, since she had not felt sure whether they could be helped by counselling.

These parents proved to be particularly concerned, committed, and keen to learn about their child's psychological functioning. They were particularly co-operative and wanted to try out new ways of relating to Craig, following our thinking in sessions and their imaginative discoveries that occurred in between sessions. Both parents were in what I have called a depressive state of mind and they could talk about their successful as well as their unsuccessful ways of dealing with Craig. Mother, in particular, could look back on her severe PND and earlier childhood without feeling totally overwhelmed and wiped out. I offered this family an urgent appointment following a telephone conversation with mother, which had alerted me to the necessity for prompt intervention. She had sounded very needy and was still rather depressed, although apparently not as depressed as when Craig was born.

Broken biscuit, broken mummy

When I first met this family in the clinic waiting room, I had a taste of the traumatic state of Craig. As soon as I entered the waiting room to introduce myself, he looked at me in terror and began screaming at the top of his voice, as if he were being slaughtered. The parents were in touch with Craig's extreme distress and tried to calm him down and to reassure him that "Maria was not a doctor." They always called me by my Christian name—which is unusual in this setting—perhaps to remind Craig and themselves that I was a doctor of a different type from those he had known so far and I would not hurt him. Eventually, he did calm down and they slowly proceeded to the therapy room with me. Once in the room, Craig, after looking wearily at me, gradually engaged with father. His demeanour struck me. He looked pale, puny, and shy and repeated few words or short sentences two or three times like an echo. When Craig eventually felt less threatened by me, partly due to his parents' encouragement to talk to me, he came nearer to me and sniffed my face, like a puppy that dares approach something dangerous. His parents told me that it was his usual way of meeting new people.

The session was spent by mother recounting the history of her severe depression, which had first manifested itself in her adolescence and had been caused by early and prolonged sexual and physical abuse, both at home and school. She spoke of the medical and psychological treatment she had tried and of Craig's birth and the effect it had had on her. She reported having improved a lot, although she still often felt on the edge and suffered from migraines and days of depression. Father, on the contrary, appeared light and jovial, supportive and sympathetic towards his wife and keen to take her and Craig to clinics when needed. Since mother was seeing a PND counsellor at the time they came to me, I decided to offer them five sessions to begin with and to focus mainly on Craig and on their relationship with him. Since Craig's reactions and his emotional and mental ways of functioning were of an early nature and more typical of a younger and unintegrated child, Craig's behaviour appeared rather unusual to his parents. I decided to embark on a journey with them, where we would try together to make sense of Craig's movements, reactions, and expressions, as we observed them during the sessions. These were similar to the way he behaved at home and nursery school. Father, in particular, was mentally free and wanted to know a lot about Craig. Mother was burdened by her guilt about having affected her son so much with her depression. I needed to address her guilt, bear the hope, and praise their commitment in coming to the clinic and willingness and desire to repair things for Craig.

In the second session, we were able to have Craig at the centre of our attention and thinking. We explored how the parents' felt lost with him and ended up overindulging him. Father, in particular, who was very proud of having a son, had a soft spot for him and always gave into him. His own father, he said in a later session, had left the family when Mr Somers was about three years old and had disappeared from his life. His mother and grandfather had brought him up and were both described as being soft, and wanting to make up for the pain caused by his father's disappearance. Mr Somers was almost excited at having a chance now of being a very present and caring father and husband. He could not bear seeing his son cry, he said.

Mrs Somers cried when Craig cried, she reported. She described a nursery situation where Craig could not interact with other children, but stood in terror when some children tried to snatch his toys from him. She felt very guilty and concerned in noticing the difference between Craig and them. As she spoke Craig watched her face closely and as soon as she became distressed, he turned to her and shrieked repeatedly and anxiously, "Sorry, sorry, sorry ... mum!" He too, began to cry and looked panic-stricken. I felt churned up inside. Mother's guilt and concern increased, while father was feeling lost at how to intervene. I said that Craig seemed to believe he was responsible for mum's upset and also scared when mum cried, as if he had made her sad and upset, hence his repeated apologies to her. I also addressed Craig and verbalized his feelings with simple words. The parents related to my thoughts, but mother struggled with her guilt, which was somehow confirmed by Craig's state of distress. I said that mother felt guilty about the effect she had had on Craig and could not contain her acute feelings. Craig immediately echoed these feelings, as he felt responsible for her distress and pleaded for her forgiveness guiltily. They had an entangled relationship, as they both fed each other's guilt and unhappiness. We needed to find a way to separate mother's and child's distress and to disentangle their mutual projections and acute sense of guilt. I asked the parents if there was a story or a TV character, which stood for "the bad one". Father came up with "the alien" and I made up a story of a little alien in mummy's heart, which made her sad and unhappy, not a little boy called Craig. Father liked this story and by the end of the session he and Craig were busy talking about the bad alien that upsets mummy and a good Craig who loves mummy. Craig repeated this in an echolalic manner. This began to free him of the excessive and almost obsessive burden of an uncommitted crime.

In the third session, the parents reported some progress in the separation process. They had become aware that Craig would become upset and apologize in the way I had described, even if mum just sneezed or coughed. Mum said to Craig that it was just a cold and mummy was fine and it was not Craig who made mummy sneeze. She also helped him to keep his toys and say "no" when children tried to snatch them off him at nursery. She was still spending the whole time with him at nursery, as separation had proved impossible up to this point. In this session, we tackled the feeding problem. Craig only ate small amounts of mushy food, as lumps made him wretch. Also he would only bite a bit of each biscuit, but never finish a whole one. He panicked if his parents tried to make him finish it and he immediately wanted another whole one. I suggested that his fear of biting and chewing could be linked with his ordinary aggressive feelings which—in his mind— had caused mum a lot of damage and made her ill and broken like a biscuit. Also, finishing a whole biscuit may have been linked with his anxieties about separation that he equated in his mind with disappearance. Perhaps he felt he had eaten up his mum, if a whole biscuit ended up inside his tummy. Primitive thinking and equating the biscuit with mother, was the level at which Craig was functioning. This thinking and language made sense to the parents. Father was particularly intuitive about these aspects of his son's mental functioning. They decided to practice talking to Craig in the sessions and at home about his fears of finishing biscuits. They reassured him that it was OK to eat it all up just like mum and dad ate whole biscuits. They emphasized that when they ate whole biscuits, they were still there and had not disappeared like the biscuit in the tummy. They used very simple sentences to convey these ideas to Craig.

In the course of our time-constrained work, Craig did improve and manage to finish biscuits, although he did not quite eat ordinary, lumpy food. The unconscious meaning of lumpy food was still too entrenched for him and would have needed a longer time to be brought in line with reality. The parents were very sensitive and never pushed him, as he became easily distressed and this still triggered off mother's distress. Craig's progress was still tied up with his mother's emotional states. In sessions, Craig looked and behaved in a different way with me. He smiled, chatted, and interacted with me freely. He showed a sense of humour as he played hide-and-seek with his hands or tapped my legs delicately, saying that my legs were lovely. Mother's appearance and moods had lifted a lot from the first session.

In the fourth session they all looked well and relaxed and Craig called out my name in a friendly manner as we met in the waiting room. We explored the issue of boundaries, which the parents were feeling more confident in "pushing", as father said. Mother had managed not to give into Craig's request to buy a toy car at every shop they met on a shopping expedition. She managed his tantrums in public on that occasion and by the fourth shop he had only protested mildly and then accepted her firm "no". The notion that

Craig had been the "King of the castle" and the parents the "dirty rascals" for all those years and with good reasons, was now in their awareness and we openly explored examples of how they had indulged his tyranny. Mother feared having damaged him and wanted to make up for the distress and deprivation that her depression had caused him. Father wished to give him the good experiences, which he had not had from his own father when he was a little boy. We had to work on the differentiation between healthy and growth-promoting limits and the depriving and growth-stifling lack of boundaries, from which Craig had unfortunately suffered. The lack of proper boundaries had unwittingly added further deprivations to this child. The Somers were receptive to this task and, as I have mentioned already, they were quite keen to try to ameliorate the actual situation.

The next psychophysical milestone we had to face in our sessions was toilet training, since Craig was still in nappies. A potty was too small and the toilet was too scary for Craig. We spoke of his fears about letting go of his wee and pooh and what happened to them if they dropped into the loo. At home he began pretending to sit on the loo or to stand in front of it, as he had seen his father doing. However, the actual functions could only take place in the safety and comfort of the nappy. This difficulty was still linked with separation and letting go and Craig's extreme need to control, presumably in order not to fall to pieces or lose himself or leak out, primitive anxieties which psychoanalysts and psychotherapists who work with autism are well aware of. Craig could not let go of his bodily products yet. To be able to keep control seemed to give him that sense of security and safety, which he still needed and which had also been jeopardized by the many operations he had undergone. The parents understood these emotional complexities of toilet training and decided not to force him. But they did not ignore the issue. They spoke to Craig about his fears, as I had done in the session, when they went home and were faced with the actual situation. Mother decided to make a hole in a pair of trainer pants, so that Craig could see the wee leaking out of his pants and into his potty. She reassured him that it was just wee, not the whole of Craig that he was letting out. He also still had the security of the trainer pants. This worked and he took an interest in his potty and wee and within a week, he was able to use the loo. I was impressed when they told me of this ingenious idea and Craig, too, looked proud. It took longer for him to use the loo to defecate and he used the nappy at night for a bit longer. However he soon managed that too.

Whenever mother relapsed into depression—although it was now happening for shorter spells of time—Craig's progress would temporarily grind to a halt. Father was also busy organizing a change of job and he was not in a position to help his wife with this task. The family had decided to move near to mother's town of origin, so that she could get the support she now felt strong enough to ask for from her extended family. Her strength came through her own counselling, our sessions, and Craig's positive response and impressive improvement. I was in contact with his nursery advisor and health visitor and they all remarked on the huge improvement which Craig and mother had gone through. Their original fear that Craig may have been autistic had given place to the joy of observing him and noticing how he was moving on in leaps and bounds. He could be left at nursery and enjoyed his time there, while mother enjoyed her time without him. Neither of the two was any longer holding on to the other for survival. Also they came to their session for the first time without Mr Somers. Craig had become more spontaneous as he played with toys, with words and short sentences, and related to me. He seemed to enjoy the pleasure of exploring and becoming more independent and learning to talk, just like a toddler.

By the time the family had arranged and organized their move, we had met for the symbolic period of nine months and—although Craig still needed to catch up with his development—it felt that a new child was being born into a new family. He could easily wave good-bye to me in our last session. Mother expressed her worries, sadness, and also excitement about the big step they were undertaking by leaving their present circumstances and returning nearer to her home. Father expressed his appreciation for the help received, at this point in their troubled family life.

Conclusion

In this piece of work with the Somers family, I had in mind Frances Tustin's style of working with the parents of autistic children, whom she saw for psychotherapy. She used to have a very close communication with those parents, as they needed a frequent input in understanding their mysterious children and she emphasized the need to ground the psychotherapeutic work with the autistic child in a solid and trusting alliance with the parents. The work with Craig was almost entirely through his parents and was based on my sharing with them the understanding of his very early modes of mental functioning, which we could observe in the sessions with him present. These parents were eager to repair things and curious to learn, just like Tustin had observed in autistic patients' parents. Tustin used to meet with them or even talk to them on the telephone very frequently. She thought it vital that these parents were kept very much in the picture about their children's therapy—without it becoming an intrusion. These parents also needed help to regain their common sense, which was likely to have got lost in the years spent living with their idiosyncratic autistic children (Tustin, 1988–1994, personal communications).

Mrs Somers was ridden with guilt, but hers was not a paralysing and persecuting guilt. She could accept her past, her depression, and Craig's congenital malformation without having to blame others excessively. She mobilized her wish and capacities to repair the situation, to make things better and to help Craig, still within the realistic limitations of her relapses into momentary depression. My work on the parent–child relationship and on understanding this child's unusual habits, was supported and made possible by mother's own counselling, which gave her the space to look at her deep-rooted difficulties and gave me the space to focus on parental issues and child development aspects.

CHAPTER FIFTEEN

Under fives' counselling as a form of assessment[1]

"The encounter with what is *not known* is at the heart of assessment"

Rustin & Quagliata, 2000

Introduction on assessment

I found the above statement by Margaret Rustin interesting when considering the general introduction on assessment. When a child and his or her family come to a Child and Adolescent Mental Health Service with symptomatic behaviour, unhappiness and disturbance, we are dealing with something that is not known to them. What is not *yet* known, I would like to stress, is something unconscious, buried within the child's or family's mind and which will, hopefully, begin to be known and made conscious during the assessment and in the following therapeutic work. The father of a one-year-old boy comes to mind. He asked for help to manage his aggressive and out-of-character feelings towards the baby, the second child in a happy, insightful family of professional parents. In the first session of under fives' counselling, what became

179

apparent was his new awareness of being stuck in an identification with his older son, due to unresolved sibling rivalry. Having been the only and cherished child in his family of origin, he had never dealt with issues of sibling rivalry. When their second baby was born, he could not deal with his feelings towards the baby and was overwhelmed by dislike and rage, thus losing his parental perspective entirely. His new *knowledge* of his unconscious feelings, which occurred in that first session, brought resolution of this conflict, which at a six-month follow-up had been maintained.

The question of assessment is an issue to which Freud (Freud, 1933) was already alerted, when he suggested using the first two weeks of treatment as a period of observation. In recent years, this topic has been written about fairly extensively. I would now like to draw attention to a number of recent publications. *Assessment in Child Psychotherapy*, edited by Rustin and Quagliata (2000), covers a range of thinking, experiences, and assessment issues explored by psychoanalytic psychotherapists from the Tavistock Clinic. Also, the chapter by Parsons, Radford and Horne, in *The Handbook of Child and Adolescent Psychotherapy* (1999), explores the aims, tools, and setting relevant to assessment, as well as the validity of the Diagnostic Profile devised by Anna Freud and her Developmental Lines, for younger and severely disturbed children. With regard to more specific assessment for parent–child psychotherapy, which encompasses pre-latency children as well as older ones, Brafman's book: *Untying the Knot. Working with Children and Parents* (Brafman, 2001) brings a Winnicottian perspective to combined therapeutic assessment work with children and parents together. Ben-Aaron *et al.* in their book, *Mother–Child and Father–Child Psychotherapy: A Manual for the Treatment of Relational Disturbances in Childhood* (2001), assess the motivation and capacity for both parents to co-participate in psychotherapeutic treatment with their problematic child.

I would like to particularly reflect on two issues, regarding assessment, that are closely linked. The first is the range of patients who can benefit from psychoanalytic psychotherapy and the second is the therapeutic alliance or consent for psychotherapy treatment. In the past, children with mainly neurotic disturbances, good verbal skills, internal conflicts, and supportive parents were part of the group to whom psychoanalytic psychotherapy would be offered (Fonagy & Target, 2001). This type of treatment was considered the treatment of choice. Nowadays, the spectrum has broadened to include children with autism and developmental delays (Alvarez & Reid, 1999; Tustin, 1972, 1990), psychopathic disturbances (Alvarez, 1992), learning disabilities and mental handicap (Sinason, 1992), severe abuse, and neglect. Similarly, the traditional type of family with children under five, who benefit from brief, psychodynamic counselling, present neurotic and depressive symptoms, belong to a more advantaged social group, and usually seek therapy of their own volition. This type of family represents the population treated in parent–infant psychotherapy by the Geneva group (Cramer, 1977; Palacio-Espasa & Manzano, 1998; Stern, 1998). However, the therapeutic scope has widened in the field of under fives and includes families where one or both parents suffer from narcissistic and borderline psychopathologies. The effectiveness of under fives' counselling, even with more disturbed families, is now being researched.

The second issue of the therapeutic alliance is an essential ingredient for treatment to take place (Hellman, 1999). Children with severe learning disabilities and developmental delays often communicate it to the therapist in puzzling or subtle ways. We have more refined techniques and tools to be able to pick this up and to offer treatment to those children, who in the past would have not been considered suitable. I have seen children with Asperger's syndrome and severe learning disabilities who were hard to reach but still somehow showed, to use Tustin's imagery, a chink in their armour, at some point during the assessment sessions. They then withdrew and rejected the chance of ongoing work in response to the end of the assessment. Such reactions had made me seriously question whether psychotherapy was the treatment of choice for those children. It was not until therapy did start that a positive answer to this question was given. Similarly, young families who notoriously flee from one Service to the other, or families with parents suffering from mental illnesses or children who are developmentally delayed, can express negativity and resistance to the work to begin with, but soon can develop a therapeutic alliance and be helped by under fives' counselling. In these cases, counselling contains parental anxieties and addresses limited areas of dysfunctional parent–child relationships without, of course, eliminating other major problems or handicaps.

Under fives' counselling can turn into an assessment for further psychotherapy for either the child or the parents, individually or as a couple. In any assessment, as well as in long-term psychotherapy, one tends to keep one's assessing eye open during sessions in order to assess the state of mind of the patient, whether s/he is in an anxiously persecuted and paranoid state or in a more anxiously depressive state. Also, we try to gauge whether the prevalent mood is dominated by love or hate feelings or by a wish to know and understand oneself. Bion introduced the vertex of L, H, and K—standing for love, hate, and knowledge—and their negative or absent counterparts (–L, –H, and –K), as a tool to comprehend the moods of the patient in each session and the movement from one state to the other (Bion, 1962a). We need to maintain a vigilant, assessing eye, to be able to pitch our interpretation in a way that reaches the patient emotionally and leads to change.

In under fives' counselling, I aim to understand the state of mind of the child and the parents, as well as their interactions, the relationship with myself in the here and now of the session, and the unconscious meaning of what is being said. I also keep close scrutiny of my countertransference, i.e. of the feelings, thoughts, and phantasies, which come to me during sessions. I do this in order to monitor how the work mobilizes understanding and changes in the family and whether the number of sessions negotiated with the family are sufficient to shift the parent's internal object and the disturbance in the relationship, which is manifested in the child's symptoms. I also monitor whether either the child or the troubled parent have changed enough for the child to continue along the previously blocked developmental path and for the parents to become more adequate parental figures. Finally, I need to assess whether a disturbance is too deeply entrenched in either child or parent or parental couple and may require further psychotherapeutic intervention. Lisa Miller (Miller, 2000) illustrates clearly, and with a wealth of clinical material, the links between under fives' counselling and assessment and how the former can become the platform for more therapeutic input.

In this chapter, I discuss a family, initially seen under the aegis of under fives' counselling, who needed further intervention. The family showed symptoms that one would think could be treatable in short-term work. It was only through a painful process that the final decision in favour of individual psychotherapy was reached.

The "Victorian pills" family

The family I have chosen to discuss is rather interesting from the point of view of assessment, as the counselling shows the uncertainties felt by the therapist and the steps, that were discussed between the therapist and the family, which were being taken during this piece of counselling. The events that led to a turning point and triggered the decision to go down the path of individual psychotherapy, for both mother and child, are also highlighted. As I write the case history, I deliberately bypass many interesting aspects of this piece of counselling, such as the inter-generational family links, for the purpose of adhering to the topic of assessment.

The health visitor described the four-year-old son as defiant, always requiring mother's attention and as being prone to disconsolate outbursts of sadness and crying. Mother, herself, seemed to be feeling depressed and it was hard for both mother and health visitor to know how much mother was affecting her son and how much the son was affecting the mother.

The first session offered was attended by the whole family, i.e. the parents, the four-year-old boy and a one-and-a-half-year-old girl. The session was taken up mainly by mother's insightful account of her long-standing anxieties, her difficulties in managing and having both children in mind and, as she called it, her neurotic worrying over anything. She saw the similarity between herself and one of her parents, in particular with regard to her depression and irritability, for example when Jonas, her four-year-old son, did not fit in with her expectations and ideals. She also spoke of her wish to be totally dedicated to child rearing, which was what her mother had happily done. It was interesting to notice that, even when she was talking about Jonas, the focus was not on the child but on herself, her difficulties, and her tendency to interfere with the children playing. In this session father and the children were on the periphery as she spoke. They partly listened, played, and occasionally chipped into what was being explored. This session and my observation of Jonas's fairly ordinary behaviour and interactions veered my thinking in the direction of mother's needs and anxieties. I offered five sessions of counselling, which were welcomed by both parents.

Mother and Jonas attended the second session alone, as father was busy at work and the toddler was left with the childminder. Mother had felt more hopeful after the first session, she said. She reported many instances of interactions with Jonas, where things had gone wrong. For example, when the younger girl would break the magic between mother and Jonas, who were busy doing things together, Jonas's mood suddenly changed, so did his behaviour and he spoilt everything for mother, as she put it and she became upset and overreacted to him. I suggested that Jonas was likely to make her feel as he had felt when the baby was born, i.e. that everything was ruined then and also every time the baby interfered with Jonas and mother being happily together. I addressed—in my suggestion—both the child's projective identification into mother, i.e. his unconscious way of making her feel the way he was feeling, and also how she was taken over by this projection and had became unable to process it. This was a first step in helping her understand his behaviour and her reaction and eventually she spoke of her fraught relationship with an older sibling, when she was a child.

Meanwhile Jonas attracted our attention as he played with toy animals. He squashed bits of plasticine on them and said they were Victorian pills, which were meant to make those animals strong. I was intrigued by these Victorian pills and asked him to tell me more. At his nursery they had just read the story about Queen Victoria being old and dying and then Queen Elizabeth coming next to the throne. He spoke competently and knowingly. I asked if Queen Victoria was strong, but he repeated that she was old and died. I dared suggesting that the Victorian pills perhaps were meant to kill those animals. He said: "We eat animals; they give animals pills to put them to sleep, then they die." I wondered aloud if he wanted to give his baby sister those pills so she would die and leave mum all to himself. No, he replied, and mother confirmed that the children played well together and the ordinary rivalry of a four year old with a new baby sibling did not seem to exist. However, he would take it out on mother, she said. I said to him that perhaps he wanted to give his mother those Victorian pills: he nodded wholeheartedly and gave her a pill. They both took this interpretation in their stride and mother, who had had counselling in the past, seemed able to accept and connect with Jonas's death wishes towards her, without being caught up in his wishful phantasies. The session continued smoothly and I felt rather surprised that we had touched on such a crucial emotional issue, such as the child's murderous feelings towards his mother, without much resistance on mother's part. This type of interpretation, which names such intense passions, is usually well received by young children, but it is likely to stir up concern or resistance in the parents, when they are faced with naming hate, murderousness etc., either in their children or themselves. However, mother's concern burst out only two weeks later in the gap before the next session. Mother telephoned me, as she was very concerned and anxious: Jonas had said he wanted to kill himself and the following day had put a plastic bag around his neck. She feared that our work would go too deep and it could be too difficult to bear. She wanted to give it a miss. However, her fears and anxieties were contained in that telephone conversation and she agreed to return with her husband for the session that was planned for the following day. In that session they expressed their worry, but did not blame me for stirring up such death wishes in their little child. Mother spoke at length about Jonas's clinginess, provocations, and callousness, when he was reprimanded and punished. His self-dislike seemed to be intense at times and mother, courageously, linked it with a telephone conversation he had once overheard. She had confided to a friend that at times, when Jonas was so impossible, she wished to kill him. Following the first assessment session, one day she lost it with him and he mentioned that telephone call and said to her: "If you don't like me, why don't you sell me?" She had felt shocked, guilty and in pieces *vis-à-vis* Jonas. In this session we worked very deeply indeed, despite mother's earlier concern. Unmetabolized death wishes, now belonging to mother too, were openly acknowledged by her. Father listened with a curious interest, but could not recognize similar death wishes in him. In this session, I became concerned about the severity of Jonas' death wishes, now turned against himself. I wondered whether it could be enough to help mother to contain him or whether he may need some individual help, since she felt so intensely guilty and caught up with him.

It felt like walking on a tightrope and I did not know which turn this work would take. At that point, though, I did not put my thinking into words, as I wanted to be a little clearer about the direction we were going and also I did not wish to increase the parents' level of anxiety.

We had planned to meet again two weeks later with mother alone, since she had felt very desperate and needy. Unfortunately, I had to cancel a session and the next time they all came but Jonas. Good progress was reported and attributed to mother having managed firmer boundaries and feeling stronger inside herself. However, later in the session, I was told that ordinary limits and frustrations produced extraordinarily intense reactions in Jonas. He hit and hurt mother physically, and now did the same to his little sister. I also learnt that he was being badly bullied by tough children at his nursery and this had alarmed both parents. In this session, Jonas' difficulties came to the fore, now that mother had managed to be more separate from him and not to react to him, as she had tended to do in the past. There was more space for thinking about him. I felt I was on a seesaw while I was taking part in and observing this up-and-down movement, in which either mother or child appeared to be very needy and troubled or more settled and able to cope. We agreed to meet again without the children.

In the last of the five planned sessions, the situation was reported as having badly deteriorated. Jonas's moods were now a problem at nursery and were also noticed by the extended family. Mother was in despair about Jonas and only able to identify with her little girl, when she was being hurt and tyrannized by her brother. We explored openly the possibility of Jonas receiving individual help at the clinic and of mother undergoing psychotherapy elsewhere, since she had expressed such need. Unfortunately there was no such facility in the clinic for more specialized, individual help for parents, so I helped mother to find a psychotherapist locally. We also negotiated more sessions for the parents to continue thinking about Jonas.

The next session took place after two months had elapsed, due to short holidays and cancellations. Mother had started to see a psychoanalytic psychotherapist three times a week and was already feeling better and calmer with Jonas. He had started full-time school and was settling in well socially and academically. He was happier in himself and able to play with his sister. In the session, I was struck by his changed behaviour and more grown-up appearance, as well as by how articulate he was in his speech. Was he being contained enough, I wondered to myself? Had he left the turmoil of infancy behind and entered latency in a not-too-bumpy way? However in the same session, mother mentioned again his wish to die, which seemed now to predominate over his outwardly expressed aggression. He also wished to hurt himself and thought he was bad and stupid. His difficulty with his aggression and the family depressive streak, also present in him, were explored openly, together with the question of psychotherapy for Jonas and its frequency. Father particularly feared that therapy might make things worse, while mother, having experienced it herself, felt keener for Jonas to have therapy. We were not ready for any decision and left it until after the long summer holiday.

They came back after a very good holiday with friends and children: Jonas had been very happy and people only expressed good comments and compliments about him. In hearing this and also that his creativity had blossomed, I thought he seemed to have finally settled. The issue of individual psychotherapy could be put aside for the time being and a review could be planned for some months later. I was, therefore, surprised when both parents said they had talked together a lot and decided they wanted him to start intensive psychotherapy as soon as possible. The main reason they gave was that they still found him very hard work and were unable to understand his sudden outbursts of intolerance and aggression, in particular towards his sister. We explored this further and realized that Jonas' improvement was still like a thin crust, which could be easily cracked under his old, unmetabolized passions. We planned an assessment for individual psychotherapy to take place with a different child psychotherapist.

Jonas did indeed start therapy three times a week and this turned out extremely beneficial and necessary for him. At last he had a place where he could work on his unmetabolized, primitive wishes, both in the area of love and life, as well as of aggression and death.

I hope this piece of work has shown how under fives' counselling can be useful as a way of assessing both the family and the child's psychological mode of functioning and to indicate what is needed next. It has also shown some of the thinking processes, the use of countertransference and the dilemmas I went through, during what I called a seesaw-like thinking. The two questions of integration, or not, of the life and death wishes in this little boy and also whether short counselling would have been enough, had a chance to unfold until the thought was born that long-term psychotherapy was the answer.

Note

1. This chapter was read, in a modified version, at the Association of Child Psychotherapist Study Weekend (A.C.P.) London, 8–9 March 2002.

CHAPTER SIXTEEN

Consultation to a nursery school[1]

Introduction

In this chapter, the understanding of the unconscious world of children under five and of their relationship with their parents and nursery teachers is applied to consultative work in a nursery school in a deprived area. The intervention, which is different from the traditional under fives' counselling with families, shows how the school began to emerge from and transform the state of disarray into which it had been thrown. The consultation was undertaken together with a colleague who had a systemic approach. Our different ways of thinking complemented each other in this situation. I will focus mainly on the psychodynamic interpretation of the school situation, when our consultation began, and on the changes that occurred as a result of this work.

A four-year-old gangster: cigar in mouth, guns in pockets

In March one year, a request for a consultation came to the clinic from an infant school. The school wanted help in managing the difficult

189

behaviour of their children and the stress that it caused to the staff, reflected in the number of absences and early retirements. The school was located next to a council estate, in a rough and deprived area, renowned for its social problems, vandalism, and delinquency. In the past the school had adopted a macho, authoritarian approach to badly behaved children, but now it wanted to adopt a more child-centred, gentle regime. The communication between the school, the parents, the Special Needs Advisory Team, and the educational psychologist had led nowhere. My colleague social worker and myself decided to respond by offering a multidisciplinary consultation.

We visited the school eleven times altogether, spread out at different intervals, over twenty-one months. At first we were asked mainly to observe two classrooms and give advice to their two teachers. These teachers were perceived as not coping and as being too demanding of the headmistress's time, as they often sent difficult children to her room. Paula was a young, attractive, recently qualified teacher who was new to the school. Petra was a very experienced teacher nearing retirement, who had worked in the school for a number of years. Both found it hard to cope with some of their children and perceived themselves as failures. Somehow they were expressing stress and discomfort on behalf of the whole school. They also presented a polarized situation. Chaos reigned in Paula's classroom, whilst strict discipline and order had been achieved by Petra with most of the children. These two teachers personified an excessively benevolent and an excessively authoritarian type of discipline, showing the split with which the school was struggling when the decision to change the style of authority was suggested.

My colleague, Jim, and myself wondered how we could help the school as a whole to reach a happy medium with proper boundaries, since the headmistress had asked us to work only with two teachers, seen separately. Paula and Petra had been singled out, while we would have liked to work with the whole school. We were aware of the unfairness of the situation and yet could only begin from where we were allowed.

We began to tackle the problem of delinquent children and families who were inclined to sabotage, devalue, and criticize any school initiative and its capacity to resolve problems with Paula, Petra, and the headmistress. We looked at the projections of incompetence and failure that were being passed down from families to children, with no understanding or containment, to the school, to teachers and to Paula and Petra in particular. We helped Paula and Petra reflect on their sense of failure, as coming from the children themselves. They felt relieved and interested in the idea and gradually began to see their children as being separate from themselves. In the third consultation, a third teacher, Hope, was introduced to us. She was joining us voluntarily, because she wanted help with her difficult kids and was not pushed by the headmistress as Paula and Petra had been. This was a sign of hope for us that things were moving institutionally and out of the rigid split and scapegoating. An interest in our intervention was spreading. Individual children, as well as general concerns, were discussed: for example, a four-year-old boy running out of school and wandering around the estate till late at night who managed to scare and paralyse both his parents and teachers, with his attitude and menacing behaviour. His teacher was touched by my metaphor that he acted like a gangster with a cigar in his mouth and guns in his pocket. He was only four and yet he projected such anxiety around. He represented the uncontained, delinquent trend in the community. There were also concerns about a five-year-old girl, possibly sexually abused, who challenged the teacher every time the latter held a fighting child. There were anxieties about the approaching end of the year and the feeling that the whole school had of being shell-shocked. There were concerns about how to prepare the children to leave and to survive the summer, which was dreaded by both the children and their deprived families. They saw the school as the giving institution, both idealized and denigrated. We also considered how to prepare the children to meet the newcomers when they returned to school in September, while old friends were no longer there and how to discuss ground rules without sounding punitive or persecuting.

It became apparent that there were difficult children in all classes. Our hope was that other teachers would join us, so that the whole school could share the issues of safe boundaries, of protecting learning, and teaching, as well as fostering social integration. However, at the beginning of the September term they had all forgotten when we were due back. Having already learnt from experience that long breaks tend to unsettle the system, not just individuals, I had telephoned the school to check if we were expected. I was reassured that they would make sure that someone would be there despite having forgotten. Paula was there and keen to start and Philippa, a new teacher in the school, also joined us. She had been in tears because a disruptive and demanding child had shattered her good intentions and hopes at the beginning of her teaching career. She did not want the child in her class at all. He seemed to be driven by an inner demon, as she described it. However, during a recent visit from the police to collect an abandoned motorbike, the boy had been fascinated and expressed a wish to become a policeman. This led to some ideas about games and themes aimed at integrating the demon-boy with the policeman-boy. Eventually, with the help of the special needs teacher, Philippa became able to achieve some integration in this boy, so that she could have him back in her classroom.

Some success with the children was reported and the teachers developed a way of handling them, which was based on acknowledgement and understanding of these difficult behaviours. They began to talk with them rather than just punish them. Firmer and clearer boundaries were also put in place. The delinquent aspect of the school had somehow been directed towards us. Our meetings never started on time and often no one was there on our arrival and people gathered around us only slowly. The headmistress kept coming and disappearing from the meetings. We felt unable and unsure how to talk about this vital group-dynamic until the fifth consultation, when the delinquent aspect in the teachers began to emerge. One of the teachers spontaneously reflected on herself and this facilitated focusing on the teachers for a change. The headmistress remembered being a rebellious child and the pleasure she got from it. Someone else remembered her brother being bad at school and a third teacher always wanted to please and behave well as a young pupil. The last teacher used to get cross when being disturbed by bad children, who would disrupt her work. This was a striking session of self-awareness during which we could openly address the delinquent side in them all. Unfortunately it was not followed by similar consultations. However, we felt they were now accepting us a little more and had enjoyed the consultation. More satisfactory contacts with families were occurring and difficult situations, such as inappropriate sexual behaviours in the children, were discussed and tackled appropriately now. The school was emerging from a state of being projectively identified with failure, delinquency, and inefficiency—aspects of that social area—and was beginning to be looked at with more respect from the families.

Delinquency in the sessions with us continued to be acted out. For example, the headmistress tried very hard to sabotage the reviewing purpose of the last session before the summer holiday. More money had to be found if the school was to continue employing our services. Positive feedback was expressed in very general terms and anxiety about the end of this school year acknowledged. After the summer, a request came for us to meet with most of the infant and nursery teachers, to offer them some proposals, and to decide how to proceed. We felt this was a hopeful movement towards a wider expansion and use of our consultation. We met once and it was like starting the work afresh, as we explained where we were coming from in terms of our work. Two children were discussed in what we felt had been a satisfactory way and people seemed engaged. However, they subsequently decided they did not want to continue and we wondered whether, once again, the need was felt mainly by the headmistress, but not shared by the school.

In the final session, a couple of months later, the three teachers who were with us at the beginning, together with the headmistress, reported a happier atmosphere in the school. Firmer boundaries were now well in place, as well as there being better integration of good and delinquent behaviours in the classrooms. Children were now occasionally expelled, or referred to the child and family clinic, or transferred to more appropriate schools. A differentiation of needs in the children and of limits in the school seemed to have taken place and decisions had followed accordingly. Paula and Petra said they could now see where the children were as individuals, and did not expect from them what they could not give. We felt and said that they seemed to have moved from blaming the children or themselves to seeing things more objectively. The most encouraging and hopeful achievement for them was that the school was now well seen, respected, and protected in the community. It had emerged from being projectively identified with failure and delinquency, to now standing for a firm, containing institution, helpful to children and families.

Note

1. This is a modified version of a paper read at the XIII International Conference of TSP, Larmor-Plage, 29th August–2 September, 2000.

CHAPTER SEVENTEEN

Parents' line

In this chapter, I describe a telephone service that has become a sort of informal Parents' Line, similar to Child Line, the telephone service for children in trouble. This is another application of the under fives' counselling described in this book.

The telephone service, which I have developed over the years, takes place when families of under fives' have been referred to the clinic. It aims at offering prompt support to parents, at a time of crisis or of ongoing difficulties and before they can be offered a more formal appointment.

The aim of this telephone counselling is to begin to explore the problem as the parents perceive it and as it affects the whole family. It is a useful way to begin to assess a number of aspects. Firstly, we can assess the parental capacity to think about the child and their mental disposition; whether the parents can reflect on their own input in the child's difficulty and try to modify their attitude; or whether they tend to blame the child or each other for the difficulties they face. Secondly, it can be used to detect the presence of maternal depression, over-involvement, excessive distance or rejection or emotional abuse, in relation to the child. Finally, we can assess the parents' availability and interest in the ideas that the therapist may, if appropriate, begin to explore on the telephone. The call is also a useful way to start screening and assessing the urgency of the problem and, if needed, to prioritize families that need to be seen as soon as possible.

Early containment of parental anxieties

The therapist, in exploring the problem with the parents, offers a sympathetic ear and a way of looking and understanding the current difficulties in a new light, which is based on the knowledge of parents' and children's deep anxieties, conflicts, and unconscious phantasies. The therapist receives and contains the raw, parental anxieties at a time of great need. On some occasions, it can be enough for a worried mother or father to talk on the telephone once or twice to embrace a new awareness, to experience relief, and even to modify the current, difficult situation with their child.

The telephone consultation provides a first form of containment of parental anxieties at a moment when parents are in the heat of a difficult situation and at the end of their tether. It is well known that the intensity of feelings and preoccupations stirred up by children at this young age can be extremely hard for the parents to bear as they can touch on unresolved, old conflicts. Therefore, the sooner containing intervention is offered, the better the outcome will be and parents, when they are seen later on, usually report how useful such conversations have been. Most of the times this telephone counselling bridges acute crises, between the time when the family is referred to the clinic and when an appointment can be offered.

I will now describe a few snippets from telephone counselling, which led to a resolution of symptoms and to an understanding of and improvement in the relationship between the parents concerned and their children.

Jimmy, aged three, had felt confused since his mother and father had separated. After a particular visit to his father, he returned to his mother feeling shaky and appearing traumatized. He had been told by father not to tell mother that he had been locked up in a room for being naughty. He eventually told his mother. Since social services, mediation, and the court were already involved with this family, I did not have to be active in any way other than to help mother understand and manage Jimmy's feelings. She could see that he was both being caught up in a loyalty conflict between his parents and fearful and confused at being treated so differently by mum and dad, when he was naughty. This was part of our first telephone conversation, in which I felt that mother was receptive to my ideas and keen to talk to Jimmy about his feelings and worries. I felt that they could wait some time before being seen and, due to the clinic's long waiting list, I offered mother the opportunity to telephone me again, if the situation worsened and she became worried, while waiting to be sent an appointment. Some months later, I telephoned her to offer an appointment with myself. Mother sounded surprised to hear that Jimmy was still on our waiting list. Since our telephone talk, she had spoken to him about his feelings of anger, upset, and confusion about mum and dad not living together and he had responded very well. He was more settled and had not shown further signs of distress. He had mastered and enjoyed the weekly visit to his father, who on his part had also modified his punitive methods of dealing with his young son.

Claire, aged four, had always been a sickly baby. She had suffered from reflux and frequent episodes of vomiting and moments of intense distress. Sleeping had also presented huge difficulties for her and her family. She had recently started to make herself sick at her beloved child minder's, who had taken on a new baby to mind. In my telephone counselling with mother, it emerged that Claire had never shown any sign of ordinary jealousy when her baby sister was born some time earlier. The parents had felt some reluctance in coming to the clinic, mother told me, as they did not wish to draw attention to the children or make Claire feel bad. However, mother was very keen to explore the problem on the 'phone. She could see that the new baby at the child minder's may have stirred up anxieties in Claire that she had not dealt with when her baby sister arrived in the family. Mother decided to talk to Claire about her feeling jealous of the child minder's new baby and her fear of losing her to the baby. Two weeks later, we spoke again on the telephone as agreed and mother reported progress in her child. Claire's symptoms had gone and she had managed to accept the child minder's baby. I think she must have felt that her mother had really understood her and mother, in turn, had felt less anxious and more able to contain her daughter's distress. Mother still wanted to telephone me a few months later, to confirm that the progress had been maintained and for her comfort and reassurance. This she did and no further difficulty was reported.

Understanding the child's mind

The parents that can benefit from this short, but thorough, guidance on the telephone are usually keen to look at ways of relating to their children and want things to be different. They do not blame other people for the problem, but are able to take on the responsibility for change. They are usually very grateful to be given a chance to vent their anxieties, worries, and doubts, as well as to explore new ideas and strategies to deal with their suffering youngsters. These ideas and strategies are grounded in the deep understanding of the child's mind, feelings, anxieties, and conflicts within the context of family relationships and nursery life.

Samuel, aged two and a half, had always been a poor sleeper and on the go all the time. The family had recently moved from another town, where they had seen a psychologist because of Samuel. Talking with mother on the telephone contributed to the shift that had already been happening since their move. He was reported as being calmer and beginning to settle at his new nursery, although tearful at being left by mother. The notion that he might feel frightened and insecure when mother left him, since so many changes had occurred in his life at that time, helped mother to see the situation from a different point of view. She was able to talk to him and the progress had been maintained, as she reported some months later when I called to offer an appointment.

Talking about worries

Asking young children *why* they act as they do is often the parents' last attempt at trying to understand and reach their children. The answer is inevitably: "I don't know" or a silent shrugging of shoulders. Defeat and despair follow as those parents have really tried their best but still failed to talk to their children. I am sometimes misunderstood, when I ask despairing mothers or fathers, to talk to their children about their children's feelings and worries. Parents usually ask their children: "*Why* are you cross?" My latest technique which I have coined to help parents, is to differentiate between asking: "*Why* are you cross" and stating: "You feel cross ... *because* ..." This second statement shows the child that his or her mum and dad understand and know how the child may be feeling. A young child needs his parents to understand and take on board his feelings, worries, likes and dislikes, pleasant or uncomfortable states etc. and put them into words. This is the way to help children to know and learn about their feelings. Naming feelings without anger, blame, resentment, scolding, humiliation or other emotional hooks on the parents' part, produces huge relief in the child and establishes a new alliance between children and parents.

If, during my telephone counselling, parents can adopt and own this new way of talking to their children, this can lead to a real modification in their response to the child, in their reciprocal relatedness, and consequently in the child's behaviour. The need to come to the clinic may then subside.

Lauren, aged four, was described as a very strong-willed and determined little girl, unable to share mother with her younger sibling. Sleep times were difficult and she also disrupted the family's happy times and outings. She would sulk for hours at home and even at nursery, if she did not want to go. They had tried many strategies suggested by other professionals, including speaking to Lauren about her feelings, her anger etc., but to no avail. I was curious to know more about how they had spoken to Lauren about her feelings and mother said: "I asked *why* she was so cross and *why* she broke her toys, but it didn't help." I suggested to mother saying to Lauren that she was angry at having to leave mum to go to nursery or that she did not like sharing mum with dad and baby; hence she broke her toys. Mother could take in this idea and finally *affirm* her daughter's feelings, without an edge or resentment. In another telephone call, she told me that Lauren had improved in all areas of her emotional development and life in general.

Concluding remarks

There is an increasing number of studies that show that many factors affect emotional development, behaviour, and the developing brain of the child in the first eighteen months and up to the third year of life. These factors include the type of attachment between the mother/carer and the infant/small child, the type of object relations between them, and the presence of traumas or other environmental factors. These experiences become imprinted on the brain and leave permanent, but not always irreversible marks, as neuroscientists are beginning to discover (Damasio, 1999; Perry *et al.*, 1995; Schore, 1994).

Early interventions with children, families and institutions have particular value, and they can often free situations and developmental blocks at an early stage before they become entrenched to the extent that they require different and longer forms of intervention. Young children are particularly vulnerable to adverse influences since their defences are less structured and established than in adults. Parents of children under five usually present particular openness and availability to being helped, as their own vulnerable, infantile selves are revived by the birth of their children and the ongoing interactions with them.

The counselling I have described can be beneficial in a short time as it relies on the special emotional availability of these parents and on the fluidity of the defences of these young children. Both children and parents can benefit enormously from a prompt and focused therapeutic intervention. The symptoms often disappear in a few sessions and the understanding of previously unconscious forces tends to bring long-lasting changes in the parent–child relationship. The child's blocked developmental path is freed and growing is resumed.

The under fives' counselling, as it is intended and described in this book, makes use of a number of theoretical strands and ideas. These include the containment of parental anxieties and reverie by the therapist, as well as the disentanglement of mutual projections from the child onto the parent and from the parent onto the child and the understanding of guilt. Guilt can be an impairing and holding-back force or a reparative and growth-promoting one. The concepts of attachment and of transmission of unresolved ways of relating and expressing feelings can also throw light on many difficulties experienced with young children in young families.

Technically, the counselling aims to bring the difficulties and symptoms into the here and now of sessions, where they can be explored, understood, linked to present or past anxious and conflictual situations, and can be contained by the therapist. The silent or verbalized analysis of transference and countertransference and the use of refined techniques to understand early and disturbed modes of functioning are part of the therapist's tool kit.

Future areas of exploration and research into this short psycho-analytic counselling will address the minutiae of the interventions between all participants including the therapist, and how they influence each other and affect changes in the parent–child relationship. The analysis of processes occurring in sessions will need to be recorded in detail or videotaped to render the process transparent and understandable to the outsider.

I hope I have managed to convey to the reader my love for this type of work, to stimulate some curiosity about the ideas that I have shared here, and to inspire practitioners and parents.

REFERENCES

Acquarone, S. (2002). Mother–infant psychotherapy: a classification of eleven psychoanalytic treatment strategies. In: B. Kahr (Ed.), *The Legacy of Winnicott* (pp. 50–78). London & New York: Karnac Books.
Ainsworth, M. D. S., Bell, S. M. V., & Stayton, D. J. (1971). Individual differences in strange behaviour of one-year-olds. In: H. R. Schaffer (Ed.), *The Origin of Human Social Relationship*. London: Academic Press.
Ainsworth, M. D. S., Blehar, R. M. C., Waters, E., & Wall, S. (1978). *Patterns of Attachment: a Psychological Study of the Strange Situation.* Hillsdale, NJ: Erlbaum.
Alvarez, A. (1992). *Live Company.* London & New York: Routledge.
Alvarez, A., & Reid, S. (1999). *Autism and Personality. Findings from the Tavistock Autism Workshop.* London & New York: Routledge.
Amini, F., Lewis, T., Lannon, R., Louie, A., Baumbacher, G., McGuinness, T., & Zircher Schiff, E. (1996). Affect, attachment, memory: contributions towards psychobiologic integration. *Psychiatry*, 59(3): 213–239.
Balint, M., Omstein, P. H.,& Balint, E. (1972). *Focal Psychotherapy.* London: Tavistock.
Baradon, T. (2002). Psychotherapeutic work with parents and infants—psychoanalytic and attachment perspectives. *Attachment & Human Development*, 4(1): 25–38.

Barrows, P. (1996). Soiling children: the oedipal configuration. *Journal of Child Psychotherapy*, 22(2): 240–260.

Barrows, P. (1999). Brief work with under fives; a psychoanalytic approach. *Clinical Child Psychology and Psychiatry*, 4(2): 187–199.

Beebe, B. (1982). Micro-timing in mother–infant communication. In: M. R. Key (Ed.), *Non-Verbal Communication Today* (pp. 169–195). New York: Mouton.

Ben-Aaron, M., Harel, J., Kaplan, H., & Patt, R. (2001). *Mother–Child and Father–Child Psychotherapy. A Manual for the Treatment of Relational Disturbances in Childhood*. London & Philadelphia: Whurr Publishers.

Berg, A. (2000). Beyond the dyad: parent–infant psychotherapy in a multi-cultural society. Reflections from South Africa. Paper presented at the 7th Congress of the Association of Infant Mental Health, Montreal.

Bick, E. (1963). Notes on infant observation in psychoanalytic training. *International Journal of Psycho-Analysis*, 45: 558–566.

Bick, E. (1968). The experience of the skin in early object relation. *International Journal of Psycho-Analysis*, 49: 484–486.

Bion, W. R. (1955). Language and the schizophrenic. In: M. Klein, P. Heimann & R. E. Money-Kyrle (Eds.), *New Direction in Psycho-Analysis*. London: Tavistock Publication.

Bion, W. R. (1962a). *Learning from Experience*. London: Maresfield Reprints.

Bion, W. R. (1962b). A theory of thinking. *International Journal of Psycho-Analysis*, 33: 306–310 [republished (1967) *Second Thoughts* (pp. 111–119). London: Maresfield Reprints].

Bion, W. R. (1963). *Elements of Psycho-Analysis*. London: Maresfield Reprints.

Bion, W. R. (1967). Notes on memory and desire. In: E. Spillius (Ed.), *Melanie Klein Today (1988), Volume 2: Mainly Practice*. London: Routledge.

Blos, P. Jr (1985). Intergenerational separation–individuation. *The Psychoanalytic Study of the Child*, 40: 41–56.

Bowlby, J. (1969). The child's tie to his mother: attachment theory. In: *Attachment and Loss. Volume 1: Attachment Theory*. London: Hogarth.

Bowlby, J. (1980). Death of parent during childhood and adolescence. In: *Attachment and Loss. Volume 3: Loss Sadness and Depression*. London: Penguin Education, 1981.

Brafman, A. H. (2001). *Untying the Knot. Working with Children and Parents*. London & New York: Karnac Books.

Brazelton, T. B., & Cramer, B. G. (1991). *The Earliest Relationship.* London: Karnac Books.
Brazelton, T. B., Tronick, E., Adamson, L., Als, H., & Wise, S. (1975). Early mother–infant reciprocity. *Ciba Foundation Symposium, 33*: 137–154.
Breggin, P. R. (1998). *Talking Back to Ritalin: What Doctors Aren't Telling You About Stimulants for Children.* Monroe, ME: Common Courage Press.
Breuer, J., & Freud, S. (1893–1895). Studies on Hysteria. *S.E., 2*: 255–305.
Byng-Hall, J. (1986). Family scripts: a concept which can bridge child psychotherapy and family therapy thinking. *Journal of Child Psychotherapy, 12*(1): 3–13.
Byng-Hall, J. (1995). *Rewriting Family Scripts.* New York: The Guilford Press.
Coates, S. W., & Moore, M. S. (1998). The complexity of early trauma: representation and transformation. In: D. Di Ceglie & D. Freedman (Eds.), *A Stranger in my Own Body.* London: Karnac Books.
Cooper, P., & Murray, L. (1997). *Postpartum Depression and Child Development.* London & New York: The Guilford Press.
Damasio, A. (1999). *The Feeling of What Happens.* London: William Heinemann.
Dante, A. (1314). Inferno. In: *The Divine Comedy.* London & New York: Penguin Classics, 1971.
Daws, D. (1989). *Through the Night Helping Parents and Sleepless Infants.* London: Free Association Books.
Daws, D. (1997). The perils of intimacy: closeness and distance in feeding and weaning. *Journal of Child Psychotherapy, 23*(2): 179–199.
Daws, D. (1999). Brief psychotherapy with infant and their parents. In: M. Laniado & A. Horne (Eds.), *The Handbook of Child and Adolescent Psychotherapy* (pp. 261–272). London: Routledge.
Di Ceglie, D. (1998). Reflection on the nature of the "atypical gender identity organization". In: *A Stranger in my Own Body.* London: Karnac Books.
Fonagy, P., & Target, M. (2001). Introduction: the historical background of psychoanalytic psychotherapy for children. In: M. Ben-Aaron, J. Harel, H. Kaplan & R. Patt (Eds.), *Mother–Child and Father–Child Psychotherapy.* London & Philadelphia: Whurr Publishers.
Field, T. M., Woodson, R., Greenberg, G., & Cohen, D. (1982). Discrimination and imitation of facial expression by neonates. *Science, 218*(8): 179–181.

Forth, M. J. (1992). The little girl lost: psychotherapy with an anal-retentive and soiling four-year-old. *Journal of Child Psychotherapy*, 18(2): 63–86.
Fraiberg, S., Adelson, E., & Shapiro, V. (1975). Ghosts in the Nursery. *Journal of the American Academy of Child Psychiatry*, 14: 387–421.
Fraiberg, S. (1982). Pathological defenses in infancy. *Psychoanalytic Quarterly*, 2: 612–635.
Freud, S. (1905). *Fragments of an Analysis of a Case of Hysteria*. S.E., 7: 7–122.
Freud, S. (1909a). *Analysis of a Phobia in a five-year-old Boy*. S.E., 10: 5–149.
Freud, S. (1909b). *Notes upon a Case of Obsessional Neurosis*. S.E., 10: 155–318.
Freud, S. (1910). *The Future Prospects of Psycho-analytic Theory*. S.E., 11: 139-151.
Freud, S. (1917a). Psycho-analysis and psychiatry. In: *General Theory of Neuroses*. S.E., 16: 243–256.
Freud, S. (1917b). *Mourning and Melancholia*. S.E., 14: 243–260.
Freud, S. (1917c). Analytic therapy. In: *General Theory of Neuroses*. S.E., 16: 448–463.
Freud, S. (1918). From the history of an infantile neurosis. S.E., 17: 9–123.
Freud, S. (1920). *Beyond the Pleasure Principle*. S.E., 18: 3–64.
Freud, S. (1923). *The Ego and the Id*. S.E., 19: 3–66.
Freud, S. (1926). Inhibition, symptoms and anxiety. S.E., 20: 87–174.
Freud, S. (1933). *New Introductory Lectures on Psycho-Analysis*. S.E., 22.
Freud, S. (1937). *Analysis Terminable and Interminable*. S.E., 23: 216–253.
Fromm-Reichman, F. (1959). *Psychoanalysis and Psychotherapy*. Chicago: University of Chicago Press.
Furman, E. (1974). *A Child's Parent Dies: Studies in Childhood Bereavement*. New Haven & London: Yale University Press.
Furman, R. A. (1996). Methilphenidate and "ADHD" in Europe and in the USA. *Child Analysis*, 7: 132–145.
Gallo, M. T. (1997). The little alien: links between mind and body in parent–infant psychotherapy. *Journal of Child Psychotherapy*, 23(2): 201–218.
George, C., Kaplan, N., & Main, M. (1996). *Adult Attachment Interview Protocol* (3rd edn). Unpublished manuscript, University of California at Berkley.
Grotstein, J. S. (1990). Invariants in primitive emotional disorders. In: *Master Clinicians on Treating the Regressed Patient*. Northvale, New Jersey & London: Jason Aronson Inc.

Hammer, E. (1990). *Reaching the Affect. Styles in the Psychodynamic Therapies*. Northvale, NJ: Jason Aronson.
Heimann, P. (1949/1950). On counter-transference. In: *About Children and Children-No-Longer*. London: Routledge.
Heimann, P. (1959/1960). Counter-transference. In: *About Children and Children-No-Longer*. London: Routledge.
Hellman, I. (1999). *From War Babies to Grandmothers. Forty-Eight Years in Psychoanalysis*. London & New York: Karnac Books.
Holmes, J. (1993). *John Bowlby and Attachment Theory*. London: Routledge.
Hopkins, J. (1992). Infant–parent psychotherapy. *Journal of Child Psychotherapy*, 18(1): 5–18.
Isaacs, S. (1948). The nature and function of phantasy. Republished (1952) in: M. Klein, P. Heimann, S. Isaacs & J. Riviere (Eds.), *Developments in Psycho-Analysis* (pp. 67–121). London: Karnac Books.
Jacobs, T. J. (1999). Countertransference past and present: a review of the concept. *International Journal of Psychoanalysis*, 80: 575–594.
Jackson, M., & Williams, P. (1994). *Unimaginable Storms*. London: Karnac Books.
Judd, D. (1989). *Give Sorrow Words*. London: Free Association Books.
Kahr, B. (1996). Donald Winnicott and the foundation of child psychotherapy. *Journal of Child Psychotherapy*, 22(3): 327–342.
Keats, J. (1952). *Letters*. M. B. Forman (Ed.) (4th edn). London: Oxford University Press.
Klein, M. (1935). A contribution to the psychogenesis of manic-depressive states. In: *MKW, Volume I* (pp. 262–289). London: Hogarth Press.
Klein, M. (1952a). The origins of transference. In: *The Writing of Melanie Klein, Volume 3* (pp. 48–56). London: Hogarth Press.
Klein, M. (1952b). The mutual influences in the development of ego and id. In: *The Writing of Melanie Klein, Volume 3*(pp. 57–60). London: Hogarth Press.
Klein, M. (1959). Our adult world and its roots in infancy. In: *The Writing of Melanie Klein, Volume 3* (pp. 147–263). London: Hogarth Press.
Kubler-Ross, E. (1970). *On Death and Dying*. London & New York: Tavistock Publication.
Kubler-Ross, E. (1983). *On Children and Death*. New York: Collier Books.
Kumar, R., & Robson, K. (1984). A prospective study of emotional disorders in childbearing women. *British Journal of Medical Psychology*, 144: 35–47.
Lebovici, S. (1983). *Le Nourisson, la Mere et le Psychanalyste*. Paris: Editions du Centurion.

Lebovici, S., & McDougall, J. (1960). *Un Cas de Psychose Infantile*. Paris: Presses Universitaires de France.

Lewis, E., & Bourne, S. (1989). *Perinatal Death Pamphlet*. Tavistock Joint Library.

Lewis, E., & Bourne, S. (2000). Pregnancy after stillbirth or neonatal death: psychological risks and management. In: *"Spilt Milk" Perinatal Loss and Bereavement*. London: The Institute of Psychoanalysis.

Lubbe, T. (1996). Who lets go first? Some observations on the struggle around weaning. *Journal of Child Psychotherapy*, 22(2): 194–213.

Lubbe, T. (2000). *The Borderline Psychotic Child*. London: Routledge.

Lucas, R. (2000). Puerperal psychosis: vulnerability and aftermath. In: *"Spilt Milk" Perinatal Loss & Bereavement*. London: The Institute of Psychoanalysis.

Magagna, J. (1987). Three years of infant observation with Mrs Bick. *Journal of Child Psychotherapy*, 13(1): 19–39.

Magagna, J. (1994). Individual psychodynamic psychotherapy. In: B. Lask & R. Bryant-Waugh (Eds.), *Childhood Onset Anorexia Nervosa and Related Eating Disorders* (pp. 191–208). Hillside, NJ: Erlbaum.

Main, M., Kaplan, N., & Cassidy, J. (1985). Security in infancy, childhood and adulthood: a move to the level of representation. In: I. Bretherton & I. Waters (Eds.), *Growing Points of Attachment Theory and Research* (pp. 66–104). Monograph 50, Society for Research in Child Development.

Main, T. (1957). The ailment. *British Journal of Medical Psychology*, 33: 129–145.

Malan, D. H. (1975). *A Study of Brief Psychotherapy* (Rosetta edn). New York: A. Plenum.

Manzano, J., & Palacio-Espasa, F. (1993). *Las Therapias en Psiquiatria Infantil y en Psicopedagogia*. Barcelona, Buenos Aires & Mexico: Ediciones Paidos.

Manzano, J., & Palacio-Espasa, F. (1998). *Curare il Bambino*. Torino: Bollati Boringhieri.

Manzano, J., Palacio-Espasa, F., & Zilkha, N. (1999). The narcissistic scenario of parenthood. *International Journal of Psycho-Analysis*, 80: 465–476.

McGuinness, D. (1989). Attention Deficit Disorder: the emperor's clothes, animal "pharm" and other fictions. In: S. Fisher & R. P. Greenberg (Eds.), *The Limits of Biological Treatments for Psychological Distress: Comparison with Psychotherapy and Placebo*. Hillside, NJ: Erlbaum.

Meltzer, D. (1978). *The Kleinian Development—Part III—The Clinical Significance of the Work of Bion.* Perthshire: Clunie Press.
Miller, L. (1992). The relation of infant observation to clinical practice in an Under Fives Counselling Service. *Journal of Child Psychotherapy, 18*(1).
Miller, L. (2000). An Under-Fives's Counselling Service and its relation to questions of assessment. In: *Assessment in Child Psychotherapy.* London: Duckworth.
Miller, L., Rustin, M., Rustin, M., & Shuttelworth, J. (1989). *Closely Observed Infants.* London: Duckworth.
Mollon, P. (1993). *The Fragile Self.* London: Whurr Publications.
Money-Kyrle, R. (1956). Normal counter-transference and some of its deviations. In: *Melanie Klein Today.* London: Routledge.
Norman, J. (2001). The psychoanalyst and the baby: a new look at work with infants. *International Journal of Psychoanalysis, 82*: 83–100.
Orford, E. (1998). Wrestling with the whirlwinds: an approach to the understanding of ADD/ADHD. *Journal of Child Psychotherapy, 24*: 253–266.
Palacio-Espasa, F., & Manzano, J. (1993). *Las Therapias en Psiquiatria Infantil y en Psicopedagogia.* Barcelona, Buenos Aires & Mexico: Ediciones Paidos.
Parkes, C. M. (1972). *Bereavement: Studies of Grief in Adult Life.* London: Tavistock Publications.
Parsons, M., Radford, P., & Horne, A. (1999). Non-intensive psychotherapy and assessment. In: M. Laniado & A. Horne (Eds.), *The Handbook of Child and Adolescent Psychotherapy* (pp. 215–232). London: Routledge.
Pawl, J. H., & Lieberman, A. F. (1997). Infant–parent psychotherapy: In: P. F. Kernberg & J. R. Bemporad (Eds.), *Handbook of Child and Adolescent Psychiatry.* New York: Wiley & Sons, Inc.
Perez Sanchez, M. (1968). *L'Osservazione del Bambino.* Roma: Borla.
Perry, B. D., Pollard, R. A., Blakley, T. L., Baker, W. L., & Vigilante, D. (1995). Childhood trauma, the neuro-biology of adaptation and the use-dependent development of the brain, how "states" become "traits". *Infant Mental Health Journal, 16*(4): 271–291.
Pincus, L. (1976). *Death and the Family. The Importance of Mourning.* London & Boston: Faber & Faber.
Pontecorvo, M. (1986). Introduzione. In: *Il Modello Tavistock* (pp. 9–44). Firenze: Psycho, Martinelli.
Pozzi, M. E. (1991). Dalle Catene del conflitto psichico alla liberta'. *Psychologos, International Review of Psychology, 0*: 5–15.

Pozzi, M. E. (1993). It is never the right time: how to help a mother separate from her young child. *Psychoanalytic Psychotherapy*, 7(2): 135–147.

Pozzi, M. E. (1995). Early problems in mother–child separation as a basis for narcissistic disturbance. In: J. Cooper & N. Maxwell (Eds.), *Narcissistic Wounds Clinical Perspectives* (pp. 31–39). London: Whurr Publishers Ltd.

Pozzi, M. E. (1999). Psychodynamic counselling with under-5s and their families: clinical and technical issues. *Journal of Child Psychotherapy*, 25(1): 51–70.

Pozzi, M. E. (2000). Ritalin for whom? Understanding the need for Ritalin in psychodynamic counselling with families of under-5's. *Journal of Child Psychotherapy*, 26(1): 25–43.

Racker, H. (1968). *Transference and Countertransference*. London: Maresfield Library.

Raphael-Leff, J. (2000). Climbing the walls: therapeutic intervention for post-partum disturbance. In: *"Spilt Milk" Perinatal Loss & Breakdown*. London: The Institute of Psychoanalysis.

Reid, S. (Ed.) (1997). *Developments in Infant Observation*. London & New York: Routledge.

Rey, H. (1994). *Universals of Psychoanalysis in the Treatment of Psychotic and Borderline States*. London: Free Association Books.

Robertson, J., & Robertson, J. (1971). Young children in brief separation: a fresh look. *Psychoanalytical Study of the Child*, 26: 264–315.

Rustin, M., & Quagliata, E. (2000). *Assessment in Child Psychotherapy*. London: Duckworth.

Schore, A. N. (1994). *Affect Regulation and the Origin of the Self. The Neurobiology of Emotional Development*. Hillside, New York: EEA Publishers.

Sharp, D. et al. (1992). Susceptibility of infants to maternal depression: effect of timing and differential impact in males and females. *Infant Behaviour & Development*, 17 (spec. ICIS issue).

Sheperd, R., Johns, J., & Taylor Robinson, H. (1996). *D. W. Winnicott. Thinking about Children*. London: Karnac Books.

Shill, M. (2000). Hyperactivity and the ego: actions as a defense against affect. *Child Analysis*, 11: 109–140.

Sinason, V. (1988). Richard III, Ephaestus and Echo: sexuality and mental/multiple handicap. *Journal of Child Psychotherapy*, 14(2): 93–105.

Sinason, V. (1992). The handicapped smile: Ali's defence against trauma. In: *Mental Handicap And The Human Condition*. London: Free Association Books.

Sinason, V. (1994). *Treating Survivors of Satanist Abuse*. London & New York: Routledge.
Smith, H. (1995). *Unhappy Children. Reasons and Remedies*. London & New York: Free Association Books.
Stern, D. (1971). A microanalysis of the mother–infant interaction. *Journal of the American Academy of Child Psychiatry*, 10: 501–507.
Stern, D. (1977). Misteps in the dance. In: *The First Relationship* (pp. 109–126). Cambridge, Massachusetts: Harvard University Press.
Stern, D. (1998). *The Motherhood Constellation*. London: Karnac Books.
Stiefel, I. (1997). Can disturbance in attachment contribute to Attention Deficit Hyperactivity Disorder? A case discussion. *Clinical Child Psychology and Psychiatry*, 2(1): 45–64.
Symington, N. (1990). The possibility of human freedom and its transmission with particular reference to the thought of Bion. *International Journal of Psycho-Analysis*, 71: 95–106.
Taylor, E. (1991). *The Epidemiology of Childhood Hyperactivity*. Oxford: Oxford University Press.
Taylor, E. (1994). Syndromes of attention deficit and overactivity. In: M. Rutter, E. Taylor & L. Hersov (Eds.), *Child and Adolescent Psychiatry*. Oxford: Blackwell Scientific.
Thomson-Salo, F., & Paul, C. (2001). Some principles of parent–infant psychotherapy: Ann Morgan's contribution. *Australian Journal of Psychotherapy*, 20(1&2): 36–59.
Trad, P. V. (1993). *Short-Term Parent–Infant Psychotherapy*. New York: Basic Books.
Trevarthen, C. (1984). Emotions in infancy: regulators of contacts and relationship with persons. In: K. Scherer & P. Ekman (Eds.), *Approaches in Emotions* (pp. 129–157). Hillsdale, NJ: Erlbaum.
Tronick, E. Z. (1989). Emotions and emotional communications in infants. In: *American Psychologist*, 44(2): 112–119.
Tronick, E. Z., Wienberg, M. K. *et al.* (1997). Depressed mothers and infants: failure to form dyadic states of consciousness. In: L. Murry, P. J. Cooper *et al.* (Eds.), *Postpartum Depression and Child Development* (pp. 54–81). New York: Guilford Press.
Tustin, F. (1972). *Autism and Childhood Psychosis*. London: Hogarth [reprinted New York: Jason Aronson, 1973].
Tustin, F. (1986). *Autistic Barriers in Neurotic Patients*. London: Karnac Books.
Tustin, F. (1990). *The Protective Shell in Children and Adults*. London: Karnac Books.

Tustin, F. (1988–1993). Personal communications occurred at Amersham.
Tustin, F. (1994). Autistic children who are assessed as not brain-damaged. *Journal of Child Psychotherapy*, 20(1): 103–131.
Watillon, A. (1993). The dynamics of psychoanalytic therapies of the early parent–child relationship. *International Journal of Psychoanalysis*, 74: 1037–1048.
Williams, G. (1997). *Internal Landscapes and Foreign Bodies*. London: Tavistock Clinic Series.
Winnicott, D. W. (1947). Hate in the Countertransference. In: *Through Paediatrics to Psychoanalysis*. London: Karnac Books.
Winnicott, D. W. (1941). The observation of infants in a set situation. In: *Through Paediatrics to Psychoanalysis*. London: Karnac Books.
Winnicott, D. W. (1954). The depressive position in normal emotional development. In: *Through Paediatrics To Psychoanalysis*. London: Karnac Books.
Winnicott, D. W. (1960). The theory of the parent–infant relationship. In: *The Maturational Processes and the Facilitating Environment* (pp. 37–55). London: Hogarth Press, 1965.
Winnicott, D. W. (1971). Case I. In: *Therapeutic Consultations in Child Psychiatry* (pp. 12–27). London: Hogarth Press.

INDEX

Adult Attachment Interview (AAI), 24, 28
abuse, 3, 21, 89, 109, 154, 181
   emotional, 98, 151, 195
   physical, 151, 173
   sexual, 26, 101, 155, 173, 191
attention deficit hyperactivity disorder/attention deficit disorder (ADHD/ADD), *see* hyperactivity
Adult Mental Health Service, 161
affective disorder(s), 22
aggression, 57, 60, 81, 97, 134, 147, 149, 155, 187
Ainsworth, M., 23–24, 203
Amini, F., 9, 27, 203
assessment, 42, 53, 150, 179–183, 185, 187
attachment, 24, 26–28, 30, 32, 51, 65, 116, 126, 151, 157, 201–202
   figure, 23, 28, 118, 122
   theory, 22–24, 32, 151

authority, 26, 44, 46, 69, 84, 86, 94–97, 139, 155, 166, 190
autism, 19, 26, 31, 56, 133, 150, 176, 181

bad mother, 45, 56–59, 117, 165–166
Balint, M., 20, 77, 203
Barrows. P., 101–102, 204
Beebe, B., 9, 204
bereavement, 51–52, 63, 79, 92–93, 121, 130
Bick, E., 7, 152, 204
binocular vision, 8
Bion, W., 4, 8, 12, 15–17, 31, 35, 40–41, 52, 79, 90, 96–97, 108, 112, 117, 151, 167, 182, 204
black hole, 29
bolt(s), 4–5, 89, 95, 98
borderline, 22, 29, 46, 53, 82, 143–144, 181
boundary, 17, 97
Bourne, S., 56, 61, 75, 128, 208
Bowlby, J., 23, 121–122, 204

213

brain, 26–31, 139, 150–151, 201
Brazelton, T. B., 21, 27, 205
Breggin, P. R., 150, 205
Breuer, J., 4, 20, 37, 205
Byng-Hall, J., 23–25, 95, 129, 163, 205

Caesarean, 116
care-giver, 23, 28–30, 32
chaos therapy, 31
character disorder(s), 22
child development, 21, 178
Child and Adolescent Mental Health Service, 179
Coates, S. W., 117, 205
Conners Questionnaire, 153
contained, 28, 43, 47, 52, 59, 78, 96–98, 137, 167, 185, 187, 202
container–contained, 4, 15–16, 117
Cooper, J. P., 27, 55–56, 80, 205
counselling, 4–5, 7, 11–12, 15, 17–18, 20–21, 24–27, 32, 35–36, 39, 41–42, 47, 51–53, 56–60, 78, 82, 85–86, 109–110, 112–113, 118–119, 127, 130, 132–134, 136–141, 144, 146, 152, 155–157, 159, 161, 171, 177–179, 181–185, 187–189, 195–197, 199, 202
countertransference, 35, 37–42, 44, 93, 105, 182, 188, 202
Cramer, B. G., 21–22, 181, 205

Daws, D., 22, 34, 90, 205
defence(s), 12, 17, 62, 82, 126, 151–152, 201–202
depressive
  position, 13, 76
  conflict, 52
  disposition, 15, 23, 36, 45, 52, 166
  feelings, 63
  guilt, 15
  moments, 53
  state of mind, 126, 148, 168, 172, 182
  streak, 187
  symptoms, 181

developmental delay(s), 52, 81, 171, 181
Diamond, B., 29
Di Ceglie, D., 118, 205
difficulty, 44, 63–64, 69, 72, 77, 81, 83–84, 86, 89, 95, 111, 117–118, 134, 143–144, 151, 156, 176, 187, 195, 198
dyad, 4, 18, 84, 96
dying, fear of, 71, 92

eating disorder(s), 44, 82
echo, echolalic, 157, 172, 174
Ekman, P., 9
ending (treatment), 20, 25, 40, 140, 155, 169
envy, envying, 76, 109, 131, 134
ethic, ethical, 33, 108

father's role, 73
family script(s), 25, 163, 167
Ferenczi, S., 20
fertility, 74
Field, T. M., 27, 205
focal psychotherapy, 20–21
follow-up, 31, 34, 62, 73–74, 102, 150, 180
Forth, M. J., 101, 206
foster parent, 151
free association, 32–33
freedom, 19–20, 26, 35, 61–62, 89–90, 94, 96–98
Fraiberg, S., 21–22, 27, 206
Freud, A., 12, 180
Freud, S., 4, 13–14, 20, 32–33, 35, 37–39, 75–76, 116, 124, 143, 180, 205–206
Fromm-Reichman, F., 150, 206
Furman, E., 121, 206
Furman, R. A., 150, 206

GP, 56, 58, 82, 158, 163
gender identity, 116, 117–119
genetic, 9, 29, 34, 112
Geneva, 22, 181
ghost(s), 21, 111

Grotstein, J. S., 29, 206
guilt(y), 4, 15, 16, 37, 45, 47, 57, 60, 86, 94, 105, 107–109, 111, 118, 121, 128–129, 130, 131–133, 135–136, 139–141, 144–145, 149, 151, 154–155 159, 162, 166, 168, 173–174, 178, 185, 202

Hammer, E., 32, 207
handicap(s), handicapped, handicapping, 34, 133–135, 138–141, 181
hate, hatred, 19–20, 39–40, 108–109, 124, 162, 167, 169, 182, 185
Heimann, P., 38–39, 41–42, 207
holding, 16, 35
Holmes, J., 23, 207
homosexuality, 116
hook(s), hooked, hooking, 4–5, 17, 46, 84, 111, 199
Hopkins, J., 22, 207
hyperactivity, 45, 52, 56, 143–144, 149–152, 162
hyper-arousal, 29

Iiro, 19–20
in vitro fertilization (IVF), 74
identification(s), 8, 14, 26, 36, 39, 44, 47, 52, 58, 59, 66–67, 92, 119, 155, 180, 184
Independent Group, 38
infant observation, 7–8, 10, 36
infant–parent, 8–9, 16, 18–19, 21–22, 177
inside baby, 16, 71–72, 75–76, 83
intergenerational pattern of attachment, 26, 32, 47, 116, 118, 122, 151, 201–202
Isaacs, S., 14, 207
Izard, C. E., 9, 215

Jackson, M., 150, 207
Jacobs, T. J., 40, 207
Judd, D., 121, 207

Kahr, B., 18–19, 207

Keats, J., 8, 207
Klein, M., 12–15, 23, 122, 207
Kleinian(s), 38, 152
Kubler-Ross, E., 121, 123, 207
Kumar, R., 55, 207

Lebovici, S., 56, 207
Lewis, E., 56, 61, 75, 128, 208
Lewis, T., 203
Little Hans, 13
Loss, *see* mourning
Lubbe, T., 7, 139–143–144, 208
Lucas, R., 56, 208

Magagna, J., 7, 208
Main, T., 24, 28, 149, 208
Main, M., 206, 208
Malan, D. H., 20, 36, 208
Manzano, G., 22–23, 41, 52, 59, 181, 208–209
Margaret, 18–19
marital therapy, 10, 25, 53
McGuinness, D., 150, 203, 208
McDougall, J., 56, 208
mechanism of defence, *see* defence mechanism
Meltzer, D., 8, 209
mental disposition, 15, 23, 82, 195
mental handicap, *see* handicap
Miller, L., 7, 12, 27, 53, 182, 209
miscarriage, *see* perinatal death
Mollon, P., 36, 209
Money-Kyrle, R., 39–40, 209
Moore, M. S., 117, 205
mother figure, 23–24
mourning, 61, 63, 68, 75–76, 78, 112, 116, 121–123, 125–127, 130–132, 159
Murray, L., 27, 55, 56, 205
mutative interpretation, 129

N.H.S., 11
narcissistic, 29, 53, 62, 80, 181
neuroendocrine, 29
neuroscience(s), 9, 26, 31
"no-entry syndrome", 82

object(s), 13–14, 18–19, 22, 24, 28, 36, 59, 71, 75–76, 78, 81–82, 101, 116, 122, 127, 131, 159, 182
object-relation(s) 26, 28, 30, 77, 151, 201
  school of, 22–23
Oedipal, 25, 91, 101–102, 127, 135, 165, 168
omnipotent, omnipotence, 16–17, 26, 61–62, 102, 124, 156, 159
omniscience, 16–17
Orford, E., 150, 209

Palacio-Espasa, F., 22–23, 41, 52–53, 59, 181, 208–209
paranoid–schizoid, 13, 15, 23, 166
parental couple, 15–16, 102, 112, 165, 182
parent–infant psychotherapy, 19, 21–22, 181
Parents' Line, 43, 53, 195
Parkes, M. C., 121, 123, 209
pateo, 3
Perez-Sanchez, M., 7, 209
perinatal death, 60–61, 65–67, 71–72, 74–77, 103, 128
Perry, B. D., 27, 29–30, 201, 209
phantasy, 13, 41, 76, 81, 83, 98, 102
Pincus, L., 121, 123, 209
Pontecorvo, M., 7, 209
post natal depression (PND), 55–57, 59, 61, 171–173
post-Freudian, 22
Pozzi, M., 44, 46–47, 149, 161, 209
pragmatic semantic disorder, 155
pregnancy, 60–61, 67, 75–76, 116–117, 129, 134–135, 138, 152, 162, 168
pre-transference, 22, 43, 52–53
projection(s), 15, 17, 19, 22, 26, 31, 41, 45, 47, 52, 57, 59, 68–69, 72, 78–79, 82–83, 96, 106–107, 112, 130, 147, 154–155, 159, 163–164, 168, 174, 184, 190, 202
psychoanalytic psychotherapy, 31, 33, 93, 180

psychotherapy, *see* parent–infant psychotherapy

Racker, H., 39, 210
Raphael-Leff, J., 55–56, 60, 210
Reid, S., 7, 181, 203, 210
reparation, repair, 15, 19, 127, 173, 178, 202
repetition compulsion, 28
replacement, 66, 78, 132
repression retaliation or Talion law, 76
reverie, 16, 30–31, 35, 96–97 108, 112, 202
Rey, H., 82, 210
Ritalin, 149–150, 152–159
Robertson, J., 122, 210
Robertson, J., 122, 210
role reversal, 14, 46, 125

San Francisco, 22
Schore, A. N., 27–32, 201, 210
script *see* family script
secondary handicap, 133–134, 139
separation, separation anxiety, 23–24, 26, 34, 51–52, 63, 67, 69–71, 76–80, 84, 97, 111, 116–119, 122, 124, 136–138, 174–176
setting, the, 22, 32–36, 172, 180
Sharp, D., 55, 210
Shepherd, R., 19, 210
Shill, M., 152, 210
Sinason, V., 36, 133, 139, 141, 181, 210
sleep problem(s), 90, 92–93, 97, 140, 147, 150
Smith, H., 121, 211
social services, 109, 196
soiling, 39, 46, 101–102, 104, 111
spatula, 18–19
spilling out, 108
splitting, 14–15, 45, 83, 130
squiggle, 19
Stern, D., 9, 21–22, 27, 35, 181, 211
Stiefel, I., 150, 211

strange situation, 24
stress hormone(s), 29
stupid smile, 133–134, 141
Symington, N., 89–90, 97, 129, 211
systemic family therapy, 24, 189

Talion law, *see* retaliation
Tavistock Clinic, 11, 92, 180
Taylor, E., 150, 206, 211
Taylor Robinson, H., 210
telephone consultation, *see* Parents' Line
toilet training, 103, 171, 176
training, 7–8, 23, 33–34
transference, 21–23. 30, 32, 35, 37–42, 44–45, 59, 70, 86, 106, 109, 112, 146, 152–153, 158, 163–164, 202
transitional space, 71
trauma(s), 3, 17, 26, 29, 201

Trevarthen, C., 27, 211
Tronick, E. Z., 27, 55, 205, 211
Tustin, F., 26, 28–29, 31, 56, 151, 177–178, 181, 211–212
twin(s), 115–117, 127–130

unconscious phantasy, 13–14, 22, 25, 196
unconscious, 3, 7, 17, 19, 24, 26, 31–32, 35, 38–39, 43, 82, 87, 90, 92, 95–96, 106, 129, 169, 175, 179–180, 182, 184, 189, 202
under fives' counselling and workshop, 21, 78, 92

Williams, G., 82, 212
Williams, P., 150, 207
Winnicott, D. W., 7, 12, 16, 18–19, 29, 31, 35, 39–40, 76, 151, 212